THE
PASTOR
A GUIDE FOR GOD'S FAITHFUL SERVANT

THE PASTOR

A GUIDE FOR GOD'S FAITHFUL SERVANT

Jim Vogel, Editor
More than 30 contributing authors

Regular Baptist Books
Arlington Heights, Illinois

Scripture quotations marked "ESV" are taken from The Holy Bible, English Standard Version® (ESV®), copyright © 2001 by Crossway, a publishing ministry of Good News Publishers. Used by permission. All rights reserved.

Scripture quotations marked "NASB" are taken from the New American Standard Bible®, copyright © 1960, 1962, 1963, 1968, 1971, 1972, 1973, 1975, 1977, 1995 by The Lockman Foundation. Used by permission.

Scripture quotations marked "NIV" are taken from the Holy Bible, New International Version®, NIV®. Copyright © 1973, 1978, 1984, by Biblica, Inc.™ Used by permission of Zondervan. All rights reserved worldwide.

Scripture quotations marked "NKJV" are taken from the New King James Version®. Copyright © 1982 by Thomas Nelson, Inc. Used by permission. All rights reserved.

The Pastor: A Guide for God's Faithful Servant
© 2012 Regular Baptist Press • Arlington Heights, Illinois
www.RegularBaptistPress.org • 1-800-727-4440
RBP5226 • ISBN: 978-1-60776-584-4

Second printing—2016

All rights reserved. Except as permitted under U.S. Copyright Law, no part of this publication may be reproduced, distributed, or transmitted in any form or by any means, or stored in a database or retrieval system, without the prior written permission of the publisher.

Contents

Contributors 7
Foreword 9
   John Greening
Introduction 11
   Jim Vogel

Personal Priorities

1. The Call to the Ministry 18
   Daniel Davey
2. Personal Spiritual Life 32
   Tim White
3. Marriage and Family 40
   Mike Peck
4. The Example of Character and Integrity 49
   Matthew Morrell
5. Pastoral Ethics and Decorum 59
   Tim Jordan

Core Responsibilities

6. Preaching and Teaching the Word of God 70
   Gary Gromacki
7. Administrating as a Bishop: Keeping the Church in Check 79
   Ken Floyd
8. Shepherding with Pastoral Care 88
   Ernie Schmidt
9. Biblical Counseling: Discipleship in the Details 96
   Jeff Newman
10. Evangelizing 106
   Pat Nemmers
11. Making Disciples: The Priority and Practice 114
   Don McCall
12. Visioneering 123
   Stephen Viars

Primary Competencies

13. Developing a Local Church Educational Strategy 135
    John Greening
14. Working with Deacons 143
    Will Hatfield
15. Guiding the Staff 152
    Don Shirk
16. Working with Volunteers 162
    Jon Jenks
17. Planting Daughter Churches 171
    Ken Davis
18. Guiding the Local Outreach Program 183
    Jim Vogel
19. Leading in Finances and Facilities 195
    George Prinzing
20. Overseeing the Church's Corporate Worship Gathering 203
    Ken Pyne
21. Ministering Effectively to Marriages and Families 213
    Scott Poling
22. Leading Effectively through Change 222
    Mike Augsburger
23. Guiding the Missions Program 231
    Gary L. Anderson
24. Dealing with Church Conflict 240
    Randal L. Gilmore
25. Sunday School: Boring or Soaring? 249
    Jack Austin
26. Dealing with the Troublemaker 257
    Duke Crawford
27. Working with Various Age Groups 263
    Dave Rockwell
28. Handling Transition with Wisdom and Grace 271
    Rich Van Heukelum

Special Situations

29. Pastoral Internships 280
    Joel Dunlap
30. The Bivocational Pastor 287
    Kevin Subra
31. The Interim Pastor 294
    Lee D. Kliewer
32. The Associate Pastor 304
    Bruce Snyder

Contributors

Jim Vogel (DMin, Trinity Evangelical Divinity School) is state representative of the Northeast Fellowship. Having spent thirty years in pastoral ministry, he served as the associate national representative of the General Association of Regular Baptist Churches.

John Greening (DMin, Baptist Bible Seminary) is national representative of the General Association of Regular Baptist Churches. For over twenty years he served as a pastor and now represents the GARBC across the country and around the world while ministering through education and writing.

Gary L. Anderson (DD, Baptist Bible Seminary) is president emeritus of Baptist Mid-Missions, after serving as president of Baptist Mid-Missions for twenty-six years and pastor for twelve years.

Mike Augsburger (DMin, Trinity Evangelical Divinity School) is lead pastor of Willow Creek Baptist Church, West Des Moines, Iowa.

Jack Austin (BA, Faith Baptist Bible College) is pastor of Christian Education at Calvary Baptist Church, Wisconsin Rapids, Wisconsin.

Duke Crawford (MA, Faith Baptist Theological Seminary) is pastor of Emmanuel Baptist Church, Toledo, Ohio, and is a member of the Association of Certified Biblical Counselors.

Daniel Davey (ThD, Central Baptist Theological Seminary) is president of Virginia Beach Theological Seminary and was previously pastor of Colonial Baptist Church, Virginia Beach, Virginia, for thirty-three years.

Ken Davis (DMin, Trinity Evangelical Divinity School) is director of Project Jerusalem at Baptist Bible Seminary and has been a church planter with Baptist Mid-Missions for over thirty-five years.

Joel Dunlap is a graduate of Faith Baptist Bible College and Theological Seminary and was an associate pastor for four years.

Ken Floyd (MDiv, Grace Theological Seminary) has thirty years of pastoral experience and is executive ministry director of the Michigan Association of Regular Baptist Churches.

Randal L. Gilmore (MA, Western Michigan University) is director of Word of Life Japan and regional director of Word of Life Pacific Rim. He was previously a pastor for thirty-five years and has taught Biblical conflict management internationally.

Gary Gromacki (PhD, Baptist Bible Seminary) is professor of Bible and homiletics at Baptist Bible Seminary. He also edits *The Journal of Ministry and Theology*.

Will Hatfield (MDiv, Baptist Bible Seminary) is lead pastor of CrossRoad Baptist Church, Ames, Iowa.

Jon Jenks (MDiv, Baptist Bible Seminary) is pastor of Calvary Baptist Church, Wisconsin Rapids, Wisconsin, where he previously served as Christian Education pastor.

Tim Jordan (DMin, Westminster Theological Seminary) is pastor of Calvary Baptist Church, Lansdale, Pennsylvania, and until 2015 was concurrently chancellor of Calvary Baptist Seminary.

Lee D. Kliewer (EdD, Nova Southeastern University) is executive assistant to the president at Summit University. He previously served in pastoral ministries for twenty years.

Don McCall (DMin, Baptist Bible Seminary) teaches pastoral ministry courses at Summit University. He has served as a pastor and interim pastor for more than thirty years.

Matthew Morrell (DMin, Northland International University) is pastor of Fourth Baptist Church, Plymouth, Minnesota.

Pat Nemmers (BA, Faith Baptist Bible College) is lead pastor of Saylorville Baptist Church, Des Moines, Iowa, where he has served since 1998. He also works with the church-planting network Engage, which has planted four churches.

Jeff Newman (DMin, Westminster Theological Seminary) teaches Bible and Biblical counseling at Faith Baptist Bible College and Theological Seminary. He also assists pastors and churches through an active counseling and speaking ministry.

Mike Peck (DMin, Luther Rice Seminary) ministers to churches and missionaries around the world involving marriage, parenting, and other counseling-related issues. Previously he was vice president of Baptist Church Planters for fourteen years and a pastor for thirty years.

Scott Poling (MDiv, Dallas Theological Seminary) has been pastor of Harvest New Beginnings, Oswego, Illinois, since 1995.

George Prinzing (BRE, Tennessee Temple University) has been in pastoral ministry since 1987 and is now pastor of Tri County Baptist Church, Lady Lake, Florida.

Ken Pyne (DMin, Northern Baptist Theological Seminary) is seminary chaplain and director of internships at Summit University. Previously he was an associate pastor of worship for twenty-seven years.

Dave Rockwell (DMin, Trinity Evangelical Divinity School) has served on the pastoral staffs of several churches and on the faculties of two Bible colleges. He has a special interest in effective Bible teaching and the sound spiritual growth of the church.

Ernie Schmidt (DMin, Central Baptist Theological Seminary) has taught at college and graduate levels for forty years, during which time he also pastored churches in Minnesota, Montana, Alaska, and Iowa and served as dean of Faith Baptist Theological Seminary.

Don Shirk (DMin, Baptist Bible Seminary) has ministered as pastor of Grace Baptist Church, Batavia, New York, since 1987. He also serves as a police chaplain.

Bruce Snyder graduated from the pastor's course at Moody Bible Institute, has pastored for fifty years, and is currently pastor emeritus at Emmanuel Baptist Church, Toledo, Ohio.

Kevin Subra (BA, Faith Baptist Bible College) is pastor of Northridge Baptist Church, Des Moines, Iowa. A bivocational pastor, he works in computer security.

Rich Van Heukelum (DMin, Baptist Bible Seminary) is pastor of Shawnee Baptist Church, Shamong, New Jersey. He previously served as pastor of churches in New York and Iowa.

Stephen Viars (DMin, Westminster Theological Seminary) is pastor of Faith Church, Lafayette, Indiana, and vice president of the Biblical Counseling Coalition board of directors.

Tim White (DMin, Reformed Theological Seminary) is dean and professor of Bible at Piedmont International University. He has also pastored churches in North Carolina since 1981.

Foreword
— John Greening

Learning to behave properly in church as a boy was no small task. That behavioral challenge was exacerbated by the reality that I was a PK (pastor's kid). My conduct was not merely an expression of my individual soul liberty, for which I was accountable. My conduct also reflected on my dad and mom in their roles as parents and as pastor and wife.

I never struggled with outright rebellion. Adolescent defiance would have (whether fairly or unfairly) impacted the credibility of my parents' ministry. My behavioral challenges instead took the form of such problems as "juvenile restless leg syndrome," a malady created by the volatile mixture of too much boyhood energy, cramped sanctuary pews, and church services that never seemed to end. That combination had explosive potential.

During sermon time, I developed overactive "mind and mouth" disease, producing witty comments that popped out effervescently to my high school age friends sitting next to me. Unfortunately my comments had little to do with the message being preached—much to my father's chagrin and older pew members' dismay.

In what was a display of divine irony (or justice), God in His eternal plan had determined that my life's vocational calling was to serve as a pastor. Though my legs continued to be restless at times, and my mind never quite stopped conjuring up some humorous thought, I found that a whole new set of behavioral challenges awaited me as I entered the pastorate.

I was not alone in facing the learning curve for pastoral behavior. The apostle Paul communicated with his young student Timothy to mentor him in the proper demeanor and execution of church ministry. Paul said to Timothy, "These things I write to you, though I hope to come to you shortly; but if I am delayed, I write so that you may know how you ought to conduct yourself in the house of God, which is the church of the living God, the pillar and ground of the truth" (1 Tim. 3:14, 15, NKJV).

The church in Ephesus that young pastor Timothy was shepherding was like any church. There were constant challenges to face. Here is a short list of what he had to navigate. It may sound similar to the laundry list of challenges confronting you.

- Dealing with deficient teachers using faulty curriculum
- Guarding the centrality of the gospel
- Handling troublemakers in the congregation
- Developing positive community relations
- Providing gender role guidelines
- Establishing leadership qualifications
- Correcting truth distortions
- Establishing credibility as a young pastor
- Maintaining discipline in personal life and ministry
- Communicating properly when under pressure
- Caring for the needs of the elderly
- Determining pastoral salaries
- Responding to criticism
- Managing finances
- Focusing on the right priorities

The ministry is not a vocation for a novice (1 Tim. 3:6). The complexity of pastoral service requires the wisdom and experience of a seasoned veteran. Every young pastor needs a "been there, done that" perspective such as the one Paul provided to inexperienced Timothy as he embarked on his pastoral career. Even veteran pastors can value from wise counsel as well as review and refinement of pastoral basics.

I have known the general editor of this book, Jim Vogel, for many years. He started his ministry under the tutelage of a trusted pastor who groomed him. As Jim gained experience, he invested in the development of young men who went from his church into ministry, and in his staff, who grew under his mentoring. Jim is now a pastor of pastors, counseling and challenging them to pursue excellence in their work.

Each contributor to this book is a seasoned veteran of pastoral ministry. The compilation of wisdom contained in the pages that follow is a rich treasure trove of ministry guidance that will further equip men for the "good work" of pastoring the church of the living God.

Introduction
— Jim Vogel

I never intended to be a pastor. My father was a successful businessman who served faithfully in our home church for many years and had a great impact for the Lord. Through most of my teenage years, I felt that I would head in the same direction. So in my final year of high school, I applied to a well-known Christian university, thinking I would pursue a business career like my dad.

But God had other plans. Using some unique influences on a student missions trip and the encouragement of a godly youth leader, God redirected me toward ministry, and I have never looked back. After Bible college and seminary, I was a youth pastor and then a lead pastor, serving for a total of thirty years. Now I pastor pastors, seeking to encourage, train, and equip them for the world's most challenging and rewarding work.

As every pastor knows, pastoring isn't easy. It's thrilling and fulfilling to be sure—but also demanding and difficult. Here's why: effective pastoring focuses on three primary responsibilities, each of which seems to require a full-time commitment to accomplish with any measure of success. Allow me to summarize.

Pastors Lead Churches

It's God's design that pastors give overall leadership to congregations. Scriptural teaching is unmistakably clear about this role under God. Peter said it well when he instructed his fellow pastors to "be shepherds of God's flock that is under your care, serving as overseers" (1 Pet. 5:2, NIV). Additionally, I believe Paul had pastors in mind when he described them as those "who are over you in the Lord" (1 Thess. 5:12, NIV), and later in his first letter to Timothy, he described elders (same office as pastors) as those who "direct the affairs of the church" (1 Tim. 5:17, NIV). God never gives this overarching leadership responsibility to deacons. In Biblical perspective, they assist pastors and serve alongside them as supportive co-laborers.

Much could be said about the nature of this pastoral leadership responsibility, but the following traits of pastoral leaders stand out to me as especially important.

Humble leadership. Biblical pastoral leadership is not harsh and dictatorial, but is instead marked by a humble spirit and a servant's perspective. Again, Peter spoke to this when he instructed pastors to be "eager to serve; not lording it over those entrusted to you, but being examples to the flock"(1 Pet. 5:2, 3, NIV). Additionally, Paul, although not directly speaking of pastors, described the manner of a servant leader and stated that "the Lord's servant must . . . be kind to everyone, able to teach, not resentful. Those who oppose him he must gently instruct" (2 Tim. 2:24, 25, NIV). Of course, compassionate leadership doesn't preclude confrontation and a willingness to address problems proactively but is always marked by a genuine concern for people and their welfare.

Godly leadership. The responsibility of giving overall leadership to a church with humility and courage requires a foundation of genuine godliness. Effective pastoral leadership is godly leadership. The pastoral task cannot be accomplished with fruitfulness out of a spiritual vacuum. Tim White's chapter in the opening section of this book appropriately emphasizes the spiritual life of the pastoral leader as a foundational priority for all that he does.

Courageous leadership. Being an overseer of a church brings added pressures and closer scrutiny. It carries with it the responsibility of making unpopular decisions at times and of dealing firmly yet lovingly with problems. It often brings criticism and resistance. Effective pastoral leadership means having the willingness to confront sin and work through Biblical principles of restoration. In short, pastors who lead effectively are men of courage.

Visionary leadership. Effective pastors are also forward thinkers. They are the lead "vision casters" for their churches. Steve Viars ably addresses this responsibility in detail in his chapter. But let me emphasize that when such leadership is lacking, churches default to maintenance ministry, continuing programs and activities without a sense of direction and purpose. Christ gave His church a mission and defined its priorities. Pastors who know how to articulate purpose and values, assess their churches' progress, and establish a goal-setting process are sure to see their churches go forward for God's glory.

How does this leadership work out practically in a church? It works when the responsibilities outlined in the chapters of this book are fulfilled. Pastors lead deacons, direct staff, oversee educational ministries, guide worship, strategize outreach, preside over meetings, supervise stewardship activities, deal with conflict, lead in discipline, and much, much more.

Pastors Communicate Truth

The pastor's priority responsibility of preaching and teaching the Word of God is emphasized throughout the Scriptures. The writer of Hebrews had pastoral leaders in mind when he admonished his readers to "remember your leaders, who spoke the word of God to you" (Heb. 13:7, NIV). Paul described pastors as those who "admonish you" (1 Thess. 5:12, NIV), and at the end of his life, he charged Timothy to "preach the Word . . . with great patience and careful instruction" (2 Tim. 4:2, NIV). While others can be enlisted and trained in this Bible-teaching task, pastors have the primary responsibility for communication. The Word of God changes lives, fuels spiritual growth, and equips for ministry. It's the foundation for all that the church is and does. A few concepts can help us clarify this task.

Expository preaching. Such preaching puts the emphasis on *exposing* the truth of a section of Scripture rather than *imposing* our ideas upon it. It's an approach that keeps the pastor focused on the Scriptural material and guards him from digression toward (or even obsession with) his own thoughts and ideas. Preparation for expository preaching requires long hours of study but yields the fruit of changed lives! (See Gary Gromacki's excellent chapter on this topic.)

Priority preaching. Beware of the danger of allowing preaching to become secondary in corporate worship. There are so many helpful and truly uplifting aspects of worship available to God's people today, and I do not denigrate the use of newer elements that truly draw our hearts to God. But the preaching of the Word of God must remain central, setting the "truth parameters" for the rest of worship, which finds its climactic expression in Scriptural proclamation.

Pastoral preaching. Keep in mind what God desires us to be: pastors, not just preachers. It's easy to get so passionate about our preaching that our preparation seems to require a weekly hibernation in our offices. If we are not intentional about our schedule, our time for sermon preparation can swallow up most of our available time, and we are then forced to neglect other aspects of our pastoral role. It's time spent with our people between Sundays—becoming aware of their struggles and helping lift their burdens—that fuels our preaching with practicality and helpful application.

Teaching. On a more personal level, may I suggest that pastors consider active involvement in the teaching ministries of the church beyond their primary preaching role in corporate worship settings. Some may disagree, but I believe that pastors who don't take advantage of the opportunity to share God's Word in smaller settings, such as Sunday School classes and small groups, miss out on another level of communication (often a more personal or intimate one) that can supplement their effectiveness in the pulpit.

Pastors Care for People

In Paul's description of the qualifications of pastors (overseers) in his letter to Timothy, he directly mentioned the responsibility of caring. Comparing the pastor's role to that of a father, he speaks of the pastor's commitment to "take care of God's church" (1 Tim. 3:5, NIV). The word translated *care* in this passage implies much more than mere governance; it emphasizes caring action. (See the only other two usages of this unique word in the New Testament in Luke 10:34 and 35.) Pastors are to be congregational caregivers!

The shepherding analogy is helpful here because it reminds us that our role as pastors is more than feeding and leading; it involves a compassionate concern that is demonstrated in caring action. Just as shepherds tend the flock, watch over the sheep, and minister to their needs for shelter, safety, and comfort, so a good pastoral shepherd recognizes the importance of responding to the needs of the sick, paying specific attention to the homebound, counseling those with special needs, providing comfort to the grieving, helping couples prepare for married life, and much more.

No pastor can afford to ignore these personal caring aspects of his ministry without consequence. They give power to our preaching and foster genuine community. In larger churches this ministry can be shared with other leaders, but I personally believe that all pastors must be involved in this to some degree.

Since leaving the pastorate, I have been occasionally asked what I miss the most about that role now that I do not have a local congregation to serve. I think I surprise some people when I mention caring ministries. But it's true. I miss visiting those in the hospital facing surgery and sharing the amazing comfort of God's Word at a memorial service. I miss working with couples preparing for their marriages and comforting those in broken ones. It is at these times when our people need us most and our words have the greatest impact.

Despite the variety of ministry approaches and philosophies in churches today, these three roles of leading the church, communicating truth, and caring remain constant for pastoral leaders who wish to follow the Biblical pattern. And in reality, the chapters that follow fall under these categories of pastoral responsibility.

About This Book

Why another book on pastoring, and what makes this one unique? For one thing, the pastoral ministry landscape is constantly changing. New challenges and opportunities call for fresh ideas and perspectives that today's pastors ought to be kept abreast of. Also, while many excellent materials are available today on specific aspects of pastoral work such as counseling and preaching, not many focus, as this one does, on a broad spectrum of subjects related to a pastor's life and work. This book is not written by a single author, but by many. It is strengthened by the involvement of more than two dozen excellent authors who each share in an area of expertise. While Scripture is referenced throughout, this volume does not focus primarily on Biblical exposition but on practical help for pastors. It's not a book of sermons, nor is it intended to be a technical volume, but a more popular treatment designed to be of value to both the ministry student and the seasoned pastor. The chapters have intentionally been kept concise to allow for addressing more subjects and perhaps for a wider usage by today's busy pastors.

The book is divided into four sections:
- The initial five chapters address the spiritual and personal foundation of pastoral ministry. An effective pastor builds his public ministry upon the foundation of his private calling and commitments as well as his personal walk with God.
- Chapters 6–12 emphasize what I believe are the seven core responsibilities of a pastor. They represent the essence of a pastoral job description. Few pastors can successfully serve without some understanding and competency in these areas.
- Chapters 13–28 address pastoral leadership in sixteen specific church

ministry areas with practical suggestions to enhance the pastor's effectiveness.
- Chapters 29–32 deal with four specialized roles that deserve special attention and are increasingly an important part of any discussion on pastoral ministries.

It is my prayer that this volume will have a wide influence and provide pastors with real help in their ministries.

Personal Priorities

1
The Call to the Ministry
— Daniel Davey

What exactly is the call of God, and how is a man to absolutely know that God has commissioned him to the ministry? Should he expect a literal, audible call from Heaven? Or perhaps, should he expect a silent but unmistakable internal impulse from the Holy Spirit? Additionally, if such an experience is necessary, should a young man aspiring to the ministry prepare himself to wait for God to directly call him, such as Old Testament men like Moses (Exod. 3; 4), Gideon (Judg. 6), and Samuel (1 Sam. 3)? Or should he expect a clarion Christ-call like New Testament men such as James and John (Mark 1:19, 20), Nathanael (John 1:45–51), and Paul (Acts 9)? Where does the Word of God fit into all of this?

By asking such questions, I am seeking to prod our minds to discover whether or not the Scriptures have a definite and seamless plan—a Biblical norm, of sorts—of calling men into ministry regardless of how sensational the initial experience may or may not be. To properly answer this question, I think we should begin with the Scriptures and focus on the Biblical term *call*.

The Biblical Term *Call*
Call in the Old Testament

An examination of the English term *call* in the Old Testament reveals that it is usually a translation of the Hebrew verb *qarah*. Our concern here is to consider only those passages where God is the One calling and mankind is the one being called. From this narrow domain, three observations may provide some helpful insight and background to our study.

God initiates the call. First and most obvious, when God is the One calling, He is clearly viewed as the initiator of the call. Though this is true without exception, this observation is most clearly validated when the man He calls is totally unaware of God's calling yet acts in accord with His purpose. Such is the case with the Medo-Persian king Cyrus the Great (see Isaiah 45:1, 4–6).

The call may be for a specific act of service. A remarkable feature of God's call is that it may be extended to someone to accomplish specific acts of service for the glory of God. In clear terms, the call of God was not just for vocational ministry roles. This was exactly the case with Bezalel, the skilled craftsman whom God called to build the tabernacle of meeting. Moses chronicled Bezalel's appointment with the following words of the Lord: "See, I have *called by name* Bezalel, the son of Uri, the son of Hur, of the tribe of Judah. I have filled him with the Spirit of God in wisdom, in understanding, in knowledge, and in all kinds of craftsmanship" (Exod. 31:2, 3, NASB; emphasis added).

The call may be for vocational service. This final observation relates to the vocational call of God that led men into a leader-prophet role. Moses (Exod. 3:1–10) and Samuel (1 Sam. 3:1–21) are examples of such a call, and both were taken completely by surprise with God's choice. Moses, an eighty-year-old man, was called by God from a burning bush left unconsumed by the fire (Exod. 3:2, 4), and Samuel, just a young boy, was called by God four times (1 Sam. 3:4–14). These two examples, as with all the prophets of the Old Testament, were given divine revelation, and that revelation was often accompanied by miraculous activity.

What is important to note from these observations is that God chooses to use men as a means to accomplish His purpose on earth, and this choice rests solely in His sovereign will. When He selects men, He both calls and equips them for either specific acts of service or vocational ministry. In so doing, He receives all the honor and glory when the work is complete.

Call in the New Testament

The abundant usages of the verb *to call* (*kaleō*) and cognate nouns *calling* (*klēsis*) and *the called ones* (*klētois*) in the New Testament seem to support the idea that a person's salvation call of God in Christ fully encompasses every detail of his life—from his spiritual birth to his future glorification. Paul expressed this very idea with great confidence to both the Roman and the Thessalonian believers. To the Romans he wrote:

> And we know that God causes all things to work together for good to those who love God, to those who are called

[*tois klētois,* "the ones called"] according to His purpose. For those whom He foreknew, He also predestined to become conformed to the image of His Son, so that He would be the firstborn among many brethren; and these whom He predestined, He also called [*ekalesen*]; and these whom He called [*ekalesen*], He also justified; and these whom He justified, He also glorified. (Rom. 8:28–30, NASB)

And to the Thessalonians he wrote: "But we should always give thanks to God for you, brethren beloved by the Lord, because God has chosen you from the beginning for salvation through sanctification by the Spirit and faith in the truth. *It was for this He called* [*kaleō*] *you through our gospel,* that you may gain the glory of our Lord Jesus Christ" (2 Thess. 2:13, 14, NASB; emphasis added).

To the Corinthians Paul also noted this breadth of God's calling with a number of specific statements that include "[you are] sanctified in Christ Jesus, saints by *calling*" (1 Cor. 1:2); "you *were called* into fellowship with His Son" (1:9); "those who are *the called*" (1:24); "consider your *calling*, brethren, that there were not many wise . . . , mighty, . . . [or] noble" (1:26); when marriages are struggling, "God *has called* us to peace" (7:15); and "as God *has called* each, in this manner let him walk" (7:17, NASB). The term *call* or *calling* relates to the effective gospel call in the Corinthians' lives, bringing them into fellowship with Jesus Christ (1:9). Paul considered this call, once received by the Corinthians, a permanent "set apart" relationship in Christ (1:2), being enjoyed no matter what situation of life the believer found himself in as he eagerly waited for the revelation of Jesus Christ (1:7, 8). What this means in practical terms is this: (1) the call of God through the gospel places one in Christ (1:1–9); (2) this gospel call fully embraces every life-detail of God's set-apart purpose for each saint (7:17–24); and (3) this sanctifying purpose of God, then, includes fitting each saint for ministry within the Body of Christ—whether formal or informal positions (12:1–31).

Assuming my understanding of Paul's usage of *call* and *calling* are accurate, there are two lingering questions to answer. First, if there is no distinct and separate vocational call to ministry, how are texts like Mark 1:20, Acts 13:1–4, and Romans 1:1 to be understood? Second, can a man absolutely know that he has been fitted by God for vocational ministry to lead the church if no additional call is required? This second question must be set aside until the first question is addressed.

The passages in question—such as Mark 1:20, Acts 13:1–4, and

Romans 1:1—are marked by the truth that certain men received a direct invitation from Jesus Christ to be a disciple and, in later days, an apostle (Mark 3:13–19; 6:30). By definition, the word *apostle* means "a delegate, messenger, one sent forth with orders." This term can be used in a broad or narrow sense. In the broad sense it may fulfill the definition as "one sent forth with orders"; however, the New Testament most often uses it in a technical or narrow sense. This narrow sense identifies a small group of men who were eyewitnesses of the resurrected Christ (Acts 1:21, 22), specifically called by Jesus Himself (Luke 6:12, 13), and identified in the New Testament as holding a special office, "an apostle of Christ Jesus" (Eph. 1:1, NASB). In his book *Systematic Theology*, Wayne Grudem explains that these "apostles had unique authority to found and govern the early church, and they could speak and write the words of God" (Eph. 2:20; 2 Pet. 3:1, 2).

Since these apostles met exclusive qualifications, their divine call into ministry is not to be considered a prototype for those who follow them into church leadership. These apostles were uniquely qualified and labeled "first" in the early church (1 Cor. 12:28). Their distinctive call to the ministry, their exceptional gifting, their direct reception of divine revelation, and their special enabling to write and speak the words of Christ were for the purpose of establishing the early church in truth and grace. Pastors and teachers today are called by the New Testament to trace their doctrine, but never their supernatural office or experiences (2 Cor. 12:12; 2 Tim. 3:10–17).

The Conclusion of *Call* in the Testaments

From the Old Testament, the call of God is acknowledged as sovereignly dispensed upon men for either particular acts of service (e.g., Bezalel, the skilled craftsman) or vocational ministry appointment (e.g., Moses and Samuel). In every case, God fulfills His own purpose as the initiator of the call and man is the responder. In the New Testament, this sovereign initiative continues unfettered, but with two significant points of clarity. First, the call of God is actually His effectual call in the gospel of Jesus Christ, and it is enjoyed by all believers. Second, this call encompasses all things within the believer's human existence: from salvation to sanctification, from fellowship to discipleship, from singleness to marriage, and from ministry to eldership. Therefore, the man desiring vocational ministry need not seek an additional call from God beyond what he has already received in Christ. So, with this being said, we may now address the second question: Can a man absolutely know that he has been fitted by God for vocational ministry to lead the church if no additional call is required?

The Ministry Call: Objective Requirements and Affirming Observations

There is no doubt that all believers are called to ministry. Paul was clear on this and used the body metaphor to explain this important truth—every member is important, and each is to do his part (Eph. 4:16; 1 Cor. 12:12–25). However, the Body needs leaders—human leaders—identified in Titus 1 as mature men (*elder*), gracious guardians (*bishop*), skilled managers (*steward*) who are appointed as leaders in the church. Paul considered these men "gifts of Christ" to His church (Eph. 4:7–11).

Not only are these men considered divine gifts, but Paul told the Ephesian elders that "the Holy Spirit has made you overseers, to shepherd the church of God which He purchased with His own blood" (Acts 20:28, NASB). This language of Paul could not be more emphatic, "the Holy Spirit *has made you*." This verb *has made* carries the idea of "to strategically place or carefully appoint." It is used in such important passages as Romans 4:17, where Paul quoted Genesis 17:5 and recalled what God had said to Abraham: "A father of many nations *have I made* you" (NASB); and in 1 Corinthians 3:10, where Paul defended his apostolic work and said, "Like a wise master builder *I laid* a foundation, and another is building on it" (NASB). This term was also used by Paul to explain that "God *has appointed* in the church, first apostles, second prophets, third teachers" (1 Cor. 12:28, NASB). In like manner, Paul used this word in his Acts message to the Ephesian elders to emphasize their strategic appointment by the Holy Spirit to oversee God's church. More weighty words could not be found in relation to the ministry.

The question remains, how does the Holy Spirit do this? How does the Spirit prepare, fit, and appoint men for church leadership? While this question is not determined by divine revelation or apostolic experiences, it may be unambiguously resolved by a careful analysis of two New Testament ingredients: objective requirements and affirming observations. These Biblical requirements and spiritual observations cooperate as a unified entity, and may both privately (within the heart of the one called) and publicly (within the body of the local church) demonstrate the call of God's Spirit upon a man for vocational ministry.

As you weigh these requirements and observations, you must not think that they are in a fixed chronological arrangement to be checked off as you would a grocery list. In fact, both parts need to be "syncretistically" viewed by the reader. What I mean by this is that each part works in harmony with the other and that within each part there is mutual dependence. So failure in one requirement will obstruct the whole. Therefore, carefully consider the five objective requirements and the five affirming observations as a unit that stands or falls together.

Objective requirements for the man God prepares and fits

The man the Holy Spirit appoints is a man who meets certain Biblical requirements. These may be accurately expressed as objective requirements because they can be seen in a man's life, as well as be evaluated by others. It is important to appreciate that these essential requirements that mark a man's life also allow room for spiritual progress and personal development. Paul made this clear to Timothy when he encouraged him to minister as "an example of those who believe," for in so doing "your progress [*prokoph*] will be evident to all" (1 Tim. 4:12, 15, NASB). In other words, these five requirements do not have to be fully developed in the life of a future church leader, but they must be evident in some form if he is to qualify for vocational ministry.

Integrity of life. The Biblical word *integrity* comes from the Hebrew term *tahm* and is often used in poetic literature such as Job 1:1, a *"blameless"* man; Psalm 37:37, "mark the *blameless* man;" and Song of Solomon 6:9, "my dove, my *perfect one*, is unique" (NASB). The idea of this term is not absolute perfection; rather, it identifies one as being whole, sound, complete, and morally innocent.

From this background, I borrow the term to identify the character of the man who is pursing the twenty-two qualifications named by Paul that are to mark an elder's life. In both 1 Timothy and Titus, Paul began the elder qualifications with an overarching term translated "above reproach" or "blameless." This term, as George Knight writes, identifies "the overall requirement" of the two passages, and "as such, a man would not be open to attack or criticism in terms of Christian life in general or in terms of characteristics that Paul goes on to name. This does not mean that an elder must be perfect, but it may be fairly said that each named characteristic marks his life." In other words, a man who is blameless is noted by his stubborn pursuit of integrity, for he knows, writes John MacArthur, that "a man is qualified because of who and what he *is*, not because of what he *does*."

Not a novice. Though this is a qualification found in the 1 Timothy list, it is also highlighted by Paul in the same book with the command, "Do not lay hands upon anyone too hastily" (1 Tim. 5:22, NASB). This idea emphasizes that new converts should not be considered for church leadership, for they must have a proven track record in their Christian life. As we have already seen in the Titus terms (*elder*, *bishop*, and *steward*), to be fit for such an office means to evince a life of maturity, grace, and skill. One vital point needs to be underscored, and this relates to the physical age of the one under consideration. Though Paul's letters do not state a minimum age for a pastor, Gene Getz observed, "It is not accidental that the word *elder* [used by Paul] in itself refers to age." However, several problems may immediately come to mind, such as, being older in age does not ensure maturity, nor does being young in age automatically signify immaturity.

While each of these problems may pose questions about the exact age of an elder, the real question is this: Is this man qualified to lead the church? The question is not about mental acumen or personal abilities, but it must be answered in light of the Titus terms meaning "mature leader," "gracious guardian," and "skilled manager." For these qualities to be observable in a man's life, it will take time, development, and local church experience. In general terms, it might be better (maybe, more Biblical) for men under the age of thirty-five to consider taking an associate position and develop under a godly, older leader. For this to happen, the local church must appreciate the immeasurable value of developing the next generation of pastors and leaders.

Skillful in teaching. The Greek term *didaktikos* is found two times in the New Testament (1 Tim. 3:2; 2 Tim. 2:24) and is best translated "skillful in teaching." This may be the only qualification of the twenty-two that relates to the actual function of the elder, and it clearly distinguishes the office of the bishop from the office of deacon in 1 Timothy 3. The ability to teach rests on three pillars.

Pillar 1: Skillful in teaching. This means that the elder evidences a lifestyle that works "hard at preaching and teaching" (1 Tim. 5:17, NASB). Any skill of life takes hard work, and no man will acquire preaching and teaching competence without a dogged pursuit of truth. This will mean late nights and early mornings. It will include at times saying no to recreation and entertainment. It will mean a firm and strong commitment to the tedious study of the words, theology, and original languages of the Bible. Therefore, a young man who desires a ministry of the Word will demonstrate a mental and emotional commitment to the study of God's Word alongside his passion to preach it.

Pillar 2: Gracious communication of God's truth. A skilled teacher has learned to couch his communication of the Scriptures with words of gentleness and in a spirit of patience (2 Tim. 2:24). There is firmness in his words by virtue of the word he is speaking (cf. 1 Tim. 1:3), but there is calmness and endurance in his delivery even with those who oppose what he says. This may seem difficult for a young man—maybe impossible—for no one likes opposition. As a young man watches his older pastor demonstrate these qualities, and as he gains ministry experience in such situations, he will learn how to effectively communicate God's truth to hurting souls.

Pillar 3: Sound doctrine and effective use of it. The elder is able "to refute those who contradict" (NASB) with "sound doctrine" just as "he has been taught" (Titus 1:9, NKJV). Paul was not mandating intellectual scholars for local church teaching positions, but he was asking for faithful students—men who hunger and thirst to know God's Word and who have proven their pursuit through study (whether formal or informal). In today's world, this can be most objectively observed in the life of a young man by reviewing his background in college and seminary. However, a college or seminary degree in itself does not qualify anyone to be a pastor. An education degree is accomplished by taking tests and writing papers. Such mental activity may earn academic favor, but it may also mask the spiritual deficiencies of the soul. Yet a plodding student in seminary who is sensitive to the Word, theology, and Biblical languages will usually continue this faithful pattern as he gains ministry experience. Time in ministry will prove the veracity of such a conclusion, but that is precisely the point for young preachers—they need time in local church ministry to develop and mature in their theological mind-set.

Marital and family considerations. Much has been written and said concerning the pastor and his family. It is significant that the New Testament considers the family a priority for the pastor. In fact Paul questioned, "If a man does not know how to manage his own household, how will he take care of the church of God?" (1 Tim. 3:5, NASB). In particular, the pastor must be "devoted to his wife," implying faithfulness in marriage. In addition, the pastor must have "faithful children" described as "not accused of dissipation or insubordination" (Titus 1:6, NKJV). Such a family will model the faith that Dad preaches and teaches. When a man seeks vocational ministry, his family will be the centerpiece of his testimony before the church. If he proves well at home in private, he will lead well in public as he manages the flock of God.

Church approval. The last objective requirement encompasses the other four. Young men who aspire to the ministry must demonstrate their life's commitment within the context of a local church. A young man's integrity, maturity of faith, skillfulness in teaching, and marital and family fidelity must all be viewed and valued by the local body. The church must witness a young man in action to verify that he fits Paul's description of a mature leader, gracious guardian, and skilled manager. The young man must establish that he can effectively lead people—working with them and not around them. He must demonstrate genuine submission to his own pastoral leadership, whether he personally agrees with every decision and action that is made. When his life displays such qualities in real-life situations, the church will gladly affirm his obvious call to ministry.

These objective requirements are the visible outworking of God's purpose in the life of a young man whom He has appointed for ministry. It is the high privilege and responsibility of the local church to evaluate and affirm these requirements as the members view the hands-on ministry of a developing elder. When a local church so operates, it works in union with its Head, and it cooperates with the larger Body of Christ preparing qualified men for church leadership.

Affirming observations for the man God prepares and fits

A final word needs to be said concerning the individual heart of the young man who desires vocational ministry. Though the objective requirements are necessary to validate the call of God upon a man, there are also private matters within the man's heart that he must consider. These are more subjective in nature, but they provide him personal affirmation that God is leading him toward ministry. These private observations work alongside the objective requirements and are subject to them. For example, a man is not called by God into the ministry by a private impression or experience without the consent of the local church. His private experiences may never trump integrity, maturity of faith, skillfulness in teaching, and family fidelity. Accordingly, because a man evidences some of the pastoral qualifications and has successfully completed seminary education does not mean he is automatically suited for a pastor role. Far from it!

We have already seen the indispensability of the objective requirements, but there must also be an internal work of the Spirit wooing and impressing the young man's heart that God is calling him into vocational ministry. It is true that this "secret call," as John Calvin called it, is subjective and will vary from person to person depending on each one's own maturity in the faith; however, as these subjective observations quietly work alongside the objective requirements, the call of God will be confirmed.

Word impression. As a man reads the Word, the Spirit begins to use it to direct his heart toward the ministry. With some men, it has been a Biblical story; with others, a short passage; and with some, a single verse. Yet through this Word impression, the man begins to sense that God's call for vocational ministry is upon his life. Over time the Word will dominate him—inexplicably capture his heart—and begin its mysterious work of perfecting him for this good work (2 Tim. 3:16, 17).

Spirit desire. As the Word begins to point a man toward the ministry, the Spirit begins to create and promote an intense desire to pursue the ministry. Paul wrote, "If any man aspires to the office of overseer, it is a fine work he desires to do" (1 Tim. 3:1, NASB). Paul used the term *aspire* (from *orego*), which is defined as "[to] stretch oneself, [or] reach out one's hand." This desire is sourced in the Spirit and seeks to exalt the glory of God in vocational ministry. Spurgeon colorfully made this point with the following words.

> Many young men have the same idea of being parsons as I had of being a huntsman—a mere childish notion that they would like the coat and the horn-blowing; the honour, the respect, the ease; and they are probably even fools enough to think, the riches of the ministry. (Ignorant beings they must be if they look for wealth in connection with the Baptist ministry.) The fascination of the preacher's office is very great to weak minds, and hence I earnestly caution all young men not to mistake whim for inspiration, and a childish preference for a call of the Holy Spirit.

Godly opinions. No one knows the heart of a man like those who are closest to him. As the aspiring young man converses with godly people around him about his deep longing for the ministry and what he seems to be sensing from the Lord, these folks will play a significant part in affirming his heart's direction. However, a caution is in order. Spurgeon once recalled a godly lady who tried to dissuade him from entering the ministry; he later wrote that others' opinions are neither "final nor infallible." Nevertheless, opinions do matter. Just as Barnabas came alongside John Mark (Acts 15:37–39), so the Lord will use people to encourage and guide young hearts seeking the ministry. It must be noted that those who love the Lord and who care deeply for an aspiring ministry candidate will be granted the privilege to speak into his life and encourage his future direction.

Providential circumstances. This category gets the most attention among those who are seeking the Lord's direction, and is often the ultimate court of appeal. Make no mistake, God is sovereign and He orchestrates "all things after the counsel of His will" (Eph. 1:11, NASB). While circumstances and experiences are valid markers in determining God's purpose, they must be weighed in concert with this entire paradigm. They may not be exalted above the other requirements or observations, and indeed they may not be used by themselves as a man's ultimate proof of decision. This is very important, especially when circumstances seem to discourage or even oppose his ministry desire. Men such as John Bunyan, Adoniram Judson, and William Cary came face-to-face with incredibly difficult circumstances that seemed absolutely insurmountable. However, none of these eminent saints took circumstances as the final appeal; rather, they appealed to the God of these circumstances. In their appeal they had to exercise patience and even pursue God's call when death seemed inevitable.

What this all means for the aspiring young man is that he will indeed have experiences—good and bad—but they must be balanced by the other components we have mentioned to properly analyze their value. Paul and Silas quickly learned that God's will includes both sweet and bitter circumstances, and their call into Europe did not depend on how easy or difficult the way might be (Acts 16). With time and experience, a young man will learn that circumstances have a part in God's will; however, just as "good circumstances" are not the leading indicator of God's call, so "bad circumstances" are not the termination of it.

Ministry experience. As stated throughout this essay, no man is prepared for vocational ministry without meaningful ministry in the local church. God uses ministry experience to shape a man, break a man, and encourage (sometimes stop) a man for local church leadership. When a young man gains experience, he develops right before the eyes of the church membership. This growth assures the hearts of all those to whom he is ministering that he is being fit by God for gospel ministry. Someone graduating from college or seminary and entering right into vocational work without having meaningful local church ministry is as strange as a medical doctor graduating from medical school and entering his chosen field without fulfilling an internship. It will not work in the medical field, and it usually will not work in the ministry. Spurgeon had a pastors' college attached to his church. He viewed it as a place to train men God had *already called*. He did not consider his college as a place where God called men to ministry. In his autobiography, Spurgeon inscribed his heartbeat for ministry-training with the following words, which need to be rehearsed by all those entering theological places of learning:

> We laid down, as a basis, the condition that a man must, during about two years, have been engaged in preaching, and must have some seals to his ministry, *before* we could entertain his application. No matter how talented or promising he might appear to be, the College could not act upon mere hopes, but must have evident marks of a Divine call, so far as human judgment can discover them. This became a main point with us, for we wanted, not men whom our tutors could make into scholars, but men whom the Lord had ordained to be preachers. [Emphasis mine.]

Vocational ministry is reserved for men whom God calls. Many are uncertain of what the call of God is, and how it actually is accomplished in the life of a man aspiring to ministry. Most notably, the New Testament does not seem to support the idea that a vocational call to ministry is separate from one's call in Christ through the gospel. So, this essay is offered to help us think through the manner in which God deals with those He has designed for leadership in the gospel ministry. There are objective Biblical requirements for ministry leaders, and there are more subjective personal observations that complement these objectives. Taken together in the context of a local church, the call of God will unambiguously be determined in the life of an aspiring minister of the gospel. Ultimately, it is God Who calls, and He will not leave Himself without a witness.

Take Action . . .
1. Evaluate yourself: Are you a man of integrity?
2. Teach a class or Bible study. Invite mature believers to participate, as well as new believers. Ask the mature believers to critique your skill in teaching, according to the three pillars.
3. Find a mentor from whom you can learn about courtship, marriage, and parenting, according to where you are in life.
4. If you are not yet a pastor, meet with your pastor or pastors to express your interest in pastoral ministry and to enlist their guidance.
5. Write your testimony of being led into the pastoral ministry. Include the portion of God's Word used by the Spirit to impress this ministry upon your heart, your Spirit-given desire, any human input, and any influential circumstances.
6. Write your "pastoral résumé." Take it to a godly leader, asking where there are holes in your experience. Pursue God's direction for filling those holes.

Discussion
1. In the opening verses of Titus, Paul used three terms to describe the man who would lead God's church: *elder* (*presbuterous*, 1:5), *overseer* (*episkopon*, 1:7), and *steward* (*oikonomon*, 1:7). What is the connotation of each word? What responsibilities are entailed in each role?
2. Do you agree or disagree that Acts 13:1–4 is the Biblical norm for a vocational call to ministry, and that this call is distinct to a man's initial call to salvation? Explain.
3. What qualifies a man for Biblical pastoral ministry?
4. How can a man know the difference between circumstantial opposition to his call to ministry and the Holy Spirit's closing the door to pastoral ministry?

For Further Study
Am I Called? by Dave Harvey, Crossway, 2012.
Autobiography by C. H. Spurgeon, volumes 1 and 2.
Brothers, We Are Not Professionals by John Piper, Broadman and Holman, 2002.
The Christian Ministry, 6th rep. ed., by Charles Bridges, Seeley, Burnside and Seeley, 1844.
The Glory of the Ministry by A. T. Robertson, Broadman Press, 1979.

Lectures to My Students by C. H. Spurgeon, Zondervan, 1954.

The Master's Plan for the Church by John MacArthur, Moody, 1991.

The Pastoral Epistles by George Knight III, Eerdmans, 1992. (This commentary belongs to The New International Greek Testament Commentary series.)

Preaching and Preachers by D. Martyn Lloyd-Jones, Zondervan, 1971.

The Reformed Pastor by Richard Baxter, Banner of Truth, 1974.

Sharpening the Focus of the Church by Gene Getz, David C. Cook, 1984.

Spiritual Leadership by J. Oswald Sanders, Moody, 1967.

2

Personal Spiritual Life
— Tim White

A teacher was helping one of her kindergarten students get his cowboy boots on before leaving for home. He had asked her for help, and she could see why. Even with her pulling and pushing, the boots just did not want to fit—they seemed too small. She persisted, and by the time she got the second boot on, she had worked up a sweat. She almost cried when the little boy said, "These are on the wrong feet."

It can be hard to tell with boots, so she looked closely. Sure enough, they were on the wrong feet. She tugged and pulled and finally pulled off the boots. She managed to keep her cool as together they worked to get the boots back on the right feet. Finally, just as she finished, he said, "You know, these aren't my boots."

She bit her tongue to keep from screaming. Once again she struggled to help him pull the ill-fitting boots off his feet. No sooner had they gotten the boots off, when he said, "See, they're my brother's boots, but my mom said I could wear them."

At that point, the teacher did not know if she should laugh or cry, but, mustering up what patience she had left, she wrestled the boots back on his feet. Finally, she finished. Helping him into his coat, she asked, "Now, where are your gloves?" He said, "I stuffed them in the toes of my boots."

If we are not careful as pastors and teachers of God's Word, we will lose our patience, burden, and love for our people. There is only one remedy for remaining effective in ministry: cultivating a spiritual life before God.

Cultivating the Spiritual Life

Charles Spurgeon, in his classic for pastors, *Lectures to My Students,* set a precedent when he titled his first chapter "The Minister's Self-watch." He based this chapter on Paul's exhortation to his apostolic representative Timothy, who was serving as a pastor: "Take heed unto thyself, and unto the doctrine" (1 Tim. 4:16, KJV). Spurgeon wrote twenty-eight chapters in *Lectures to My Students* on pastoral ministry. But before he instructed on the call to the ministry or sermon preparation or the use of gestures and illustrations in preaching, Spurgeon warned each pastor not to "neglect the culture of yourself."

How can you and I as pastors "take heed" to ourselves? How can we stay spiritual? How can we love God with all our heart? How can we love our people as ourselves? A fellow minister who was recently in the process of writing his resignation said to me, "My heart is no longer in this ministry." How can we keep our heart in what God has called us to do?

Conversion

Before we talk about what some writers call the "spiritual disciplines" or the "means of grace," I want to start where Spurgeon started in his first lesson to his pastoral students. Before all other advice, Spurgeon wrote of the need for the pastor to be regenerated, saying, "It should be one of our first cares that we ourselves be saved men."

Hopefully, few who read this chapter will need to trust Christ as their Savior, but most pastors know pastors who preached for years the good news without having received it themselves. I rebaptized one such pastor who had preached for decades and had sinners come to Christ under his preaching before he was converted. The first and most obvious means to cultivating the spiritual life is salvation.

Spiritual Disciplines

Next, to cultivate our spiritual life we must "exercise," or "train," ourselves in godliness. In 1 Timothy 4:7 Paul instructed Timothy to enter God's gym and spiritually work out. Paul used an athletic word when he wrote *exercise*. This English word comes from the Greek word *gumnazo*, from which we get *gymnasium* and *gymnastics*.

R. Kent Hughes based his book *Disciplines of the Godly Man* on 1 Timothy 4:7. He wrote:

> The statement from Paul to Timothy regarding spiritual discipline in 1 Timothy 4:7—"train yourself to be godly"—takes on not only transcending importance, but personal urgency.

> There are other passages which teach discipline, but this is the great classic text of Scripture. The word "train" comes from the word *gumnos*. . . . By New Testament times it referred to exercise and training in general. But even then it was, and is, a word with the smell of the gym in it—the sweat of a good workout. "Gymnasticize (exercise, work out, train) yourself for the purpose of godliness" conveys the feel of what Paul is saying. In a word he is calling for spiritual sweat.

The gym where I exercise has a wide range of ways to physically work out. Likewise, different spiritual exercises produce godliness. There are private spiritual exercises, such as private Bible reading, study, memorization, meditation, and prayer. Some would include fasting, silence, and solitude. There are also corporate spiritual disciplines, which include the public preaching of God's Word and worship. In *Systematic Theology,* Wayne Grudem discusses ten additional means of grace within the fellowship of a church: teaching of the Word, baptism, the Lord's Supper, prayer for one another, church discipline, giving, spiritual gifts, fellowship, evangelism, and personal ministry to individuals.

Before the Greek athletes competed, they removed every encumbrance. The writer of Hebrews exhorted believers "to lay aside every weight" (12:1, NKJV) so we can run the spiritual race God has set before us.

In their book *Spiritual Leadership,* Henry and Richard Blackaby discuss a series of sins that easily weigh down pastors. They point out that "every year thousands of leaders shipwreck their careers, their organizations, and their families by making careless, foolish choices," and they discuss ten pitfalls: pride, sexual sin, cynicism, greed, mental laziness, oversensitivity, spiritual lethargy, domestic neglect, administrative carelessness, and prolonged position holding.

I want to focus on only one: mental laziness. Homer Kent's commentary *The Pastoral Epistles* comments on Paul's request that Timothy bring books to Paul (2 Tim. 4:13) when he comes to see him in prison. Kent wrote: "Books are tools. The quality of some sermons heard today makes one suspicious that some preachers haven't read a serious book since they graduated from seminary." *Spiritual Leadership* provides an example from the ministry of D. L. Moody. Although Moody was having an enormously successful evangelistic ministry and was one of the most famous religious leaders of his day, "he had grown spiritually and intellectually malnourished. He had been continually preaching, but he had not been learning. . . . Moody realized he had told people everything he knew and that he had nothing new to say." So he went home and took on no major speaking engagements "until he felt he had studied enough to have fresh, new insights from God's Word to share with people. He set a rigid schedule that included six hours of study every morning. Even after he began traveling once again, Moody carried a small library with him. He was determined that despite the press of people and responsibilities upon his time, he could not afford to stop learning and still be effective as a spiritual leader."

D. L. Moody overcame mental laziness. He was willing to make serious lifestyle and schedule changes in order to spend time in God's Word for his own spiritual advancement and so he could advance others spiritually. Do you need to make this life-altering change?

The Spiritual Discipline of Taking in the Word of God

One of the spiritual disciplines that God uses, and the most important, as a means of grace in our lives is the intake of His Word. We cannot be spiritual without the Holy Spirit–inspired Word of God, which is "profitable . . . that the man of God may be perfect, throughly furnished unto all good works" (2 Tim. 3:16, 17, KJV). Are we using every tool available to us to learn and grow with the passion of Paul for the Word of God? Paul wanted to finish his last few days studying and feeding his soul with the researched Word of God and books. What precious times Paul must have experienced with God's Word as he faced imminent martyrdom in that cold, damp prison in Rome.

Benjamin Breckinridge Warfield (1851–1921) was professor of theology at Princeton Theological Seminary from 1887 to 1921. Warfield is considered the last of the great Princeton theologians before the split in 1929 that formed Westminster Seminary under the leadership of J. Gresham Machen. Warfield delivered a sermon to the pastoral students at the Autumn Conference of Princeton Theological Seminary on October 4, 1911. The sermon was titled "The Religious Life of the Theological Student." What Warfield preached to the pastoral students needs to be heard by pastors today who are still students of God's Word.

Warfield began his sermon: "A minister must be both learned and religious [after reading the sermon, one knows that by *religious* Warfield meant *godly*]. It is not a matter of choosing between the two. He must study, but he must study as in the presence of God and not in a secular spirit. He must recognize the privilege of pursuing his studies in the environment where God and salvation from sin are the air he breathes." Oh, that all of us students of the Word, whether students in preparation or pastors in their studies, had this appreciation. The theological student is training to be "apt to teach." This requires learning. But he must also be godly.

There should be no antithesis between being able to teach and being godly. Warfield quoted someone who said, "Ten minutes on your knees will give you a truer, deeper, more operative knowledge of God than ten hours over your books. . . . Why should you turn from God when you turn to your books, or feel that you must turn from your books in order to turn to God?"

Warfield warned theological students (and pastors) of the danger of constant contact with divine things. They can become like the Old Testament priests who handled and moved the tabernacle furniture, around which God manifested His glory, as just mere earthly materials. If our study of theology and God's Word has become commonplace, then we have become "weary of God."

The Word of God is not a worker's manual with which we become skilled technicians. Paul called what he preached "the word of his grace, which is able to build you up" (Acts 20:32, KJV). The Word is a means of God ministering His all-sufficient grace into our lives. If our theological studies or sermon preparation is not causing us to grow in holiness, then we are hardening. Warfield noted that our study of God's Word should be a "religious exercise out of which [we] draw every day enlargement of heart, elevation of spirit, and adorning delight in [our] Maker and [our] Savior."

The Word Feeds Meditation

How can our study of God's Word—either in devotions, sermon preparation, or even in our general reading—usher us into the presence of God? How can our study and preaching of God's Word actually be a means of grace as it was in Paul's life (Acts 20:32)? One answer is meditation on God's Word. It is easy for us who are bombarded with information *not* to meditate on or process all the input to which we are exposed. We are inundated with news from our car radios, e-mails at work, texts and tweets from friends, website surfing, podcasts, TV, and endless cell phone calls.

How can we overcome the endless competitors for our time and attention and grow in the grace and knowledge of God's Word? Meditation! Donald Whitney in *Spiritual Disciplines for the Christian Life* defines meditation as "deep thinking on the truths and spiritual realities revealed in Scripture for the purposes of understanding, application, and prayer." He illustrated it this way:

> Hearing God's Word is like one dip of the tea bag into the cup. Some of the tea's flavor is absorbed by the water [you], but not as much as would occur with a more thorough soaking of the bag [God's Word]. In this analogy, reading, studying, and memorizing God's Word are represented by additional plunges of the tea bag into the cup. The more frequently the tea enters the water, the more effect it has. Meditation, however, is like immersing the bag completely and letting it steep until all the rich tea flavor has been extracted and the hot water is thoroughly tinctured reddish brown.

Spiritual success according to the Bible is promised only in relationship to the Bible and specifically in regard to meditating on God's Word (Ps. 1:1–3; Josh. 1:8).

Jonathan Edwards, the eighteenth-century theologian and pastor, cultivated his spiritual life through meditation on God's Word. Whitney related an example: Edwards wondered how he could best use the time he had to spend on horseback. So "he worked out a plan for pinning a small piece of paper to a given spot on his coat, assigning the paper a number and charging his mind to associate a subject with that piece of paper. After a ride as long as the three-day return from Boston he would be bristling with papers. Back in his study, he would take off the papers methodically, and write down the train of thought each slip recalled to him."

Just like Jonathan Edwards, we have to discipline ourselves to creatively use our time wisely to meditate on God's Word.

Meditation Feeds Prayer

Meditation equips us to apply God's Word. Just as meditating should take place after hearing, reading, studying, and memorizing God's Word, prayer should be the practical application of meditation. Thomas Manton wrote of this process, "The word feeds meditation and meditation feeds prayer."

Daniel, in the Babylonian Captivity, was meditating on Jeremiah 25, as Daniel 9:1 and 2 record. When he understood the significance of the passage to his life and circumstance, he set his face "unto the Lord God, to seek by prayer and supplications, with fasting, and sackcloth, and ashes" (KJV). Meditation fed one of the most remarkable prayers in God's Word, found in Daniel 9:3–19.

David also benefited from his meditation, which led to this outburst of praise: "Oh, how I love Your law! It is my meditation all the day. You, through Your commandments, make me wiser than my enemies; for they are ever with me. I have more understanding than all my teachers, for Your testimonies are my meditation. I understand more than the ancients, because I keep Your precepts" (Ps. 119:97–100, NKJV).

One on my favorite psalms is Psalm 103, which is a praise psalm. In this psalm of pure praise (there is not one negative comment or complaint), David praised God for what He has done and Who He is. Sometimes at night I join David in praising God. I simply meditate my way through the psalm, praising Him for His works (forgiveness, healing, deliverance, and spiritual satisfaction; 103:1–5) and for His attributes (holiness, justice, mercy, eternity, and sovereignty; 103:6–22).

When I remember what God said through Asaph in Psalm 50:23, praising God becomes an act of worship: "Whoever offers praise glorifies Me" (NKJV). It is the meditation on God's Word, however, that leads to the prayer and praise that enable me to bring glory and delight to God.

As a result of his recorded meditations, Jonathan Edwards' words still impact our lives to this day. If we would commit ourselves to this lost art of concentration, God could use us to be agents of change in the lives of those to whom He has called us to minister.

We pastors have the greatest advantage in cultivating our spiritual lives because we are privileged to study God's Word as a major part of our ministry. We spend more time in God's Word than in administration or counseling or visitation. When we study God's Word as in the presence of God, mediate on it, delight in it, and then pray it back to Him in praise, the Word truly is "the word of His grace, which is able to build you [us] up" (Acts 20:32, NKJV).

Take Action . . .
1. Be sure you are a born-again Christian (John 3).
2. Evaluate your private spiritual "training program." Where are you strong? weak?
3. Evaluate your faithfulness to corporate spiritual disciplines.
4. Set up safeguards to protect yourself from the ten leaders' pitfalls into which too many leaders crash.
5. Ask yourself if your study has given you fresh, new insights from God's Word to share with people. If not, do what you must to make a change.
6. If you do not have one, design a plan for reading, memorizing, and meditating on specific passages from God's Word.

Discussion
1. Robert Murray M'Cheyne said, "Remember you are God's sword. . . . A holy minister is an awful weapon in the hand of God." How is a pastor God's sword?
2. How does a pastor balance sharpening his professional skills with "taking heed" to his likeness to Christ?

For Further Study
Disciplines of a Godly Man by R. Kent Hughes, Crossway, 1991.
Knowing Scripture by R. C. Sproul, InterVarsity Press, 1977.
Lectures to My Students by C. H. Spurgeon, Zondervan, 1954.
The Religious Life of Theological Students by B. B. Warfield, P and R Publishing, 1992.
Spiritual Disciplines for the Christian Life by Donald S. Whitney, NavPress, 1991.
Spiritual Leadership by Henry and Richard Blackaby, Broadman and Holman, 2001.
"Surprised by the Appearances of Love" by Stephen Davey, 2007, available at wisdomonline.org.
Systematic Theology: An Introduction to Biblical Doctrine by Wayne Grudem, Zondervan, 1994.
The Works of Thomas Manton by Thomas Manton, Maranatha Publications.

3

Marriage and Family
— Mike Peck

Ministry, home, and family rank highest in priorities for pastors who love the Lord. Actually the pastor's family and ministry share a lot in common. The Lord Jesus must be the center and builder of both. Following Him requires the pastor's intentional involvement and unmistakable diligence. Carelessness brings eventual ruin to both home and ministry.

The good news is that the pastor's marriage and parenting do not have to be perfect! The bad news is, if the pastor and his wife have a poor marriage or if their parenting skills are deficient, his failure in the ministry is almost certain. The bishop must be "blameless" (1 Tim. 3:2, KJV), which means there must be no blatant, obvious defects in his character, marriage, parenting, or ministry. This sad truth really hit home for Pastor Mark early on a Sunday morning.

It was going to be a great Sunday! Then an early morning phone call left Pastor Mark shattered and stunned. He listened in disbelief as Jim, a good friend who pastored a church downstate, told him that he would be resigning in the morning service. His adulterous relationship of seven months had been discovered. Mark was devastated and wondered, "How could this happen?"

Several hours later another morning service was well under way, with Pastor Mark seated on the platform. Behind him the choir powerfully sang of the greatness and glory of God. The congregational song that followed was a strong declaration of determination to be faithful to this glorious God. As the singing continued, Mark spotted his precious wife and two little boys. His youngest son waved and grinned at him. A sudden tsunami of emotion swept over the young pastor. He was visibly shaken and wept softly. Folks in the congregation knew something was terribly wrong.

A hush swept over the church family as Pastor Mark stepped to the pulpit. He nearly crumpled as he told them of the phone call. Gaining his composure, he took the church family to 1 Timothy 3:1–7. Tenderly he explained that the office of pastor demands blameless leadership both in public ministry and private living in the home. He vowed with the Lord's help to be the best pastor possible by first becoming the best husband and father he could be.

By now, most were tearful. Pastor Mark continued, "I know that strong ministries and strong marriages are vitally connected. So I want everyone to know how much I love my wife and treasure my children. I promise to seek the Lord's guidance and wisdom as I lead my precious family and shepherd this dear church."

That morning service was stirring. Many couples made commitments to the Lord and their families. The journey of a lifetime began.

Many years later, Pastor Mark remembers well that bittersweet day. While still saddened by the sinful failure of his friend, he now quietly reflects, "From the ashes that morning, God worked in my heart and home. Today my wife is still my very best friend, and my children know how much I love them."

There would be no shortcuts. No one living in the parsonage would be perfect. However, a wonderful work began that Sunday morning long ago. It is the same consistent, diligent work every wise pastor undertakes. Here are a few of the powerful things Mark purposed in his heart that day and lived out over decades of pastoral ministry.

His Office as the Overseer

Paul spoke tenderly but pointedly in 1 Timothy 3:1–7. He reminded Timothy of the vital link between being a loving leader at home and a legitimate leader at church. Strong, successful ministries and loving, consistent leadership at home go hand in hand. Thankfully the pastor does not have to be perfect, only blameless (3:2).

His call is inescapable (3:1a). The "desire" or call of God upon the life of a man is that pull that overrules all the excuses and overcomes all the obstacles. It is the overwhelming conviction that God has called him to that good work that he absolutely must do. This wonderful work requires right leadership at home, which qualifies his ministry in public (3:5).

His office is overseeing (3:1b). While most pastors do not go by the title of bishop, this truly describes his role as the "overseer or superintendent." The overseeing pastor must develop a keen eye to spot situations that demand his attention both at home and in the church. He leaves nothing important to chance, hoping problems will somehow go away.

As the bishop at church and at home, he is intentionally involved. This does not mean that he micromanages everything. It does mean, however, that he is not withdrawn or disinterested.

His work is good (3:1c). Few positions in life compare to that of the bishop or pastor. Sometimes he experiences frustration, heartache, joy, and gladness all wrapped up in just one day. In the lives of many people, he shares in their deepest of tragedies as well as in times of greatest joy. Often exhausting, the ministry is still a good work.

His home life legitimizes his ministry (3:2, 4, 5). Paul clearly expressed a foundational truth with which every blameless pastor must come to terms. To be a good and successful pastor at church first requires a man to be a good and successful husband and father at home. Timothy was asked the probing question, "For if a man know not how to rule his own house, how shall he take care of the church of God?" (3:5, KJV). His house and God's church are the two places that cry out for the pastor's loving, consistent, intentional involvement and leadership.

I had a lot to get done, as radio scripts were due, my schedule was nearly packed, and, of course, Sunday was coming! The messages were started, but had a long way to go! An emergency counseling situation demanded my immediate attention and left me emotionally drained. A dear person who just needed "a moment" to speak with her pastor kept me on the phone a long time. I remember wanting to scream, "Help! What a day You and I are having, Lord!"

Just then, at the open door of my study, a quiet voice said, "Hi, Dad." There stood one of my young sons. His voice quivered as he said, "Well, Dad, I finally hit the ball. But it flew backwards and landed on the hood of your car." Tears gushed as he choked out the words, "Sorry, Dad."

The demands of ministry and the delight of family met that day in a moment locked in my memory. If I were to successfully oversee and shepherd the church, I must first oversee and shepherd my family. Here was a teachable moment that any overseeing dad had to seize. Often it is the little moments that count the most. By the way, it was a pretty good dent!

When such teachable, sometimes interrupting moments come, godly pastors and wise dads do not act frustrated and respond in anger. Intentional oversight demands loving attention and involvement, characterized by godliness and graciousness.

His Marriage as the Model

The straightforward, easy to understand teaching given to Timothy and Titus requires lifelong commitment. If the pastor is married, he must be "the husband of one wife" (1 Tim. 3:2; Titus 1:6, KJV). The counsel is good for every husband, but essential for the bishop. His heart is captivated by one woman only—his wife. He is a one-woman kind of man.

He implements safeguards, refusing to fantasize about other women. He is concerned about and appreciates the ladies in the church, but he never even approaches the line of being inappropriate, because in his heart there is room for only one. His wife knows she is cherished. She is reassured by his love and devotion. His ministry may be busy and demanding, but she knows, "My beloved is mine, and I am his" (Song of Sol. 2:16, KJV).

While there are no perfect marriages, a fun, vibrant, close, godly, and growing marriage modeled before the congregation is a very powerful illustration that is hard to ignore. This kind of pastoral marriage is never flaunted. Rather, the genuine love and commitment to the Lord and to each other are quietly and faithfully lived out daily.

A model of knowing. "Likewise, ye husbands, dwell with them according to knowledge" (1 Pet. 3:7a, KJV). Literally, the husband makes his abode by actively, intentionally knowing his wife in greater and more intimate ways. The wise pastor must ask himself, "How much do I really know my wife?" A man often assumes he knows his wife well. Usually he doesn't. A wise husband invests time and energy learning more about the desires, fears, concerns, and dreams of his wife.

A model of honoring. "Giving honour unto the wife" (1 Pet. 3:7b, KJV). This goes far beyond just opening the car door for her, although that is not a bad idea! It is grasping the preciousness of his wife being a gift from the Lord. Her value goes beyond just what she does. It is who she is and the special person God intends her to become.

Such honor will be consistently demonstrated in appreciation ("I thank God for you"), affection ("I want to grow closer to you and become more intimate with you"), and affirmation ("I cherish you; I want you to find fulfillment in our marriage, strength in our team role as parents, and joy in growing into your opportunities as a pastor's wife").

In his typically hectic week, the wise pastor regularly stops long enough to ask himself, "Do I daily honor my wife in these three areas?"

A model of building. "Being heirs together of the grace of life; that your prayers be not hindered" (1 Pet. 3:7c, KJV). An heir has part in the inheritance. Here a husband and wife are called "heirs together." What a beautiful picture of life being tenderly connected and sharing together, which results in unhindered prayers.

Every day married couples build either walls or bridges. Thoughtless actions, hurtful words, and growing resentment build walls, pushing couples farther apart. On the other hand, intentional kindness, emotional connection, and unconditional love that reach out to each other are bridges bringing couples closer together. Walls are wonderful for prisons, but not for marriages.

Hundreds of years ago Malachi cried out to the couples whose marriages were failing. They presented their offerings with real tears (Mal. 2:13). Yet God didn't regard them because they were dealing treacherously in their marriages (Mal. 2:14). Callously they built walls resulting in the tragedy of divorce.

God told Malachi, "Because the LORD hath been witness between thee and the wife of thy youth, against whom thou hast dealt treacherously: yet is she thy companion and the wife of thy covenant" (2:14, KJV). Beautifully God used two key words to describe the building of a bridge that intentionally reaches out to the marriage partner. He speaks of the oneness (2:15) of marriage through the pictures of companionship and covenant.

Malachi reminds the husband that his wife is his companion (2:14). A companion speaks of "being united, or closely associated with another." It is an emotional connection that grows through touches of endearment, actions of thoughtfulness, moments shared together, words that speak of value and worth, carefulness in listening as well as communicating, memories made together, and, most certainly, times of worship and prayer together.

Meaningful, intimate companionship grows from viewing marriage as a covenant. In premarital counseling, pastors remind couples that marriage is not a contract with loopholes and ways to escape. It is a covenant (2:14), which means "the pledging of one's life and giving it to another." The husband and wife give themselves to each other with no strings attached or contingencies to be met. Daily this covenantal companionship must be reinforced by deliberate acts of building bridges to each other. Wise pastors take inventory asking, "Today did I build a bridge of emotional connection with my wife, my covenantal companion? If I didn't build a bridge, then probably I built a wall."

A model of loving. "Husbands, love your wives, even as Christ also loved the church, and gave himself for it" (Eph. 5:25, KJV). Paul painted a striking picture of Christ's awesome unconditional love. This is how the godly pastor must love his wife!

Such unconditional love moves him to give himself without reservation to her (5:25). Though he has many clamoring for his attention, his dear wife holds a place held by no one else (5:26a). His love reassures her. She will not become a bitter pastor's wife, but will grow into the godly woman the Lord wants her to be (5:26b, 27).

How does the pastor demonstrate such love? There are several things loving pastor-husbands consistently do. Schedules are managed wisely. Conflicts are quietly resolved. Forgiveness and fellowship flourish. Good communication takes place. Dating occurs regularly. Laughter abounds. Memories are made. Dreams are shared. Intimacy is created. Intimacy is not so much a specific act of sexuality, although that is important. It is, rather, the closeness of being totally exposed emotionally as well as physically. Solomon bluntly said, "Be thou ravished always with her love" (Prov. 5:19, KJV).

A model of leading. "For the husband is the head of the wife" (Eph. 5:23, KJV). This obviously does not mean that he is the dictator and she salutes as she snaps to his command! Rather this headship is the loving leadership of the man under the headship of Christ of whom Philippians 2:7 says, He "took upon him the form of a servant" (KJV). Such servant-like headship makes the spiritual leader a delight to his wife and family.

The servant leader seeks the well-being of his loved ones. He reads the Word and heeds it. He not only leads in times of devotion and worship with the family, he prays with his wife apart from the children. She senses that he protects her by guarding his heart from spiritual enemies that would harm his marriage and home. He encourages her with the joy that they are traveling together on the journey of a lifetime. He is a spiritual leader at church and at home.

Nothing is as heart wrenching and confusing as the failed marriage of the pastor who gave wise advice at church and lived unwisely at home. Likewise, nothing compares to the joy that comes in years of faithful, consistent godly living in the pulpit as well as the parsonage!

His Parenting as a Pattern

The way the pastor raises his children will either enhance his ministry or detract from it. While the pastor's children are not going to be perfect and must not be held to a different standard from other Christian homes, successful parenting is a requirement for successful pastoral ministries. How does the pastor's parenting become a pattern for others?

He manages his house. "One that ruleth well his own house" (1 Tim. 3:4a, KJV). The word pictures in this brief statement are compelling. The idea of "ruling" is "superintending, protecting, guarding, as well as managing by being intentionally involved in the life of each child." This superintending is to be done "well," which means "beautifully or excellently." Last, the word "house" is the precious "abiding place of persons forming a family."

The directions are very clear. The pastor is to manage his family in an excellent and beautiful manner. He does not use his children's failures as sermon illustrations, nor does he flaunt their successes. He protects his home. Together they grow as a family.

He controls his young children. "Having his children in subjection with all gravity" (3:4b, KJV). What a great concept. But how does it work practically? The heart of the issue lies in the picture of the words "children," the pursuit of "subjection," and the practice of "gravity."

Paul's use of the word "children," *teknon,* is that of "a little born one." Here young children are the focus of attention. "Subjection" is the consistent, relentless, sometimes seemingly never-ending pursuit of bringing the young child into compliance and obedience. "Gravity" has to do with the practice of teaching his child to respect Mommy and Daddy as well as the Lord. This must be learned early in a child's life. Such respect will continue into adulthood.

Someday the pastor's children will grow up and talk about their dad. What are they going to say? Frightening, isn't it? They should be able to say the following things: My dad really has me in his heart (Mal. 4:6). My dad loves not only me, he really loves my mom as well (Eph. 5:25–33). My dad taught me that the true meaning of success is to do God's will (Ps. 143:10). My dad insisted on my obedience because he delights in me. I am of great value to him (Prov. 3:11, 12). My dad never treated me as an inconvenience or expense. He often tells me that I am a gift from God to him (Gen. 33:5; Ps. 127).

He sees the connection. "If a man know not how to rule his own house, how shall he take care of the church of God?" (3:5, KJV). The connection between his parenting skills at home and good leadership at church is inescapable. He is intentionally overseeing and involved. "A one-woman kind of man" describes his vibrant marriage. The godly pastor wisely manages his household as he wisely cares for the church.

The Lord Jesus said, "If ye know these things, happy are ye if ye do them" (John 13:17, KJV).

The Pastor's Heart and Prayer

> Lord, at times I feel overwhelmed.
> Your call is incredible. Really!
> My wife and children bless me.
> I so want to be a good husband, father, and pastor.
> I listen to the incredible prayers of my little children.
> They're so full of faith and excitement.
> I want to trust You in the same way.
> Everything I have really belongs to You.
> Lord, keep me from sin and failure.
> You are awesome!
> Guide and guard me, Lord, for Your glory.

"As for me and my house, we will serve the LORD" (Josh. 24:15, KJV).

Take Action . . .

1. Make both a written and a spoken commitment to your family to be the best husband, father, and pastor possible.
2. Recall the last time a family member spoke to you. Were you listening and involved, or withdrawn and disinterested?
3. Summarize the last teachable moment you had with one of your children.
4. Plan a fun outing for just you and your wife.
5. Tear down any walls between you and your wife.

Discussion

1. What characterizes a growing, vibrant marriage? Does that describe your marriage?
2. What safeguards can a husband implement in his life and ministry, assuring his wife that he is a one-woman kind of man?
3. What are ways to express to your teenage children your gratitude that

the Lord brought them to you? your adult children? your school-age children? your preschool children?
4. How can a pastor wisely manage his schedule to ensure quantity and quality time for his family?

For Further Study

Connecting: Developing Closeness on the Journey of a Lifetime by Michael Peck, Baptist Church Planters, 2011.

Family Matters: Marriage (2009), *Family Matters: Parenting* (2009), and *Family Matters: Family Life* (2008) by David and Carolyn Culver, Regular Baptist Press.

Impact Parenting: Equipping Children to Navigate Life by John and Daria Greening, Regular Baptist Press, 2002.

When Sinners Say I Do: Discovering the Power of the Gospel for Marriage by David Harvey, Shepherd Press, 2007.

Visit RegularBaptistPress.org for additional marriage and parenting resources.

4

The Example of Character and Integrity
— Matthew Morrell

In the early days of my pastoral ministry, I was very conscious of my youth. Because of my youth, I did not have the experience of other local church pastors. Because of my youth, I did not have the expertise of my Bible college and seminary professors. Because of my youth, I felt I must rely upon my education and my energy and my eloquence.

However, none of those properties is a Biblical priority for the pastor. Rather, Paul charged the young pastor Timothy regarding his example, "Let no one despise your youth, but be an example to the believers" (1 Tim. 4:12, NKJV). Similarly, Paul told the young pastor Titus, "In everything set them an example by doing what is good" (Titus 2:7, NIV). In fact, Paul's instruction to Timothy and Titus regarding their example was the very practice of Paul himself. To the Philippians Paul wrote, "Join with others in following my example, brothers, and take note of those who live according to the pattern we gave you" (Phil. 3:17, NIV), and "the things which you learned and received and heard and saw in me, these do" (Phil. 4:9, NKJV). To the Corinthians Paul said the same: "Follow my example, as I follow the example of Christ" (1 Cor. 11:1, NIV; cf. 4:16). Paul also repeated this theme to the Thessalonians: "You know what kind of men we were among you for your sake. And you became followers of us and of the Lord" (1 Thess. 1:5, 6, NKJV). Finally, lest one believe this idea is strictly Pauline, it was Peter who exhorted pastors to be "examples to the flock" (1 Pet. 5:1–3, NKJV).

Confronted with this priority for my ministry, I was forced to consider what my example would look like and what shape my example would take. My example would not be seen in the charisma of my personality, but in the character of my person. My example would not demonstrate all that I could do, but would reveal the core of who I was. My example would be the external validation of my internal character and integrity, whether good or bad. Ultimately, my example would qualify or disqualify me from pastoral ministry, for a pastor must be blameless and above reproach (Titus 1:6, 7; 1 Tim. 3:2).

For this reason, Paul called the young pastor Timothy to be an example "in word, in conduct, in love, in spirit, in faith, in purity" (1 Tim. 4:12, NKJV). These six prepositional phrases were not meant to coerce Timothy's habits, but to convict Timothy's heart. The priority of Timothy's example was not just a matter of his practice, it was a matter of the character and integrity of his person.

First Timothy 4:12 makes it clear that a pastor must be an example to his people in speech, conduct, love, faith, and purity.

Example in Speech

For the pastor who spends his days preaching, teaching, speaking, counseling, and talking with people, the statistical probability of erring with his tongue is high! In fact, James 3:2 says it is only the perfect man who does not err in what he says.

Even the most careful pastor is prone to slip with his speech, for "out of the abundance of the heart the mouth speaks" (Matt. 12:34, NKJV; Luke 6:45). Consequently, the pastor's character and integrity are critical to the governing of his tongue.

Often the pastor is privy to a lot of information about his people's faults and failures. It takes discretion to maintain confidences with that information, and it takes discipline to not speak freely. Who should be told? How much should they be told? When should they be told? Why should they be told?

Often the pastor is motivated to exaggerate the truth to impress his peers with the success of his ministry. At conferences and fellowships, a pastor is tempted to spin his story and stretch the truth to assure others that his ministry is successful.

Often the pastor is quick to speak when he would be wise to listen. The impulse is to talk. After all, the more a pastor talks, the more effective he will be, because the more he can communicate truth! However, the Bible's mandate is to "be swift to hear, slow to speak" (James 1:19, NKJV). In fact, there have been many times when my silence has been commended as my wisdom (Prov. 17:28).

Often the pastor is prone to grumble and complain about the grumbling and complaining of his people. Alas, Moses was guilty of this very thing in Numbers 11 when he expressed his displeasure to God over Israel's displeasure of him (vv. 11–14).

Whether Paul was referring to a man's personal conversations or to his formal teaching, 1 Timothy 4:12 demands that the pastor must be an example in his speech.

Example in Conduct

There are few things worse than a discrepancy between the pastor's words and his works. That is a classic case of hypocrisy—talking the talk, but not walking the walk. Jesus warned people about this error in Matthew 23:1–3: "Then Jesus spoke to the multitudes and to His disciples, saying: The scribes and the Pharisees sit in Moses' seat. Therefore whatever they tell you to observe, that observe and do, but do not do according to their works; for they say, and do not do" (NKJV).

The problem of hypocrisy among spiritual leadership has persisted over the centuries of church history. For that reason Charles Spurgeon wrote in his *Lectures to My Students,* "Actions . . . speak louder than words, so an ill life will effectually drown the voice of the most eloquent ministry. After all, our truest building must be performed with our hands; our characters must be more persuasive than our speech." It is easy to stand behind a pulpit with boldness and charge a congregation with its moral obligations before God. It is an entirely different thing to model those convictions in a pastor's personal and public life. This endeavor demands true character and integrity.

The story is told about a preacher from many years ago who was traveling by bus. Upon boarding the bus, he gave the bus driver a dollar. While the rate was seventy-five cents, the bus driver gave the pastor thirty-five cents in return, and the pastor made his way to his seat. Once seated, the preacher noticed the ten-cent error in his favor. After pausing for a moment, he got up and approached the bus driver, stating that he had been given more change than he was owed. The bus driver said, "I knew I gave you too much change. I was in your church last week and heard you preach on honesty, so I just wanted to see if you practice what you preach!"

If the pastor's public pulpit ministry does not square with his private personal life, his integrity is lost and his credibility is destroyed. Rather, his conduct ought to be "honorable among the Gentiles" (1 Pet. 2:12, NKJV). His conduct ought to be marked as "a good testimony among those who are outside, lest he fall into reproach" (1 Tim. 3:7, NKJV). His conduct ought to "be worthy of the gospel of Christ" (Phil. 1:27, NKJV).

In his book *The Reformed Pastor,* Richard Baxter said:

> It is a palpable error of some ministers, who make such a disproportion between their preaching and their living; who study hard to preach exactly, and study little or not at all to live exactly. All the week long is little enough, to study how to speak two hours; and yet one hour seems too much to study how to live all the week. They are loath to misplace a word in their sermon, or to be guilty of any notable infirmity, (and I blame them not, for the matter is holy and weighty,) but they make nothing of misplacing affections, words, and actions, in the course of their lives. Oh how curiously have I heard some men preach; and how carelessly have I seen them live!

Example in Love

In 1 Corinthians 13 Paul stretched the limits of our imagination to illustrate that nothing is more important than agape love. Even the most eloquent (v. 1), educated and effective (v. 2), or effacing and enduring (v. 3) pastor is nothing without agape love.

For that reason, Paul shined the light of agape love through a prism to show us a spectrum of that love—fifteen colors and hues, each ray a facet or a property of love. In the Greek language these properties are expressed as verbs. They do not focus on what love *is,* so much as on what loves *does* or does not *do*. Agape love is active, not abstract. For instance, as outlined in the following chart, love doesn't simply feel patience, it practices patience.

	The Character of Love in 1 Corinthians 13	
13:4a	Is patient	The patient man is long-suffering, or long-tempered. The patient man is one who has been wronged and who has the power to avenge himself but does not.
13:4b	Is kind	Just as patience will endure anything from others, kindness will give anything to others—even to its enemies.
13:4c	Is not jealous	While Jonathan had every cause to be jealous of David, the Bible says he would have willingly sacrificed his life for David: "He loved him as he loved his own soul" (1 Sam. 20:17, NKJV).
13:4d	Does not brag	Bragging is the other side of jealousy. While jealousy is my wanting what you have, bragging is trying to make you want what I have.
13:4e	Is not proud	The Corinthians were spiritual show-offs, puffed up in their own wisdom and boastful of their own giftedness. One who loves another is not concerned with his own importance.
13:5a	Is not rude	When the Corinthians met to celebrate the Lord's Table, it was "first come, first served," leaving some without anything, while others became drunk (1 Cor. 11). At other times, the Corinthians acted rudely toward each other by interrupting each other in their exercise of the gift of tongues (1 Cor. 14).
13:5b	Is not self-seeking	The man of love does not promote his own rights among those around him, but ought to think of his responsibilities toward those around him (Phil. 2:3, 4).

The Character of Love in 1 Corinthians 13

13:5c	Is not angered	Because love is not jealous, proud, rude, or self-seeking, love cannot be angered.
13:5d	Does not record wrongs	It is amazing how long a person can carry a grudge and how quickly and specifically he can remember the wrongs suffered at the hand of another.
13:6a	Does not delight in evil	Love never takes satisfaction in sin—one's own sin or another's sin.
13:6b	Rejoices in the truth	Love cannot tolerate that which is false, but celebrates that which is righteous and true.
13:7a	Bears all things	Love covers, supports, and protects another person rather than allowing harm or injury to occur to that person.
13:7b	Believes all things	Love is willing to give another person the benefit of the doubt. While some hedge themselves against being hurt, true love chooses to trust another even if it leaves him vulnerable to betrayal.
13:7c	Hopes all things	Love waits for the lost or wayward spouse or child to be saved or restored. As one man has said, "As long as there is life, love does not lose hope."
13:7d	Endures all things	For better or for worse . . . in sickness and in health . . . love is committed no matter what the cost.

Only when a pastor is characterized by this love can he model it before his people and expect to have an effectual and fruitful ministry.

I find it easy to love the lovely: the wealthy church member who showers me with gifts, the talented church member whose ministry in the church makes me look good, the strong personality that takes up my cause and convinces the congregation that my proposal for change is a good idea!

On the other hand, I find it is difficult to love the unlovely: the poor, the misfit, the dysfunctional-always-needy-never-contributes-awkward member. The constantly-complaining-thorn-in-the-flesh-"we've-never-done-it-that-way-before"-stick-in-the-mud member. Yet how can a pastor ever call his people to Christlike love for one another if he is selective with his love? For a time, the pastor may feign this love, but eventually, the people under his care will discern the shallow and hollow nature of his character and integrity in this area.

Example in Faith

The "faith" in 1 Timothy 4:12 (NKJV) does not refer to belief in the salvific sense. Rather it refers to faithfulness to one's personal responsibilities and commitments. A pastor of character and integrity is a pastor who is found faithful (1 Cor. 4:2).

Practically, this virtue demands that a pastor be responsible in every way. While few pastors would fail to file their taxes responsibly, many might be careless with other deadlines and details. While few pastors would dare to step into the pulpit on Sunday unprepared, many might stand before the people to preach underprepared.

Faithfulness demands that a pastor pray when no one else is praying, study when he is tired, give when it is inconvenient, forgive when it is hard, and preach in season and out of season. In 2 Timothy 4:2 Paul charged Timothy to preach, convince, rebuke, and exhort, with all long-suffering and teaching, anticipating a time when the hearers would not heed the truth that was being preached to them. Paul's charge to Timothy was to "fulfill your ministry" as he had fulfilled his own (2 Tim. 4:1–6, NKJV). A pastor must be faithful.

Example in Spirit

"In Spirit" refers to the attitude and enthusiasm with which a pastor discharges his duties. There is no doubt that a pastor sets the tone for his people. The pastor cannot expect his people to exceed his own excitement for evangelism or compassion for the lost. The pastor cannot expect his people to be motivated beyond his own commitment to a cause. This spirit demands depth of character and integrity from the pastor, for there are many times when it is difficult to be positive, optimistic, energetic, and inspiring before the congregation. Many times the pastor is tired, discouraged, fearful, or unhappy.

R. Kent and Barbara Hughes relay this story in *Liberating Ministry from the Success Syndrome*:

> On an unforgettable Sunday morning in 1866, the great C. H. Spurgeon stunned his five thousand listeners when from the pulpit of London's Metropolitan Tabernacle he announced, "I am the subject of depressions of spirit so fearful that I hope none of you ever gets to such extremes of wretchedness as I go to." For some of his audience, it was incomprehensible that the world's greatest preacher could know the valley of despair. Yet twenty-one years later in 1887 he said from the same pulpit, "Personally I have often passed through the dark valley."

How then does a pastor demonstrate a good example in spirit when he battles the lows of life? It must be the character and integrity of his inner man that is renewed day by day because of his eternal focus (2 Cor. 4:16ff.).

Example in Purity

While a pastor may be a strong preacher or a gifted administrator, if he cannot maintain his own moral purity, he threatens his Biblical qualification and fails to set the necessary example before his people. For that reason Paul wrote, "I discipline my body and bring it into subjection, lest, when I have preached to others, I myself should become disqualified" (1 Cor. 9:27, NKJV).

Unfortunately, a pastor can demonstrate moral purity in public while perpetually failing in private. A pastor may set a high standard for purity in his example before those watching, but then indulge in his sin when the doors are closed and the shades are drawn.

Conventional wisdom demands that the pastor have Internet filters and firewalls to protect him from any wickedness on the Internet. Conventional wisdom demands that a pastor not be alone in an office or vehicle with a woman other than his wife. Conventional wisdom demands that a pastor have an accountability partner to ask him difficult questions. However, the barriers set up by conventional wisdom can never achieve what character and integrity must. For that reason, Joseph experienced victory in his temptation with Potiphar's wife (Gen. 39) and David suffered failure in his temptation with Bathsheba (2 Sam. 11).

Ultimately, it is the personal character and integrity of the Spirit-filled man of God that is going to gain the victory over the assaulting impurities of the world.

In conclusion, John MacArthur, in *Titus,* issues this fitting charge to pastors:

> God does not call all elders to be entrepreneurs, men who begin ministries and build them. Nor does He call all elders to be producers, men who accomplish a great amount of work in the church, although those are worthy things. Neither does He call all of them to be managers, adept at mobilizing others in the Lord's service, although that, too, is a worthy thing. The Lord does, however, call all elders to be godly leaders, men who by their exemplary lives as well as their sound teaching and preaching set a pattern of virtue and devotion to the Lord for other believers to follow.

In my youth or in my old age, I must first take heed to myself before I give attention to the flock of God (Acts 20:28). It is my personal character and integrity that become my example before them. If my character and integrity are not sufficient to present a right example before those I shepherd, may I have the courage to dismiss myself from the pastorate.

Take Action . . .

1. Define "character" and "integrity" in your own words. Compare your definitions to a dictionary's.
2. Being completely honest with yourself, rank your character with a scale of your own. Now rank your integrity. Will they be godly examples for your congregation?
3. Ask someone you trust to tell you if you have a tongue problem—with gossip, exaggeration, speaking instead of listening, and the like.
4. Evaluate your life—are you failing to "walk the talk" in some area?

Discussion

1. What do people see me to be?
2. What do I know myself to be?
3. What internal changes need to occur for me to be a man of integrity and character?
4. What external changes need to occur for me to be an example to the people of God under my care?

For Further Study

Brothers, We Are Not Professionals by John Piper, Broadman and Holman, 2002.
Lectures to My Students by C. H. Spurgeon, Zondervan, 1954.
Pastoral Ministry by John MacArthur, Thomas Nelson, 2005.
The Reformed Pastor by Richard Baxter, Banner of Truth, 1979.
Titus by John MacArthur, Moody, 1996.

5

Pastoral Ethics and Decorum
— Tim Jordan

Whatever happens, conduct yourselves in a manner worthy of the gospel of Christ" (Phil. 1:27, NIV). Paul was expressing a specific and significant concern: that Timothy, and all of those who shepherd God's flock, must develop and display a lifestyle fitting, worthy, and appropriate for the glorious gospel of Jesus Christ. Such a fitting lifestyle is incredibly important, even eternally important.

Consider this: if someone takes the most dazzling and valuable diamond ever mined and places it in a cheap, gaudy plastic setting, the diamond's apparent value (not its actual value) will be greatly diminished, at best held suspect. An artificial setting for a genuine gem will cause most to consider the gem a fake as well. In the same way, a pastor's life can in no way enhance the real value of the gospel, but it can certainly diminish, distort, and even destroy its apparent value in the eyes of someone viewing his life and ministry. Herein lies an essential value of the study, development, and display of pastoral ethics and decorum. Titus 2:10 calls pastors to make sure their manner and message match "so that in everything they may adorn the doctrine of God our Savior" (ESV).

Essentially, a Biblical study of pastoral ethics and decorum addresses the specific and practical ways in which the ethical character of God, revealed in His Word, is displayed in the pastor's day-to-day personal and professional choices, actions, and attitudes. When his personal and professional life is in real (although never perfect) harmony with God's moral excellence, God is pleased and is glorified in that pastor's life and ministry. His life becomes a fitting setting for the display of God's glorious grace for all to see. God is honored.

A second serious implication of pastoral ethics and decorum is pastors' credibility with those they serve. When what God says and what pastors say *and do* as shepherds are seen to be in real practical harmony, they are credible shepherds, inspiring trust and confidence in the hearts of God's sheep. Such credibility is essential in Biblical shepherding. In one sense, if pastors don't have credibility, they don't have anything! Without credibility pastors will not be heard, believed, or followed—a serious problem for a shepherd! Certainly God can and does choose to honor His Word in spite of the "earthiness" of the earthen vessels He chooses to use. However, He clearly charges pastors to avoid confusing, obscuring, or distorting His truth with actions and attitudes that don't reflect His character, that don't match His Word.

So, in order that the Chief Shepherd is honored and the undershepherd is credible or trustworthy, a pastor must be careful that his day-to-day ethical touches with people within the church and community are marked by truth and love. Truth and love must inform and direct a pastor's actions and choices; that is, his day-to-day interactions with all people must be true, in genuine obedience to the genuine teachings of God's Word. A pastor's interactions must be motivated and marked by genuine Biblical love to God and to the people He loves. "For the whole law is fulfilled in one word: You shall love your neighbor as yourself" (Gal. 5:14, ESV). So what does truth and love in action look like in specific life and ministry situations?

The study of pastoral ethics and decorum must then focus on specific situations and applications that face all pastors. The list of topics varies a bit in different articles, books, and denominational traditions. Surprisingly, there is a fairly significant commonality in the many different lists that I've seen and read. So whether the codes of "ministerial conduct" came from Presbyterian, Baptist, Methodist, Congregationalist, Brethren, or even Unitarian denominations, or whether they came from churches or parachurch organizations, there appears to be a core of essential considerations. These topics include the pastor's work ethic, confidentiality in pastoral care, impartiality in pastoral care, integrity in relationship to women/sexual purity, financial integrity, and respect in relationship to other pastors and churches. While volumes can and have been written on each of these topics, this chapter can only briefly touch on each of them.

The Pastor's Work Ethic

So, what do truth and love look like in connection with the pastor's work ethic? As to intensity, how hard and long should a shepherd work? I'm reminded of Paul's words to the church at Thessalonica: "But we were gentle among you, like a nursing mother taking care of her own children. So, being affectionately desirous of you, we were ready to share with you not only the gospel of God but also our own selves, because you had become very dear to us. For you remember, brothers, our labor and toil: we worked night and day, that we might not be a burden to any of you, while we proclaimed to you the gospel of God" (1 Thess. 2:7–9, ESV). Paul and his team worked long, hard, sacrificially, and passionately. He compared his work ethic to a nursing mother, not to a clock-punching, clock-watching employee. He used words to describe his work that speak of extended and intense physical exertion, laboring at times to exhaustion. Truth and love demand that a pastor work long and hard.

For a pastor's work ethic to "adorn" the gospel of Christ, it must also be focused—focused on the priority tasks assigned by God, not by a committee or public opinion. A pastor should not be working himself to death or a divorce court in the pursuit of greasing the countless and incessant squeaky wheels of felt needs. With specific and intense focus a pastor should be laboring in the study, preaching, teaching, and counseling of the Word. A pastor must never allow the priority of time and effort demanded by the pastoral task or a healthy personal relationship to God and to his family to be given or stolen away by lesser priorities.

A "fitting" work ethic in a shepherd's life will also include intentional times of rest. While I don't believe in a strict New Testament Sabbath, I do believe in the timeless principle of Sabbath rest. Since, in fact, a pastor's body is the temple of the Holy Spirit, he should neither worship the temple (being either nutrition or fitness obsessed) nor abuse the temple by running it into the ground, eating or working it into uselessness. Scripture refers to the body not only as His temple, but as an instrument or tool to be used by Him or by sin. A tool is meant to be used in productive work, not to be abused or broken by carelessness nor to be polished and pampered as some ornament or trophy for display. The shepherd's work ethic should be an appropriate setting for the gospel.

Confidentiality in Pastoral Care

What about confidentiality in pastoral care? How should truth and love inform a pastor's daily choices? Certainly this is of great concern in the area of pastoral counseling, and not only has implications for the church family, but has legal implications as well in this very litigious climate. A pastor must tell the truth, but love demands that he tell the truth with a heart and mind to honor God and bless His flock. While it is unwise to promise unconditional confidentiality to someone a pastor counsels, there still must be a reasonable expectation that what is said in private remains private unless there is a moral or legal "must" to do otherwise. I assure the person I am counseling that I won't say anything that I don't have to say morally or legally. If in fact I must say something, I won't say it without letting that person know I must, giving him or her the opportunity to say it. A competent Christian attorney is a valuable resource in deciding the right path forward in these delicate matters.

Certainly the people of the church should never hear their personal story as a sermon illustration or topic of hallway conversation. Care should be given so that even if the name is never mentioned, the details of the anonymous story don't betray the identity of the people involved or humiliating and unnecessary details. Even in the Biblical practice of church discipline, great care must be taken in this area. The truth must be spoken in love, the sin must be addressed openly and honestly, but unnecessary details given to people who have no business knowing them is a breach of confidentiality that may be both spiritually and legally damaging.

Impartiality in Pastoral Care

What about partiality in pastoral care? I am convinced this is an area where misunderstanding and misinformation abound. A childish and perhaps uniquely American sense of entitlement often defines any action viewed as unfair as "partiality." "Fair" to many equates to giving the same time, same attention, same opportunities to all people in the church at the same time and in the same way. So if it's not "fair," you are guilty of partiality.

God defines partiality quite differently in James 2:1: "My brothers, show no partiality as you hold the faith in our Lord Jesus Christ, the Lord of glory" (ESV). To be direct, sinful partiality is the practice of giving or withholding spiritual service on the basis of someone's face, identity, or appearance. The book of James addresses the giving or refusing of true Christian love to a person based on that person's appearance as being wealthy or poor. The specific condemnation is not against making discriminating choices, rather it forbids making a distinction on factually and morally flawed criteria. Specifically James condemns judging someone's heart by his appearance. James clearly identifies people who do so as "judges with evil thoughts" (2:4, ESV). So then, should a pastor be treating everyone in the church the very same way? The honest answer is yes and no. Will a doctor spend equal time and resources treating someone with a common cold as he would with heart failure or an acute infection? Will a mom devote the exact amount of time and energy to her seven-year-old child as to her seven-week-old baby? Spending more time with the one with more need may be called unfair, but it is not partiality. It is in fact an impartial response to a person's request for help based on real need—not on who they are, not on their "face."

All pastors will be accused of partiality. A pastor should not summarily dismiss such accusations, but neither should he mindlessly accept them. He should examine his heart for the real basis of the decisions and distinctions he makes in his day-to-day service to the Lord's church. He should teach an accurate Biblical definition of partiality, being open and honest about how to live and serve without being "a respecter of persons." However, he must avoid being intimidated by an immature and inaccurate "fairness doctrine."

Relationship to Women

So, here's a provocative question. What do truth and love look like in a pastor's relationship to women in the church? Is this a matter of clear moral Biblical instruction or the consideration of various and changing cultural norms and perceptions? The answer is yes. Scripture demands that the pastor be a one-woman man, sexually and emotionally devoted to one woman, his wife. Giving or seeking satisfaction in either of these areas outside of marriage is sin and is damaging on many levels. Obviously, the most critical issue is objective moral purity. However, while that is the most important issue, it is not the only issue.

Not only must a pastor maintain and cultivate objective moral purity, but he must also give serious consideration to the appearance of impropriety. It's at this point that cultural norms, sensitivities, and perceptions come into play. Clearly a pastor shouldn't be sending inappropriate signals to the women he ministers to or with. He must guard himself from sending flirtatious signals, intentionally or unintentionally. Physical displays of affection are required in certain cultures and situations, but are offensive and suggestive in others. What further complicates this situation is that many and varied cultural expectations exist in every church simultaneously. While I can't take the time to say everything that should be said at this point, let me say this: your very best day-to-day coach or guide in such matters is your wife! Her God-given perspective (the other 180 degrees you can't see) is essential for navigating this most thorny issue. Listen to her. Believe her.

Another essential issue in this matter is strategic. What is the character and nature of your plan to grow in and maintain sexual purity? Should a pastor be relying on internals or externals to keep him pure? The right answer is not an "either or," but a "both and." Clearly a pastor should give attention to external "fences" in his day-to-day life. Such fences—like having windows in an office door, not traveling with a woman alone, and giving one's wife complete access to one's electronic communications— are wise practices. They do have true value in maintaining both purity and a reputation for purity. However, a primary reliance on externals will ultimately fail you.

The most critical issue in maintaining sexual purity is genuine fullness, health, and growth in your relationship to God and to your wife. Serious consideration should be given to a profound spiritual principle found in Proverbs 27:7: "He who is full loathes honey, but to the hungry even what is bitter tastes sweet" (NIV). Someone who is "full" is in a very strong position to resist even the sweetest of temptations, while someone who is "hungry" is vulnerable to the weakest. This explains why people are willing to pay an arm and a leg for a shriveled-up, fat-filled, slimy hot dog at a ball game, and scarf it down in a moment and want more! They're hungry! For the pastor, "staying full" is of the utmost importance. However, people don't "stay full" by getting. Self-indulgence just leads to greater desire and greater emptiness. Ask Solomon! Pastors get full and stay full by investing in their essential relationships, sacrificially sowing the seeds of truth and love that produce a harvest of devoted love, true fullness that satisfies their soul and fortifies them against temptation.

Financial Integrity

We talked about sex. We might as well talk about money! What do truth and love look like in the way a pastor handles money? A life that is a suitable setting for the gospel of Christ must be marked by financial integrity. It is specifically mentioned in 1 Timothy 3:3, "not a lover of money," and 1 Peter 5:2, "Shepherd the flock of God that is among you, exercising oversight, not under compulsion, but willingly, as God would have you; not for shameful gain, but eagerly" (ESV). A life characterized by either spending recklessly for one's own pleasure or hoarding for one's own security is an expression of sinful materialism. It is a deformed setting for the gem of the gospel. A man's life as a pastor should be an honest, growing model of spending and saving intentionally, with God's priorities in control. A pastor should be paying his bills on time, exercising care and discipline to avoid crippling and enslaving debt, and saving for the future. Regular, proportionate, and sacrificial giving should be a cornerstone of his financial life.

A particularly thorny test of financial integrity is the pastor's financial relationship to people in the church. The church is commanded in Scripture to generously support its pastors (1 Tim. 5:17). Showing affection and support in tangible ways fulfills God's command to love in deeds, not just words. However, when is a member's generous kindness meant to influence a decision or court special favor? Should a pastor never accept gifts (money, meals, vacations, tickets, etc.), or accept them without a thought? Clearly believers are commanded to demonstrate true love to their pastors. Clearly that love must be graciously received. Clearly that love must never buy favor or influence.

Here are five considerations that I weigh, pray about, and discuss with my circle of counselors/friends in such situations.
- How large is the gift?
- How public is the gift?
- How frequent are the gifts?
- Is there something potentially suspicious about the timing of the gift?
- Is there an expectation of some type of return on their investment, spoken or implied?

Pastors do and will always need God's wisdom in this matter.

Other Pastors and Churches

The final consideration normally included in the discussion of pastoral ethics and decorum is the pastor's relationship to other pastors and churches, particularly other Bible-believing churches in surrounding communities. My personal experience is only that—my personal experience. However, it is my experience that this is the area that shows the greatest and most glaring disparity between what pastors say and what they do.

Again, truth and love must determine practice. A pastor should honor the autonomy and authority of other Bible-teaching churches. He should publicly and privately speak of pastors and churches with the respect that comes with knowing they are the Lord's, purchased with His blood. He should honor and support their practice of discipline and insist that their members seek to reconcile their differences with their pastor face-to-face before beginning any relationship to his church. To do this, he must avoid isolationism, cultivating true fellowship when Scripture permits. A genuine ongoing personal relationship will go a long way in keeping ethical dealings clean and healthy. A pastor must refuse to entertain rumors and spread gossip, remembering that even though it may be electronic, as he writes or reads a blog, it's still gossip!

Pastoral ethics and decorum that reflect the Lord's moral excellence please the Master and provide the only suitable setting for His gospel. Truth and love must rule a pastor's real-life choices. "We put no obstacle in anyone's way, so that no fault may be found with our ministry, but as servants of God we commend ourselves in every way: by great endurance, in afflictions, hardships, calamities, beatings, imprisonments, riots, labors, sleepless nights, hunger; by purity, knowledge, patience, kindness, the Holy Spirit, genuine love" (2 Cor. 6:3–6, ESV).

Take Action . . .

1. Evaluate your work ethic. Where does it lose balance to one extreme or the other? What specific adjustments need to be made?
2. Practice not sharing everything you know, even if you could share it without gossiping.
3. Explain the difference between "fairness" and partiality to someone you lead. Discuss it with them.
4. Avoid the appearance of impropriety—have a specific unhurried conversation with your wife about this.
5. Write out your plan to grow in and maintain your sexual purity.
6. If you need to do so, get help with financial planning, budgeting, and the like.
7. Give serious thought to what you say about other pastors. Edit out anything you wouldn't say with them in the room.

Discussion

1. How can a pastor know and maintain proper balance between relying on internal versus external safeguards in maintaining both the reality and reputation for sexual purity?

2. What specific ethical dilemmas do pastors face in pastor-to-pastor, church-to-church relationships in their communities?
3. What additional action steps might a pastor take to avoid both the reality and appearance of financial impropriety in his dealings with members of the church and community?

For Further Study

The Effective Pastor: A Practical Guide to the Ministry by Robert C. Anderson, Moody, 1985.

God on Sex: The Creator's Ideas about Love, Intimacy, and Marriage by Daniel Akin, Broadman and Holman, 2003.

Ministerial Ethics: Being a Good Minister in a Not-So-Good World by Joe E. Troll and James E. Carter, Broadman and Holman, 1993.

The Total Money Makeover by Dave Ramsey, Thomas Nelson, 2007.

Core Responsibilities

6

Preaching and Teaching the Word of God
— Gary Gromacki

God has called pastors to preach and teach His Word to the church. The apostle Paul told Timothy to "preach the word" (2 Tim. 4:2, NKJV). Like Timothy, pastors have a responsibility before God to accurately preach and teach His Word. A pastor's message is the inspired inerrant Word of God (2 Tim. 3:16, 17; 2 Pet. 1:20, 21). The Bible is a pastor's message and source of authority.

Definition of Expository Preaching

Expository preaching is the persuasive communication of the intended meaning of a Bible text based on historical/grammatical exegesis and the explanation of its significance, relevance, and application by a preacher to a specific audience.

The essence of expository preaching is explaining the meaning of a Bible text in its context. Your sermon should come from the Bible and not from a movie or a newspaper article. A preacher of the Word of God must be concerned about accurate interpretation.

Expository preaching involves analysis (explaining key words) as well as synthesis (explaining the argument of the Bible book). Expository preaching is more than just giving a verse-by-verse commentary. It also involves sharing relevant illustrations and applications that help the listeners relate Bible truth to their lives. Expository preaching involves challenging people to be doers of the Word and not just hearers. It is essential that a pastor knows his audience so he can preach for life change.

Biblical Expository Preachers
Ezra
Ezra prepared his heart to seek the law of the Lord, do it, and teach it (Ezra 7:10). He read the book of the Law while all of the people stood and listened attentively (Neh. 8:1–6). He and other godly men helped Israel understand the Law (Neh. 8:7, 8). As a result of the reading and preaching of the Word, Israel experienced revival, celebrating the Feast of Booths for the first time since Joshua (Neh. 8:9–18). Expository preaching involves reading and explaining the Word of God with the goal of helping people obey the commands.

Jesus
The risen Jesus explained the meaning of the Old Testament to two discouraged disciples on the road to Emmaus. And then "beginning at Moses and all the Prophets, He expounded to them in all the Scriptures the things concerning Himself" (Luke 24:27, NKJV). The word *expounded* means He explained and clarified the Old Testament Scriptures. Starting with Genesis, Jesus explained how the Old Testament points to a Messiah Who would suffer and die for the sins of the world and be resurrected from the dead. Expository preaching focuses attention on what the Scriptures say about Jesus.

Paul
During his third missionary journey, Paul went to the synagogue of Ephesus and "spoke boldly for three months, reasoning and persuading concerning the things of the kingdom of God" (Acts 19:8, NKJV). When opposition arose, he took the new converts to the school of Tyrannus, where he taught daily. As a result of his ministry, all who lived in the Roman province of Asia heard the word of the Lord Jesus (Acts 19:9, 10). Later Paul told the Ephesian elders, "I have not shunned to declare to you the whole counsel of God" (Acts 20:27, NKJV). From Paul's preaching, we learn the importance of explaining Biblical history and prophecy in the Word of God.

Steps in Sermon Preparation
As a pastor, I made preaching through books of the Bible a priority in my ministry. Select a book of the Bible to preach or teach. Read through the book several times in several different translations. Divide the book

into preaching sections. See if you can come up with a title for each section in the book.

Study the background of the book

Research the background of the book. Consult study Bibles (e.g., Ryrie, MacArthur, ESV), survey books, and commentaries. Here are nine areas to research:

Writer: Who wrote the book?
Recipients: To whom did he write the book?
Message: What is the book about?
Place of Writing: Where did he write the book?
Purpose: Why did he write the book?
Outline: What are the main points of the book?
Characters: Who are the main people in the book?
Key Words: What are the key words of the book?
Key Verses: What are the key verses of the book?

Read the Hebrew/Greek text

Read the Scripture text in the original language: Hebrew, Aramaic (Old Testament), and Greek (New Testament). As you read the text, note any key words you would like to study in depth. *Analytical Key to the Old Testament* by Owens (four volumes) is an excellent resource to use in translating the Hebrew Bible, as it gives definitions of words, parsing of verbs, and page numbers to the *Brown-Driver-Briggs-Gesenius Hebrew Lexicon*. *Linguistic Key to the Greek New Testament* by Rienecker and Rogers defines Greek words and gives parsing of Greek verbs to help you in translating the Greek New Testament. You could also use the exegetical guide in Logos to translate the Hebrew and Greek text.

Use the inductive method of Bible study

Study the Bible using the three key steps of the inductive method of Bible study: observation, interpretation, and application. (1) Observation answers the question, What do I see? Observe content (what is written) and structure (how it is written). Be sure to identify the genre, or type of literature. (2) Interpretation answers the question, What does it mean? Write down your initial questions. Put yourself in your listeners' shoes. What questions would they ask about this text? In your sermon, ask some of these and answer them. (3) Application answers the question, How does it apply to my life? Applications to look for in the text include sins to confess, promises to claim, examples to follow, commands to obey, warnings to heed, prayers to pray, attitudes to have, motivations for obedience.

Do word studies

Select key words in your text to study. Check the definitions of words in lexicons and Bible dictionaries. Examine the historical and cultural aspects of your text. Identify places in the text in Bible maps and atlases.

Examine the Biblical theology

Examine the Biblical theology of your text. Look up cross-references on key words and verses. Use a concordance to trace how the writer used a word or phrase throughout his book. Look for direct quotations or allusions to the Old Testament in the New Testament.

Preparing and Preaching a Sermon

After studying the text, you are ready to write out your sermon.

Introduction

The introduction of your sermon should grab your audience's attention and interest. Telling a personal story, quoting a famous saying, or sharing a related story from the news can capture their attention. You should explain the context of your Bible text before you preach. At the end of your introduction, ask the key question; it should contain the subject of your sermon. The main points of your sermon outline will answer the key question.

Sermon outline

The sermon outline should contain short sentences that answer the key question. It should closely follow the outline of the Scripture text. You may want to use your exegetical outline in preaching historical narratives and give applications in your conclusion.

Sermon idea

The sermon idea is the sermon in a sentence. It can be stated as an imperative or an action step. You should be able to state in one sentence what your sermon is about, and that sentence should reflect the big idea of the Biblical writer of the text.

You will have to decide whether to use an inductive or deductive approach to your sermon. An inductive sermon reveals the sermon idea in the conclusion of the message. A deductive sermon reveals the sermon idea in the introduction or first main point. The main outline points then explain, illustrate, or apply the sermon idea to your audience.

Audience analysis

Many preachers can exegete the Scripture, but they don't know how to exegete their audience. Who is your audience? What is the spiritual condition of your audience? How old is your audience? What life stages are they in? Think about the spiritual needs and problems your listeners face. What illustrations would relate to them? It is important to examine the possible differences in interests and attitudes. Failure to recognize differences can result in a failure to relate and to communicate the truth in a relevant way.

Real-life illustrations and applications

Any pastor who preaches regularly knows the importance of illustrations. He should use a variety in his sermons: Biblical stories, parables, personal stories, and news events. Illustrations have several purposes in a sermon: they clarify a point, show a real-life application, convict of sin, inspire and move people to action, and make truth memorable.

Where do you find illustrations? Your personal experience is a great source. Keeping a short journal of your experiences lets you draw on this well again and again. Television and movies, biographies, magazines, and newspapers are also great places to find illustrations. It is best to file them by text (Bible book, chapter, verse) and alphabetically by topic. Keep a file folder with your illustrations on your laptop for repeated use.

Sermon series and sermon titles

A good restaurant has a menu with a wide variety of appetizers, salads, entrées, and desserts. It is essential for you as a pastor to provide a balanced spiritual diet for your people. Your church needs to hear messages on books of the Bible. They also need to hear what the Bible teaches about marriage and the family, living the Christian life, core values of the church, and the doctrines of the faith.

Decide on a sermon title. The title should relate to the subject of your Bible text. It should be short and creative. If you are preaching a series of messages from a book, see if you can relate the titles to one another.

Creative communication

Work on creative methods of preaching the sermon. Many pastors like to use PowerPoint. Pictures are powerful ways to communicate your message. Use three to five pictures in a sermon, but limit the number of words on a PowerPoint slide. You don't want your audience to focus on reading the PowerPoint slides. You want them to listen to you. Object lessons could be used instead of PowerPoint. Handouts with sermon notes, questions, and applications are an effective way of keeping your audience on track with you. Video clips can be effective ways to grab an audience's attention or to conclude a sermon.

Sermon delivery

Think through the delivery of your message. Where will you stand to give the introduction to your message? Will you read the Scripture first, pray, and then introduce your message? Where will you stand to share that personal illustration? What gestures could you use to communicate your message? Could you use a prop to teach an object lesson from your text? Will you use PowerPoint?

Every preacher has his own unique style and delivery. Your speech should be clear and easy to understand. The tone of your voice should be authoritative but not authoritarian. How you look will make an impression on your audience. You want to look sharp, not sloppy. It is important to develop rapport with your congregation. Maintain eye contact and smile. Preach the Word of God with spiritual power and conviction. The more you know your message, the better you will be able to communicate it. Work at preaching without notes or with few notes.

Conclusion

Use variety in how you conclude your sermons. Challenge your church to put the Word into action. Preach the gospel and challenge lost people to be saved. Encourage Christians to obey the commands of Christ.

Small group discussion questions

Many churches have growth groups to discuss the pastor's sermon and application of the Scripture text. Write out an ice breaker question to help the group get acquainted. Type out a short outline or review of your sermon for the small group leader to use. Next write out some application questions based on your Scripture text.

Get your message out

Smart pastors know the importance of getting their Biblical messages out in different formats: DVDs, CDs, and the Internet. Church websites should have links to written notes/outlines as well as recordings of sermons you have preached.

Different Types of Sermons

It is good to preach a variety of types of expository sermons to keep your audience's interest. Here are four sample sermon outlines.

Paragraph exposition

Many Bible expositors preach through a paragraph each week on Sunday.

Sermon title: Spiritually Wealthy
Scripture text: Ephesians 1:3–6
Key question: How has God the Father made us spiritually wealthy?
Outline:

I. God the Father has blessed us with every spiritual blessing in Christ (Eph. 1:3)

II. God the Father chose us in Christ before the world was created (Eph. 1:4)

III. God the Father has adopted us to be His sons (Eph. 1:5)

IV. God the Father has made us accepted in the Beloved (Jesus) (Eph. 1:6)

Verse exposition

If time is limited, you may want to do an exposition of a key Bible verse.

Title: Preaching to Change Lives
Text: 2 Timothy 4:2
Key question: How can preaching change people's lives?
Outline:

I. Preach the Word of God

II. Be ready at all times to preach the Word of God

III. Convince people of the truth from the Word of God

IV. Rebuke people who sin with the Word of God

V. Exhort people to live for God from the Word of God

Topical exposition

Topical exposition is preaching on a topic by explaining two or more texts of Scripture that deal with the same subject.

Title: Faithful Man
Text: Selected Scripture
Key question: What are the characteristics of a faithful man?
Outline:
I. A faithful man cares for the interests of others (Phil. 2:19–22)
II. A faithful man has right values (Prov. 28:20)
III. A faithful man lives a blameless life (Dan. 6:4)
IV. A faithful man is obedient to God's will (1 Sam. 2:35)
V. A faithful man demonstrates wise stewardship (1 Cor. 4:1, 2)
VI. A faithful man teaches others what he has learned (2 Tim. 2:2)

Biographical exposition

Biographical exposition is preaching on the life or key characteristic of a Bible person.

Title: Barnabas the Encourager
Text: Selected Scripture from Acts
Key question: How can we encourage others today?
Outline:
I. Give sacrificially to the Lord's work (Acts 4:32–37)
II. Believe in new converts and introduce them to your friends (Acts 9:26, 27)
III. Challenge Christians to grow in Christ (Acts 11:19–24)
IV. Mentor Christians and give them opportunities to serve the church (Acts 11:24–26)
V. Get involved in church planting and missions (Acts 11:27–30; 13:1–3)
VI. Give Christians who fail a second chance (Acts 15:36–40; 2 Tim. 4:11)

Take Action . . .

1. Learn to read Hebrew and Greek or to effectively use translation resources, both paper and digital.
2. Make it a habit to do word studies. Don't assume you already know a meaning or that your audience knows the Biblical meaning of a word.
3. List steps you will take to improve your preaching.

4. Practice writing sermon outlines, collecting information and illustrations to help you flesh them out.
5. Preach as often as the Lord gives you opportunity. Ask for objective feedback.

Discussion
1. What is expository preaching? Why is it important?
2. What steps do you take in preparing a sermon?
3. How do you preach for life change?
4. How do you discover the big idea of the Bible text?
5. What areas do you struggle within your preaching?
6. How can listening to expository preachers help a pastor with his own expository preaching?

For Further Study
12 Essential Skills for Great Preaching by Wayne McDill, Broadman and Holman, 2006.

Biblical Preaching, 2nd edition, by Haddon Robinson, Baker, 2001.

Impact Teaching: Pursuing Instructional Excellence by John and Daria Greening, Regular Baptist Press, 2000.

The Moment of Truth: A Guide to Effective Sermon Delivery by Wayne McDill, Broadman and Holman, 1999.

Power in the Pulpit by Jerry Vines and Jim Shaddix, Moody, 1999.

Preaching: How to Preach Biblically by John MacArthur, Thomas Nelson, 2005.

Success in Bible Teaching by Don Anderson, Regular Baptist Press, 2007.

Internet resources for sermons and illustrations: Bible.org and PreachingToday.org.

Commentaries: *The Bible Knowledge Commentary, Expositor's Commentary,* the NIV Application Commentary series, and the Wiersbe Bible Commentary series.

Illustrations: Roy Zuck's *The Speaker's Quotebook* and R. Kent Hughes's *1001 Great Stories and Quotes.*

7

Administrating as a Bishop: Keeping the Church in Check
— Ken Floyd

While a primary emphasis of pastoral ministry rightly focuses on the significance of preaching and teaching, the administrative role of "bishop" carries critical ramifications for the healthy functioning of a church. "This is a faithful saying: If a man desires the position of a bishop, he desires a good work" (1 Tim. 3:1, NKJV).

Biblical Foundation

In secular Greek culture, the bishop functioned as a commissioner who regulated various activities of the colony, including technical and financial responsibilities. *Bishop* referred to a person holding a definite function or fixed office within a group, including religious groups. In Biblical literature, the Septuagint (LXX) uses the word to describe officials involved in examination, contemplation, and judgment (Num. 4:16; Job 31:14; Isa. 24:22; Jer. 11:23). The word is also used in 1 Peter 2:25 to refer to Christ's spiritual administration: "the Shepherd [*poimena*] and Overseer [*episkopos*] of your souls" (NKJV).

Since the early church had a growing segment of Gentile converts, the apostles utilized the word *bishop* to convey an important aspect of Biblical leadership. They acknowledged the necessity of effective pastoral administration. While Paul and Peter used the terms *elder* and *bishop* somewhat interchangeably, they seemed to make a distinction as to what the terms imply. *Elder* seems to speak of the respectable positional status a man received because of his proven experience, while *bishop* defines the responsibility inherent in that position.

In Acts 20:28 the apostle Paul emphasized the official nature of this role when addressing those he had discipled for pastoral ministry: "Therefore take heed to yourselves and to all the flock, among which the Holy Spirit has made you overseers [*episkoposu*, bishops], to shepherd [*poimainein*, shepherd] the church of God which He purchased with His own blood" (NKJV). They in turn acknowledged this official designation by their assembling at his request. Paul also utilized this title in his writings when referring to the bishop's official ministry (Phil. 1:1; 1 Tim. 3:1), his administration in the home (1 Tim. 3:2ff.), and his public testimony (Titus 1:7ff.).

The apostle Peter acknowledged the distinctiveness of this pastoral role in his first letter. "The elders [*presbuterous*] who are among you I exhort. . . . Shepherd [*poimanate*] the flock of God which is among you, serving as overseers [*episkopountes*], not by compulsion but willingly, not for dishonest gain but eagerly; nor as being lords over those entrusted to you, but being examples to the flock" (1 Pet. 5:1–3, NKJV).

Dynamics of the Administrative Pastor
Personal dynamics

Systematic time management is critical to the pastor's effectiveness in all areas of his ministry. He doesn't need *more* time; he needs to manage *current* time wisely (Ps. 90:12). So effective pastors learn how to exercise rule over their own priorities and schedules. To paraphrase Paul's comments to Timothy, "If a man does not know how to rule [himself], how will he take care of the church of God?" (1 Tim. 3:5, NKJV). When people in leadership resist personal change, they limit their own future as well as that of the ministries they lead. Deep ministry relationships are formed not only because of a leader's administrative ability but because of his character credibility. The effective pastor recognizes that "the speed of the leader is the speed of the team" and seeks to be diligent in his own responsibilities. In their book *The Leadership Challenge,* James Kouzes and Barry Posner share five dynamics consistent with competent Christian leadership: credibility is the foundation of leadership; leadership is personal; leaders serve; leaders sacrifice; and leaders keep hope alive.

Leaders possessing these dynamics have one other thing in common: willing followers. This modeling of ministry excellence is contagious to the rest of the ministry team.

I have observed that people who are content to go with the flow regarding their time management will inevitably get stuck on a sandbar, be demolished on the rocks, or go over a cliff. The other extreme of time administration is "paralysis by analysis." Leaders dealing with this symptom are never satisfied with the information gathered, are reluctant to move forward, and have an unbiblical fear of failure. I appreciate the leadership maxim that declares, "Progressive improvement is better than delayed perfection." Effective pastors value consistent progress over unachievable perfection.

Here are seven key areas that I have made a priority in administering my ministry:

Master calendar. The master calendar serves as the "air traffic control" system for the pastor's life and aids him in establishing his overall ministry strategy. It should reflect the personal priorities of his life. He should review this calendar weekly to ensure a clear sense of purpose as well as to evaluate balance. Please remember that while it is called a "master" calendar, it should be your servant, not your master!

Time management. Administrative oversight involves intentionality in scheduling the time segments of a week.

It is essential to intentionally set aside time for prayer and thinking. A pastor must take time to reflect upon the effectiveness of the work of the ministry, as well as envision the direction of the ministry. As a pastor, I set aside all of Tuesday as a day for prayer, sermon preparation, and personal growth. This priority was communicated to the church family and protected by the church secretary. I took no phone calls unless it was a clear emergency that no one else could appropriately handle.

Another important emphasis in time management should be the pastor's marriage and family. He should regularly schedule time for this critical area and protect it, just as he would for ministry. When asked about his availability for other needs or events, the pastor can honestly respond, "I already have something important scheduled at that time. What other dates are you available to meet?"

Appropriately scheduled time for leisure is also an essential part of the pastor's time stewardship. The rubber band that is continually stretched to its limit will lose its resiliency or break. In addition to scheduling rest and relaxation, learn the discipline of saying no. Johann Wolfgang von Goethe said, "Things which matter most must never be at the mercy of things which matter least." Allow your wife and others who know you best to assist you in remaining accountable in this area.

To-do list. Henry Kaiser accurately observes, "Every minute spent planning will save two in execution." Regularly review and refine the to-do list to determine what is necessary and should be done, when it is appropriate to do it, and what can be delegated to others. Early in my ministry I found that some of my most productive times were just before leaving my office for an extended ministry trip or personal vacation. In those urgent moments, I would quickly prioritize what was essential for me to accomplish and what was not. I later made it my goal to practice this good habit of prioritizing every day.

Filing. I thank God for a seminary professor who emphasized this to his first-year students. He would often state, "An idea that cannot be placed immediately will be lost eventually." A major focus of the class was the establishing of an extensive filing system. Compared to learning Hebrew, studying Biblical texts, and addressing critical areas of theology, this assignment seemed an unscholarly, tedious, and mundane time investment. I did not realize that this wise professor was helping me recognize an important aspect of administration. Even though paper-filing systems are becoming a thing of the past, today's pastor may continue this good discipline with today's technology.

Sermon preparation. The aforementioned professor taught homiletics. He emphasized filing primarily for the preparation of sermons. He helped students understand the importance of planning ahead for regular and special-event sermons by systematically filing thoughts and resources for sermon formation.

Leadership development. Invest time in personal development. Read synopses of books when possible and appropriate. Utilize travel time by listening and praying.

Environment. Make sure your workspace is an enhancement and not a distraction. Good lighting and ventilation, quietness, and adequate storage enhance the pastor's ability to create and administrate.

Pursuing goals in these seven areas helps the administrating pastor fulfill the dynamics the apostle Paul shared with his protégé in 1 Timothy 4:13–16: "Meditate on these things; give yourself entirely to them, that your progress may be evident to all" (v. 15, NKJV).

Corporate dynamics

The effective administrating pastor identifies what is necessary to help a church understand and successfully implement its mission through the personal involvement of its members. This requires specific oversight by the pastor in three main processes: establishing strategic direction, developing leaders, and implementing effective ministries.

Discipleship. An effective administrating pastor recognizes that his job is not to *do* the ministry but to *mentor* others to minister (Eph. 4:11, 12). As the Good Shepherd, Jesus knows His sheep and they know Him (John 10:14). This wonderful model by the Chief Shepherd on behalf of His undershepherds implies a familiarity with those in the flock and an awareness of their abilities, giftedness, personality, availability, and experience.

Development. The administrating pastor exercises good stewardship by ensuring that time and resources are available so that each servant will have the opportunity to successfully fulfill his responsibility. Scheduling regular training seminars is helpful in strengthening both specific church ministries and those serving in them. The camaraderie experienced during both the travel to and attendance at seminars is invaluable for team building.

Delegation. Jesus described effective delegation as being like "a man going to a far country, who left his house and gave authority to his servants, and to each his work, and commanded the doorkeeper to watch" (Mark 13:34, NKJV). Used in tandem with discipling, delegation offers the opportunity to learn "the work of ministry . . . by which every part does its share" through practical experience (Eph. 4:12, 16, NKJV). The tutelage of a skilled pastor offers a measure of safety, and the effective administrating pastor can identify those who show giftedness and spiritual enthusiasm toward the ministry.

Long-term effectiveness, rather than short-term relief, must be the goal of delegation. There are too many stories of willing servants who have received last-minute assignments and then been left on their own to both understand and accomplish them.

Descriptions. Clearly articulate in writing the goals of the particular ministry and practical steps toward accomplishing those goals. The description should clearly state how a particular ministry connects within the church's other ministries and where it fits with the church's overall mission.

Dialogue. Effective administration recognizes that patience is a virtue, and allows proper time for people to understand, implement, and accomplish their responsibilities. A platform that facilitates effective dialogue should be established for all who are accountable for the particular ministry.

Diligence. The effective pastoral administrator does not assume that those ministering will immediately understand the proper processes and results. Rather, he will lead the team to "inspect what it expects" in a godly manner through appropriate accountability. Meetings that repeat expectations and review progress are important for both the leader and the disciple.

Due diligence will include elements of correction and/or praise. A God-honoring pastor will heed the instruction of 1 Peter 5:2, taking care not to lord it over those assigned with a responsibility. Nor will he do a task for the one responsible. When correction is necessary, he will speak the truth in love. An angry man delivering the truth causes more problems than he seeks to resolve.

Administrating church meetings

It is important for the pastor to set the focus and tone of official leadership meetings. His primary goal in administrating such meetings should be to bring glory to Christ, the Head of the church, by ensuring that all aspects of the meeting are done "decently and in order" (1 Cor. 14:40, NKJV). He helps establish the tone of the meeting by his gracious approach, enabled by the Holy Spirit. He should not be focused on winning the vote or ruling the day, but on the growth of a healthy church body that honors God. He should demonstrate the grace of self-control by welcoming questions and dialogue as an opportunity for discipleship and growth.

Meetings should start with a Biblical and prayerful focus. This sets a proper tone by drawing attention to the fact that the church is the Lord's work and His servants need to submit to His wisdom and direction.

Pastoral staff and deacon ministry meetings. In both kinds of meetings, the pastor is responsible to organize ones that emphasize clear communication, interchange of information, opportunity for exchanging ideas, declaring differing perspectives, the assignment of action plans, and accountability for assigned tasks.

- Agendas should be prepared and distributed ahead of the meeting so all involved have an opportunity to review each item and prayerfully anticipate the meeting. The names of those responsible for presenting a report should be listed next to the agenda item. This ensures good preparation on the part of those responsible for the assignment.

Placing the time allotted next to each agenda item helps guide the discussion.
- Minutes of previous meetings should be included to review prior discussion and the rationale for proposed action items. A motion index is helpful for keeping track of past action items. This helps prevent unnecessary discussion and duplication.
- Start and end meetings on time. Resist the temptation to go off on tangents by sticking to the agenda. Regularly restate meeting guidelines and procedures so that no one is tempted to derail the agenda or promote an idea without proper research and prayerful consideration.
- At the conclusion of each agenda item and at the end of the meeting, be sure every person understands his assigned responsibilities and what is expected from him at the next meeting. Ensure that proper resources are known and available for accomplishing the tasks.

Church business meetings. The pastor must also give godly leadership in his planning and leading of church business meetings.
- He should prepare well for the meeting and ensure that discussion items are communicated to the church body well in advance whenever possible. The business meeting should not be viewed as a necessary evil, like a dreaded medical procedure. Rather, such meetings should be welcomed as opportunities for sharing vision, implementing ministry, measuring effectiveness, and celebrating spiritual fruit.
- Effective, meaningful meetings are the result of strategic planning for a series of meetings, not just one meeting. Rather than pushing for a quick vote, proposals of significant consequence are given in writing, presented, and discussed a few meetings in advance.
- Discussions that result from such presentations often yield wonderful suggestions to enhance a proposal and diffuse any notion of power plays or hidden agendas. By the time actual votes are taken, there is little discussion before the call for a vote because ample time has been given for interactive dialogue.

Commit to agreed upon guidelines for Christ-honoring meetings. Here are five: (1) The Head of the church, Jesus Christ, is present in the meeting. He hears everything that is said and knows every motive. (2) Pastors are servants of the church, not sovereigns over it. (3) The Biblical office of the pastor is always to be honored. (4) Each member must speak courteously at all times. (5) There must be no personal attacks made on anyone.

Administrating documents

The pastor should give oversight to and possess a working understanding of the documents necessary to properly guide the local church. Such documents bring unity regarding the purpose and function of the church, clarity of various convictions and responsibilities, and legal declaration of the church's faith and practice. A suggested order of priority for documents includes the Scriptures, statement of faith, church covenant, constitution, and church policies.

The pastoral administrator should follow wise methodology when leading a church through proposed changes to established policies. Care should be given to share reasons for making changes, keeping in mind that a deliberate pace is better than a speedy process. Take the opportunity to teach the Biblical and practical rationales for the proposal. Emphasize effective and thorough communication.

Take Action . . .

1. Evaluate your effectiveness in these key areas of administrative leadership: vision, personnel, communication, focus, feedback, and finances.
2. Choose mentors who can help you become effective and disciplined in the area of administration.
3. Make a master calendar for the next week. At the end of the week, evaluate its usefulness, any problems, possible solutions or tweaks, and your ability to follow it.

Discussion

1. What are the Biblical distinctive nuances between "bishop," "elder," and "pastor"?
2. How does this agricultural principle apply to a local church: "A soil tiller knows the soil well but knows the tools better"?
3. What would be the value of attending a training session with leaders and workers in your church, rather than conducting the training yourself?
4. What are the benefits of delegation?

For Further Study

Being Leaders: The Nature of Authentic Christian Leadership by Aubrey Malphurs, Baker, 2003.

Building Leaders: Blueprints for Developing Leadership at Every Level of Your Church by Aubrey Malphurs, Baker, 2004.
The Business Side of Ministry by Michael Nolan, Regular Baptist Press, 2011.
Christian Reflections on The Leadership Challenge by James M. Kouzes and Barry Z. Posner, Jossey-Bass, 2004.
Church That Works by Gary L. McIntosh, Baker, 2004.
The Doctrine and Administration of the Church by Paul R. Jackson, Regular Baptist Press, 2003.
Execution: The Discipline of Getting Things Done by Larry Bossidy and Ram Charan, Crown Business/Random House, 2002.
First Things First by Stephen R. Covey, Free Press, 2003.
The Leadership Challenge by James M. Kouzes and Barry Z. Posner, Jossey-Bass, 2002.
Leading Leaders: Empowering Church Boards for Ministry Excellence by Aubrey Malphurs, Baker, 2005.
A Performance Pattern for Pastors and Churches by W. Wilbert Welch, Kregel, 2002.
A Primer for Pastors by Austin B. Tucker, Kregel, 2004.
Principles and Practices for Baptist Churches: A Guide to the Administration of Baptist Churches by Edward T. Hiscox, Kregel, 1980.
The Seven Habits of Highly Effective People by Stephen R. Covey, Simon and Schuster, 1989.

8
Shepherding with Pastoral Care
— Ernie Schmidt

"My pastor is the best. I never have a challenge that he does not address in just the right way. I never have a need he does not meet. In fact my pastor is perfect!" David clearly shared these thoughts in Psalm 23. He assured his readers that the Lord was his pastor (shepherd). Consequently, he never faced a situation that his pastor did not see him through. Although pastors are not perfect, as men of God they are to emulate the Chief Shepherd in their ministry. The Scriptures show what is expected of pastors.

The Philosophy of Caring
In the Old Testament

The shepherd model is one of God's choice illustrations of Biblical leadership. A quick survey of the Old Testament reveals that the word *shepherd* is a frequent title for human leadership. While the model is used of the Lord and of good leaders, it is startling to note that much of the Old Testament treatment is negative and focuses on Israel's sinful leaders, as seen in Ezekiel 34 (NKJV).

The leaders were living for themselves, not for the flock (Israel). The shepherds "feed themselves" (v. 2) but "do not feed the flock" (v. 3). They had not strengthened the weak, healed the sick, bound the broken, brought back ones driven away, or sought the lost (v. 4). Instead, they ruled with "force and cruelty" (v. 4). As a result, the sheep "were scattered," "became food for . . . beasts," "wandered through all the mountains" with "no one . . . seeking or searching for them" (vv. 5, 6). The dreadful phrase in verse 5, "so they were scattered because there was no shepherd," captures a deplorable situation. It shows the situation could not get any worse than it was at that time. Ezekiel's negative critique of Israel's leadership laid the foundation for a growing awareness of the need for leaders who cared.

In the Gospels

The New Testament introduces the Lord Jesus Christ as that caring leader. He was heralded as the king, but it was soon apparent that He was not the type of leader first-century Israel desired. He taught with authority, but He was not authoritarian. He led, but He led as one who serves. Externally, Christ consistently met physical needs and demonstrated great power, but His priority was people's inner condition and development. The common people loved Him, but the traditional power structure of the day hated Him. He contradicted both their view of the world and their view of leadership.

Christ not only displayed leadership, He also prepared future leaders. A blatant example of selfish ambition (Matt. 20:20–28) provided the occasion for Him to deliver the heart of His leadership philosophy. Essentially He said, "Don't be a dictator. Be a servant leader." His instruction was supported by His example. "The Son of Man did not come to be served, but to serve, and to give His life a ransom for many" (v. 28, NKJV). The culmination of His ministry was the giving of His life as a ransom for sin. His ensuing resurrection and ascension led to the giving of the Holy Spirit and the establishment of a new channel for His worldwide work to be accomplished.

The coming of the Holy Spirit instituted the church (sometimes called the universal church or the Body of Christ) that the Lord introduced in Matthew 16:18. The universal church is manifested in local churches, which require appropriate leadership. As the Chief Shepherd, Jesus Christ, through the Holy Spirit (Acts 20:28), appoints shepherds as leaders.

The prototype for the Chief Shepherd–shepherd leadership model is described in John 21. The Lord used two words to describe the future ministry of Peter and other church leaders. Both words refer to the work of a shepherd. *Feed* focuses on providing nourishment, and *tend* connotes the all-encompassing task of shepherding: feeding, leading, and guarding. Thus, those who lead churches are to follow the shepherd model.

In the Epistles

Early in his ministry Paul shared his shepherding philosophy, using two illustrations to present it (1 Thess. 2:1–12, NKJV): a mother (vv. 7–9) and a father (vv. 10–12). Compassionate leadership is reflected in Paul's "maternal" model: he was "gentle . . . as a nursing mother cherishes her own children." His affectionate "longing" led him to "impart" his own life, because the Thessalonians were "dear" to him. Hence, he was involved in "laboring night and day" for them. As a father, Paul modeled godly character identified as living "devoutly and justly and blamelessly." He further "exhorted, and comforted, and charged" them that they "would walk worthy of God."

Later, addressing the qualifications of a pastor, Paul again employed a domestic image. In 1 Timothy 3:5 he reminded Timothy that proper leadership in the home prepares one to exercise care for the church of God. The word *care* in the phrase "take care of the church" (NKJV) is the same word used of the Good Samaritan. Luke 10:34 says the Samaritan "took care of him" and promised to reimburse the innkeeper, who was to "take care of him." Thus, the care of a pastor is to be practical.

In both the Old and New Testaments, the shepherd is presented as one who concentrates his life and energy on the well-being of the flock. A real shepherd cares. One who is in it only to make a living (a "hireling") "does not care about the sheep" (John 10:13, NKJV). The life of a shepherd is a sacrificial, not a selfish, lifestyle. "The good shepherd gives His life for the sheep" (John 10:11, NKJV). Hence, the pastorate is not a job or a chosen vocation; it is a calling to serve the Chief Shepherd by serving others. The pastor is successful when he shepherds so that the flock is successful.

The Practice of Caring

How can we practice pastoral care in the twenty-first century? Other chapters in this book will deal with such matters as vision, goals, methods, and administration. The question before the pastor in this chapter is, How do I minister to people with a shepherd's heart? Methods and programs change, but human nature and basic needs do not. Everyone needs spiritual encouragement and guidance. The Holy Spirit is given to all believers to comfort, guide, and convict. Yet, as I stated, the Holy Spirit selects men to shepherd God's people (Acts 20:28). The Lord uses pastors as His instruments to minister to His flock both publicly and privately.

Public care

The public ministry of a pastor functions in two priority areas: example and preaching.

Example. Paul was not embarrassed to refer to the need for role models. He expressed the value of modeling godliness in ministry (Acts 20:18; 1 Cor. 4:16; 11:1; Phil. 3:17; 4:9). He was not promoting himself; he was stressing the necessity of fleshing out Christian living and serving. Long before the phrase "much is caught as well as taught" was first stated, Paul unveiled the principle.

The Lord Jesus' last words concerning disciples were not, "Teaching them all things I have commanded you," but rather "teaching them to *observe* all things I have commanded you" (Matt. 28:20, NKJV, emphasis added). To do this, pastors must practice what they preach. They must be men of God. Paul instructed the leaders of the church of Ephesus to "take heed to" themselves before he said to take heed to "all the flock" (Acts 20:28, NKJV).

Authentic pastoral ministry begins with the shepherd's love for the Lord, not love for ministry and its tasks (John 21:15–17). People want to know that God is at work in their pastor's life. This realization gives them hope and confidence that following their pastor's example and teaching will draw them closer to the Lord. Paul encouraged the Philippians with the assurance that "the God of peace will be with you" as they followed His model (Phil. 4:9).

Preaching. Preaching should be pastoral. This does not mean a pastor gives psychological pep talks that address temporal "felt needs." Pastoral preaching according to God's plan is the only preaching that really addresses people's true needs. Pastoral preaching explains and applies God's Word as God's Word. It is not presented as a good alternative or the best option for the congregation's concerns. It is given as God's truth, which provides "all things that pertain to life and godliness" (2 Pet. 1:3, NKJV).

Pastoral preaching involves provision and protection. A shepherd's primary task is to provide nourishment. Thus, the pastor's primary public task is to "feed the flock." This feeding ministry demands hours of studying the Bible and people to provide legitimate messages that offer appropriate nourishment. Pastors should study the Bible so they can be accurate in presenting God's truth. They should study the flock so they will be able to accurately apply the truth. Both interpretation and application must flow from the passage. Pastors should study the congregation in general and the members individually in light of the passage to shepherd them properly. The contemporary emphasis on healthy diets should remind pastors of the necessity of providing a balanced serving of the milk and the meat of the Word. They should labor to provide sound (healthy) messages that build mature, God-focused, Christ-centered believers.

A good shepherd not only provides nourishment, he also protects the flock. It is not a lack of love to warn sheep of wolves (Acts 20:29). A pastor who has a heart for the well-being of the flock will warn them of what is harmful. This is not a negative attitude that is constantly looking for something or someone to criticize. Rather, a pastor must address and expose real threats to the flock, whether it be a troublesome trend or a subtle erosion of truth. Supporting his instructions to take heed to the flock, Paul stated, "I did not cease to warn everyone night and day with tears" (Acts 20:31, NKJV). This was not a calloused, pugnacious practice, but a compassionate ("with tears") concern for the well-being of the people throughout his three-year stay at Ephesus.

Private care

While repeated many times, it is not trite to say, "People do not care how much you know until they know how much you care." The words are certainly not inspired, but they reflect life today and emphasize the need for one-on-one contact with people. The pastor's private care may be summarized by the words "interest" and "involvement."

Interest. Interest implies a serious, genuine desire to know people and their concerns. It is an active interest. Pastors make a genuine effort to know each person's individual needs and circumstances. This is the opposite of what happens on a typical Sunday morning. Before Sunday School or the morning service, someone may ask, "How are you?" and receive the expected response, "Fine." This ritual is consistent with people's comfort zones. But things really go south when the one questioned replies, "Not so good," and then shares a heavy burden. The questioner probably thinks, *Hey, wait a minute. That's not how we play the Sunday game. Your response put me in a bind. I want to act interested, but please don't drag me into your problem.* Real interest does not end with polite conversation. It wants to know so it can help.

Nehemiah is a classic illustration of genuine interest. His book opens with a question. He asked his brother about conditions among the Jews and in Jerusalem. The report he received was negative and depressing. Nehemiah could have said, "I am sorry to hear about that. I will pray for you," and left it at that. He did pray for them, but this was not the extent of his involvement. He prayed for the Lord to make a way for him to be personally involved. The rest is history, as recorded in Nehemiah 2—13. Similarly, pastoral care does not end with interest, but it must begin there.

How can a pastor show genuine interest? By getting to know the flock, following the example of the Good Shepherd, Who said, "I know My sheep" (John 10:14, NKJV). This kind of interest takes time and purposeful effort; it is not an accident. It begins by learning the names of the congregation. Hearing one's name from a leader, when he or she is one among many, has a positive impact. It deepens that person's respect and commitment to follow him. The Lord reminds us that the shepherd "calls his own sheep by name" (John 10:3, NKJV). Pastoral interest does not stop with knowing their names; it extends to knowing their needs.

Discerning needs can occur spontaneously or intentionally. Spontaneously, a question before or after a service or a quick phone call can alert a pastor to needs. Even a casual comment by or about a member can reveal concerns. The key is to be so interested in people that even casual comments alert the pastor to the needs that require spiritual assistance. While this spontaneous approach may give him some awareness of the needs of those he shepherds, a scheduled approach will open doors and provide greater insight.

What does scheduled interest look like? It is all about personal contact with people. The passive approach is availability. The pastor may tell the church that he sets aside scheduled time for spiritual disciplines and sermon preparation as well as for family time. At the same time, he will also let them know he is available 24/7 for emergencies. While sharing his priorities for time, he should assure the congregation he is available. By his words and demeanor he sets them at ease to approach him with their concerns.

The active approach takes the initiative. Phone calls and personal contact are the heart of showing interest. A pastor should be in phone contact with people on special occasions. He can call them on their birthdays and anniversaries. The conversations can be brief, but it is a significant relationship-builder. It's helpful to find out the date of a spouse's death and call the widow/widower on that day to let them know he is thinking about and praying for them. He may want to call them on the date of their anniversary as well. There may be times when he senses a member is down or disturbed. A phone call asking if there is a challenge and offering help may be just what they need to take a crucial spiritual step.

We live in a day of smartphones, texting, e-mail, Facebook, and Twitter. As much as technology can legitimately save time in ministry, nothing replaces face-to-face communication. A pastor's warm, caring conversation can be a balm to a hurting soul. Purposeful calls in the home, if even for an hour or less, will create a bond that nothing else can produce. A pastor can also plan to visit his men at their places of work. Such contacts will show he is really interested in their lives and will provide him with expanded opportunities to build evangelistic relationships. As he can, he can visit such things as sporting events, recitals, and awards ceremonies. He can be creative in scheduling—even a few innings sitting with the parents and cheering for their child reveals his care and will provide great insight into application in preaching.

Involvement. As in the case of Nehemiah, pastors must translate interest into involvement. No doubt the interest a pastor expresses will unveil needs. When it does, he has the opportunity to shepherd that sheep. One of his first responses is a promise to pray. If the environment permits, he can pray right then. Prayer is a ministry, but it is seldom the only aspect of service a pastor renders when he is involved in the lives of his people. There is no one-size-fits-all approach to any challenge. The situation provides the context of his involvement. Thus, his participation is "custom designed" and personal.

One of the best ways to show he cares is to be there in times of need. Probably the best comfort Job's "friends" offered was to sit with him "seven days and seven nights, and no one spoke a word to him" (Job 2:13, NKJV). While this is not a paradigm, it indicates that times of special need demand a pastor's presence. When his members face surgery, hospitalization, or death in the family, he needs to be right there with them. Whether it is sorrow or bad news about one's physical condition or the joy of childbirth, the pastor should be there to "rejoice with those who rejoice, and weep with those who weep" (Rom. 12:15, NKJV).

Pastors will face many occasions for caring involvement. A pastor must look for them and get involved in the lives of his people! In an airborne military context, candidates are to earn their wings. A pastor earns his wings when he expresses interest in and becomes involved in the lives of the members of his congregation. Such a ministry is not intended to elevate him above others, but it does establish his credibility and creates a greater hunger for his pulpit ministry. When he is involved in the lives of his members, they see him not merely as the one paid to perform ministry, but they see him as their pastor.

Take Action . . .
1. Constantly seek to improve your preaching.
2. Schedule interest in someone, both passively and actively.
3. Create an efficient way to pray regularly for the people in your congregation.
4. Learn the schedules of the students in your church and attend some of their extracurricular activities, including recitals and shows, as well as sporting events. Be sure to greet the students and their parents.
5. Visit someone at work; do it regularly to meet his coworkers and establish rapport with the hope of sharing the gospel with them.

Discussion
1. How do the responsibilities of an Old Testament shepherd compare with those of a New Testament pastor?
2. How do feeding and tending the flock translate into church life today?
3. Why is a mother a good illustration of a pastor? Why is a father a good illustration of a pastor?
4. How does a pastor know whether his sermons are nourishing his congregation?
5. How does a pastor balance his family's needs with emergency or unexpected needs among members of his congregation?

For Further Study
10 Power Principles for Christian Service by Warren W. Wiersbe and David W. Wiersbe, Baker, 1997.
Commentary on 1 & 2 Timothy & Titus by Ronald A. Ward, Word Books, 1974.
Escape from Church, Inc. by E. Glenn Wagner, Zondervan, 1999.
A Greek-English Lexicon of the New Testament by Walter Bauer, University of Chicago Press, 1979.
The Minister as Shepherd by Charles Jefferson, Scripture Truth Book Co.
The Pastor's Covenant by H. B. London and Neil Wiseman, Regal, 2005.
On Being a Pastor by Derek Prime and Alistair Begg, Moody, 2006.
Rediscovering Pastoral Ministry by John MacArthur, Word, 1995.
Shepherding God's Flock by Jay E. Adams, Baker, 1984.
Shepherding the Church by Joseph M. Stowell, Moody, 1994.
Shepherding the Small Church by Glenn Daman, Kregel, 2002.

9

Biblical Counseling: Discipleship in the Details
— Jeff Newman

The public proclamation of the Word is the centerpiece of a pastor's leadership. Through this proclamation, and through prayer and his example of godly living, the pastor leads the flock (Heb. 13:7–9; 1 Thess. 1:5, 6). In Biblical counseling, the pastor seeks the lost and builds up the sheep in the context of a personal relationship of Biblical friendship and trust. He helps people connect the truth of the Word of God to the details of living life in the midst of a broken world (Acts 20:18–36).

In His Word, God outlined the qualifications for counseling. Jay Adams, in his book *Competent to Counsel,* points out that Paul summarized these qualifications when he wrote to the Roman believers, "I myself am confident . . . that you also are full of goodness, filled with all knowledge, able also to admonish one another" (Rom. 15:14, NKJV). He declared that they were "competent to counsel." These qualifications of integrity and knowledge challenge the pastor to give clear Biblical definition and direction to his counsel, to cultivate his own character and ability in counseling, and to conduct an effective counseling ministry that points people to Christ in the midst of the challenges of life.

Constructing a Counseling Foundation
Making disciples, not solving problems

The average person's understanding of counseling has been shaped in large part by the culture of modern secular psychology. Many Christians view counseling in a way that ignores or marginalizes the wonderful Counselor and His sufficient direction on the topic. The result: counseling becomes the almost exclusive work of those trained in various secular models of psychology and subsequent therapies; people generally view counseling as only for those with really big problems, and thus, as a sign of weakness. Therefore, counseling takes place mostly outside the church as a service believed to be empirically based, rather than theory laden.

However, viewed through the lens of the Word of the wonderful Counselor, what our world calls *counseling*, He calls *discipleship*. In Biblical counseling, the pastor and others engage in the ministry of focused discipleship, bringing together their knowledge of the Scriptures with their knowledge of the people they are seeking to help. Those engaged in counseling see themselves as disciple makers for Christ: (1) integrating evangelism and discipleship into every aspect of life—"Go therefore and make disciples of all the nations"; (2) identifying believers with Christ and the local church through baptism—"baptizing them in the name of the Father and of the Son and of the Holy Spirit"; and (3) instructing believers in all of the truth of God's Word, leading them to see and live life from God's perspective—"teaching them to observe all things that I have commanded you," while doing all of this with complete reliance on Christ—"I am with you always, even to the end of the age" (Matt. 28:19, 20, NKJV).

In one sense, this type of counseling happens in every interpersonal interaction and in every observation of another's life. A wise pastor views every conversation as a counseling moment. The chief aim is to glorify God through purposeful disciple making in the context of a local church. In an article titled "Discipleship in the Details," published in *Faith Pulpit*, I wrote, "Biblical counseling is discipleship in the details—bringing together the richness of the Word of God with the intricacies of people's lives in such a way that God is glorified through producing disciples who live out the truth of the Word of God in the details of life."

Building faith, not coping with the problems

The pastor's counseling ministry affords him the opportunity to do discipleship in the context of conversations about problems without allowing those problems to upstage the God Who is at work in the midst of those problems. Christ transforms sinners into saints, enemies into children, slaves of sin into sons of God, and victims and violators into victors. His goal is far more beautiful than simply assisting His children to cope with life in this sin-cursed world. He desires to make them look more and more like members of His family as they walk with faith in His Word.

Having this faith-building focus for his counseling provides the pastor with great hope. Not every problem encountered can be solved in this life, but God's goal for counseling can always be attained. The woman facing a lifetime of chronic pain can be led to trust the One Who will certainly remove her pain in the eternal future. The man estranged from his wayward adult daughter can be encouraged in his relationship with a Savior Who suffered alone while deserted by those He had poured His life into. The woman abandoned by her unfaithful husband can rest in her relationship with the One Who endured being forsaken by His Father, knowing that He will never forsake her.

Having this focus also produces perseverance in the work of counseling. As the pastor and others under his leadership reach out in love, purposing to help people through God's Word, some problems of daily living will be solved, and suffering will be relieved. But when the pain and suffering of this fallen world continue their ravages, all involved in counseling can continue to live faithfully for Christ. He alone makes true sense out of suffering and offers the sure hope of an end to all suffering. Even when the pastor encounters those who reject the counsel of God's Word, he can rejoice because God uses those experiences to strengthen his own faith and polish him into a clearer reflection of the Savior.

Cultivating Personal Counseling Growth
Fostering transparency in life and ministry

Often, people do not come to their pastor for help. The Internet, television, self-help books, and hotlines seem to offer help and hope without the embarrassment of self-disclosure. Christian culture often fosters a stereotype of the pastor as untouched by the problems of day-to-day living. So individuals confused by the shame or guilt of their problems will often hide from, rather than seek out, the pastor.

While much of this challenge lies outside his control, the pastor who cultivates appropriate transparency will instill hope and will help draw in those who need his special care. The apostle Paul's transparency in the opening chapters of 2 Corinthians provides a model to follow. Notice that he quickly declared his need for God and his own inability to help himself: "We had the sentence of death in ourselves, that we should not trust in ourselves but in God who raises the dead" (2 Cor. 1:9, NKJV). He confessed that he was "hard pressed on every side, . . . perplexed, . . . persecuted, . . . struck down, . . . [and] always carrying about in the body the dying of the Lord Jesus." The goal of this openness was to point them beyond himself:

"We have this treasure in earthen vessels, that the excellence of the power may be of God and not of us. We are hard pressed on every side, yet not crushed; we are perplexed, but not in despair; persecuted, but not forsaken; struck down, but not destroyed—always carrying about in the body the dying of the Lord Jesus, that the life of Jesus also may be manifested in our body" (2 Cor. 4:7–10, NKJV).

Studying Scripture for personal growth and change

A pastor who approaches the Word prayerfully as a needy learner himself will grow in his walk with God, treat others with love and humility, and minister the Word with precision in his counseling ministry. He ministers out of the well of his own soul. If the well is dry, his ministry is parched. This dryness shows up quickly in the ministry of counseling-discipleship. The dynamic interaction of the conversations of counseling calls for a well that is filled with the Word of God, both known and lived.

Observing people through the lens of God's Word

Effective counseling demands a love for people, and loving people well requires knowing people well. Knowing people well demands a robust Biblical anthropology and an ability to connect that anthropology to everyday life. Cultivating such connection develops as the pastor spends time considering his own growth and as he counsels others. It can also grow as the pastor becomes a people watcher. Whether walking the mall, reading a newspaper or biography, coaching Little League, or simply enjoying an evening on the porch—opportunities to become a student of people abound. Taking advantage of these opportunities to consider human thought and behavior in the light of God's Word provides the pastor with unlimited occasions to provoke his thinking on God's interpretation of life.

Equipped with God's view of people, the pastor sees every person as created in the image of God and as someone for whom Christ died. He can consider every word and action he observes as being related to God, whether the person being observed is aware of the connection or not. The pastor can allow his observations to provoke his thinking about how he might minister to the people he observes. What questions might he ask to gain more information and provoke thoughtfulness? How would he connect the truth of the Word of God to this person's life? With such activity, the pastor sharpens his personal discipline to be a careful observer of people and to think Biblically about the breadth and depth of human experience. It will help him minister wisely in ways similar to Christ's ministry to the woman at the well (John 4:6–42).

Continuing education in Biblical counseling

Thirty years ago only a handful of good, Biblical counseling resources existed. Today, books, journals, blogs, classes, and conferences abound. While few of these resources are presented from a distinctively fundamental Baptist and dispensational perspective, many of them provide beneficial Biblical teaching, helpful insight, and thought-provoking case studies. Others' study of the Word and their experiences of the ministry of the Word afford today's pastor opportunities to grow in knowledge and practical ability. The effective pastor will avail himself of some of the rich resources available to him on the topic of Biblical counseling. He will naturally be drawn to read on the topics most pressing among the people he currently counsels (anxiety, depression, addictions, etc.), but he will also avail himself of opportunities to investigate the unifying questions of counseling and discipleship—questions of mind-body (the interaction of the material and immaterial aspects of man), questions of Biblical human motivation (why do people do what they do?), and questions of how people grow and change. He will read and listen thoughtfully and critically, understanding the theological perspectives of the author/presenter and connecting what he is learning to his past and present ministry experiences. The result will be a growing understanding of God, self, and the people to whom he ministers.

Networking with pastors and professionals

A pastor who desires to grow in his ability to counsel others will cultivate relationships with people he recognizes as effective in the ministry of counseling. Most people with both a burden for and an ability in Biblical counseling desire to help others develop in their own abilities. Multiple means of communication—e-mail, phone, video-conferencing, etc.—provide today's pastor with the ability to link personally with these people around the world. The resultant conversations about the blessings and challenges of counseling benefit both the one seeking and the one giving help.

Observing counseling or co-counseling with a more experienced fellow pastor or counselor affords the opportunity for a pastor to see firsthand how God's Word is wisely ministered to people in a variety of life contexts. The time invested will bring long-term dividends. Referring a person to another pastor or Biblical counselor in the area and attending the sessions with that person often result in all involved receiving life-changing help.

In addition to building a network of pastors and counselors to go to for help and advice, a pastor should also cultivate relationships with other professionals. Establishing rapport with local law enforcement, emergency responders, firefighters, and other community leaders before emergencies arise fosters trust and even opens doors for ministry in the community. Establishing relationships with local medical personnel can provide a much-needed starting place for referrals. The counsel of a lawyer can also prove helpful at times and often is indispensable. The pastor should never presume upon personal relationships with these types of professionals, and he should expect to pay for services as would anyone else.

Conducting Effective Counseling

A pastor should allow his counseling ministry to develop as a natural extension of his public ministry. As this takes place, the pastor will find occasion to reach out to others, and others will reach out to him. Over time, the pastor will also involve other spiritually mature believers in assisting him in this work of focused discipleship.

Reaching out to others

Community involvement and befriending unbelievers in the community allow the pastor to build trust with those who need Christ. When challenges come into these people's lives, the pastor can naturally offer to pray for and with those in crisis. He will also find opportunity to talk with them about the challenges. The pastor then has opportunity to listen carefully to the person's descriptions and interpretations of the problem, and to learn of the individual's various responses to the problem. As he learns more about the person and the problem, the pastor will be afforded opportunities to connect the richness of the gospel to the details of the person's life. Counseling becomes here a ministry of evangelism. When the object of an unbeliever's hope proves unworthy of the trust invested in it, the pastor can accurately represent Christ as the only enduring hope amidst life's challenges.

As the pastor and his wife demonstrate hospitality to the members of the church, the pastor will naturally have opportunity to get to know his flock and to build trust. When the challenges of life overwhelm, or when the pastor sees concerns for the safety of a member of his flock, he can then reach out to pray, talk, and search the Scriptures with the person. Some of these matters call for beginning to counsel at the coffee shop; many will move from there to the dining room table; some will move to the study or counseling room. But always, the pastor will demonstrate the relevancy of the Word of God for interpreting and living life, and often the result will be a member of the flock staying on or returning to the path of faith, taking steps of strengthened faith.

The pastor who reaches out to others in time of need will find that he establishes a reputation of care and competency. Those who have received help will encourage others to reach out for help, and others will reach out on their own as they sense the pastor's care.

Reaching back to the pastor

When a person seeks help, the pastor then has wonderful opportunity to represent his Savior. Representing Christ well demands several ongoing responses from the pastor as he carries on the conversations of counseling. First, he listens. "He who answers a matter before he hears it, it is folly and shame to him" (Prov. 18:13, NKJV). The pastor who listens well and patiently asks wise questions emulates the love of Christ. Second, the pastor ponders his own life before God and this person. He will ask himself, "What does this person need to see of Christ lived out in my life as I counsel?" Third, the pastor prayerfully and wisely considers what God's agenda is in the person's life at the moment and seeks to be a part of that work of God. The pastor considers what God would want the person he is helping to know of God, self, and others, and how God would want that knowledge to be lived out. Fourth, the pastor prayerfully and compassionately communicates this agenda—God's way of seeing and living life—to the person seeking help. Finally, the pastor helps the person walk by faith, building the truth of the Word of God into life, confessing sin, and turning from it through specific steps of obedience.

Involving others

As the pastor reaches out to others, and others to him, opportunities to involve people in the ministry of counseling will come. The widower who followed Christ faithfully through the valley of the shadow of death, the parents who clung to Christ and each other when their wayward college-age daughter forsook the faith, the older couple who faithfully loved Christ and each other through the blessings and burdens of life, the couple who came back from the brink of divorce to cultivate a marriage that well reflects Christ—all of these people become potential fellow servants with the pastor in his work of counseling.

From the pulpit and in the counseling room, the pastor's ministry to these people began the process of training these individuals to counsel others. The process continues as the pastor, with the permission of all involved, encourages targeted fellowship among these people and others. The pastor provides direction to the fellowship, and, in some instances, shifts some of his counseling to those who are themselves competent and interested. All the while, he meets regularly with those who assist him in the counseling ministry and provides them with ongoing training and accountability. The ministry of focused discipleship comes full circle, the disciples become disciple makers, and all "grow up in all things into Him who is the head—Christ" (Eph. 4:15, NKJV).

Take Action . . .
1. Write out your understanding of Biblical anthropology.
2. Learn to watch people; consider their thoughts and behavior in light of God's Word.
3. Think about questions you could ask the people you observe and how you would connect Biblical truth to their lives.
4. Build a network of pastors and counselors to go to for counseling help and advice.
5. Prayerfully consider who you can ask to become your fellow servants in the work of counseling.

Discussion
1. What attitudes toward counseling have you encountered among pastors? Why do you think such a variety of attitudes exists?
2. How does viewing counseling as focused discipleship (discipleship in the details) help shape a pastor's attitudes and responsibility for the ministry of counseling?
3. Do you see ways that the world's definition and goal of counseling have shaped your thinking? How has reading this chapter challenged you to reshape your thinking?
4. Choose one of the methods given in this chapter for cultivating

personal counseling growth. Discuss specific ideas for putting it into practice in your own life.
5. Discuss an example of transparency that you have observed in the life of a pastor. What can you learn from that example?
6. What do you see as your greatest personal challenges as you consider the counseling ministry of a pastor? Discuss them along with ways to address the challenges.

For Further Study

Association of Certified Biblical Counselors website, biblicalcounseling.com, offers links to conference, training, and certification information; finding a counselor; and additional resources.

Biblical Counseling Coalition website, biblicalcounselingcoalition.org, has a wealth of information and resources available for counselors.

Blame It on the Brain?: Distinguishing Chemical Imbalances, Brain Disorders, and Disobedience by Edward T. Welch, P & R Publishing, 1998.

Changed into His Image by Jim Berg, BJU Press, 1999.

Christian Counseling and Education Foundation website, ccef.org, provides valuable information and resources for counselors.

The Christian Counselor's Manual by Jay E. Adams, Zondervan, 1986.

Competent to Counsel by Jay E. Adams, Zondervan, 1970.

Conflict under Control by Jeff Newman, Regular Baptist Press, 2007.

Counseling: How to Counsel Biblically by John MacArthur and Wayne Mack, Thomas Nelson, 2005.

Insight and Creativity in Christian Counseling: A Study of the Usual and the Unique by Jay E. Adams, Baker, 1982.

Institute for Nouthetic Studies website, nouthetic.org, allows counselors to benefit from the tutelage of Dr. Jay E. Adams, "the founding father of the modern Biblical counseling movement."

Instruments in the Redeemer's Hands: People in Need of Change Helping People in Need of Change by Paul D. Tripp, P & R Publishing, 1998.

Pastor and Deacons: Biblical Qualifications, Scriptural Roles, and Right Relationships by John Hartog II, Trafford Publishing, 2008.

Seeing with New Eyes: Counseling and the Human Condition through the Lens of Scripture by David Powlison, P & R Publishing, 2003.

Speaking the Truth in Love: Counsel in Community by David Powlison, New Growth Press, 2005.

"What Is Biblical Counseling, Anyway?" by Edward T. Welch, *Journal of Biblical Counseling,* 16:1, 1997.

Women Helping Women by Elyse Fitzpatrick and Carol Cornish, Harvest House, 1997.

10

Evangelizing
– Pat Nemmers

Recently a friend in ministry called me. He wanted to share with me a thought on leadership that had captured him. He said, "Pat, you know the old adage 'Everything rises and falls on leadership'? Well, I think it's somewhat inept. I think it would be better stated: Everything rises and falls on leadership—and 'followership.'"

It was an awkward moment. I love this guy. He has blessed my life on a number of occasions. But I could not have disagreed with him more.

Leadership by definition engenders followers. No followers, no leader. I told my friend that if he gave me twenty rebels and one Christ-honoring leader, I'd show him a bunch of former rebels—and maybe a few leaders out of the group—in a relatively short period of time.

So what's this have to do with evangelism in pastoral ministry? Pretty much everything. Since Solomon put it best, I will agree with him. There really is nothing new under the sun, and the adage is as true now as it was when first expressed: "Everything rises and falls on leadership." Every pastor or pastor wannabe reading this chapter wants a church that wins people to Jesus. Well, here is another general truth: it will not happen if it is not happening with you. Yet if it is happening with you, it will happen in your church. Joy, anticipation, and genuine holiness will begin to pervade your services. And the naysayers? Well, they'll go into hiding because they've started sounding ridiculous against all that God is doing.

The Reasons . . . Some of You Will Need Convincing

On my first Sunday in the first church I pastored, twenty-seven people showed up. The next Sunday only twenty-one came! I called my brother who had led me to Christ and was still very instrumental in my life. I told him this thing was going backwards. He told me to "get out there and preach like you're preaching to 2,100!" I took his advice and the church began to grow. But it was not because I preached with great power. I quickly learned that even passionate preaching could not be heard in other homes, so I would have to go to those homes. I did. And over time, souls came to Christ, we had regular baptisms, and the pews started to fill up.

Yours will too. But you will need to make some changes, and those changes must start with you. If you are a pastor, you will need to concede this general fact: you set the tone, atmosphere, joy, passion, love, and example to your church. If your church is joyful, it is likely because you are joyful. If it is joyless, it is likely because you are not exuding joy. If your church is compassionate, it is likely because you are compassionate. If your church is heavy into doctrine and theology, again, it will probably be because you are. And if your church is evangelistic, it will likely be because you are evangelistic. If it's not, it is likely because you are not.

To be clear, I have never met a Baptist pastor who was not for the idea of evangelism. Interestingly, of all the themes our churches and association conferences choose, evangelism in one form or another is always one we come back to. The subject serves like a homing device, and that's a good thing. Yet even after a soul-stirring set of meetings, when the dust settles, we usually return to what got us to where we are.

Speaking of dust, I once was invited to be the keynote speaker in a state meeting on the subject of evangelism. When I arrived, the host pastor took me for a tour of his church. It was an old church with a small congregation, but he had been there many years. History was his love, and every room had a historical theme. I admit it was impressive. In the sanctuary, I walked to the platform to get a feel of things before the meetings. I walked up to the baptistry, which was noticeably dusty. But I was not prepared for what I would see inside. Looking down, I was shocked to discover a sofa. The pastor, following close behind and clearly embarrassed, leaned on the rail of the baptistry and said, "I'll bet the waters of your church are stirred all the time."

I answered, "Apparently more than these."

"We haven't seen many come to Christ. That's why we invited you here!" he said with a sly smile.

I had a great time there. I met some tremendous young pastors with a true zeal for evangelism. Yet I could not help but wonder if that brother would comfortably slide into the things that had gotten him to where he was.

Here, dear friend, are the simple reasons to commit to personally evangelizing the lost.

It's your calling

Imagine a firefighter who never fought fires. A police officer who never patrolled. An architect who never designed. You get the point. If you're not evangelizing, start doing so. If you are, keep it up! If you're struggling doing so, you're not alone. Be encouraged. God loves it when we attempt to spread the good news of His Son. Fruit will come. But if you're under the impression that evangelism is only for the specially gifted, you're wrong. Paul commanded Timothy to "do the work of an evangelist, fulfill your ministry" (2 Tim. 4:5, ESV). I take it that evangelism was not Timothy's dominant gift. Yet Paul, in his last will and testament, exhorted his beloved son in the faith to get out of his comfort zone and preach Christ to the lost.

It's your joy

Longing to return to the fruitful ground of Thessalonica, Paul burst out his heart reason to get back to the believers there when he said, "For you are our glory and joy" (1 Thess. 2:20, ESV). My two greatest joys of a quarter century of pastoring have been leading souls to trust Jesus and planting churches from the fruit of evangelism. Dear pastor friend, embrace your calling. It's your glory and joy.

It's your influence

"Let no one despise you for your youth, but set the believers an example in speech, in conduct, in love, in faith, in purity" (1 Tim. 4:12, ESV). Someone has said, "He who calls himself a leader but has no one following him is just taking a walk." If you are a pastor, to one degree or another you are a leader. If you are not leading anyone, you might want to reexamine your call. If you are leading, I have a question: Where are you taking your people? It will not be enough for you to cast a vision of the lost and fields white for harvest unless you can from time to time show them an actual sheaf from those nearby fields.

It's the only way the church truly grows

It's always encouraging when a Christian family moves into your area and decides to join your church. It's also cool when someone leaves an unsound church to come to yours because they long for solid food. Yet the hard truth is this: while your numbers might have increased, the church has not grown. Technically, the church grows only when someone comes to Jesus in faith. Luke put it succinctly: "The Lord added to their number day by day those who were being saved" (Acts 2:47, ESV).

It keeps Biblical priorities in place

In His powerful denunciation of the scribes and Pharisees, Jesus provided an equally powerful insight into human nature, which inverts His priorities. "Woe to you, scribes and Pharisees, hypocrites! For you tithe mint and dill and cumin, and have neglected the weightier matters of the law: justice and mercy and faithfulness. These you ought to have done, without neglecting the others" (Matt. 23:23, ESV). Jesus was not condemning what they were tithing. He was condemning the fact they had "neglected the weightier matters."

As I view it, the gospel should be the hub, the center of your ministry. The gospel wins people. People fill your church. They also end up filling positions like evangelists, teachers, youth workers, ushers, greeters, helpers, cooks, deacons, and dozens of other ministry opportunities in your church. Evangelism literally becomes the feeder of virtually every other position in the church—including the pastorate. At this writing, I am involved in a third church plant, the pastor having been converted right here nearly ten years ago.

The point is that evangelistic ministry done simply and faithfully actually helps keep your priorities straight. I love creativity, but I have seen some pretty bizarre tactics used to win people and draw others to church. The farther we get from the simplicity of gospel outreach, the stranger we must look from Heaven. Keeping evangelistic outreach as your highest ministry priority will help keep other things in line.

The Resolutions . . . Let's Assume You're Convinced

Pastors are constantly calling people to make resolutions. Before starting the next chapter of this book, why not make a few personally, especially in the realm of gospel outreach? Here are some simple yet life-changing promises I encourage you to make.

I will pray daily for personal opportunities

I know of no other prayer in my life that God has answered more often and more quickly than the prayer for personal opportunities. (And who isn't thrilled when God answers prayer?!) Yet like you, my ministry, apart from evangelism, is so busy it is easy to omit, forget, or just squeeze out this responsibility we are called to do. Here's a solution—pray about it every day. Ask God to place opportunities in front of you and give you the boldness and grace to take them.

Not long ago I was studying at a coffee shop. It occurred to me I had not personally spoken to anyone about Jesus in quite some time. I was convicted, humbled, and overwhelmed with the need to share Christ. So I paused, prayed, and asked God to give me an opportunity to talk to someone that day. As I opened my eyes and looked up, there was a young man literally staring at me. He asked, "Are you a pastor or something?" I said, "Well, yes." He went on to completely open up to me and, upon a subsequent meeting, trusted Jesus. Why not make a promise to pray for evangelistic opportunities each day, then watch God move?

I will begin to meet with lost people

Some of the greatest advice ever given me came from the pastor who discipled me. He, too, was a busy man. He told me no matter how busy things got, he always wanted to have a study going with lost people. That stuck. And while I've not always accomplished this, it is my desire and resolution to meet regularly with non-Christians. Besides the opportunity, I find it keeps me current with the worldviews of others and helps me better relate with those outside the faith.

Meeting with the lost has also helped me to increase my genuine love for those bound by sin. When Jesus "saw the crowds, he had compassion for them" (Matt 9:36, ESV). Should we be any different? Pastors should be more "high touch" than "high tech." People are people in every generation. They want—they need—contact. Real, sit-down, look-you-in-the-eye, handshake or hug, I-really-care-about-you kind of contact. Brother, determine to meet with lost people who need Jesus. If Jesus was "a friend of sinners," we should be too.

I will reject moralistic preaching

In 1992 President George H. W. Bush was riding one of the highest approval ratings in presidential history. Having led a great victory in Iraq during Desert Shield, he looked invincible in attaining a second term. But Bill Clinton had other plans. He would succeed in turning the tide of Bush's popularity by turning the issue to the economy. And he would do it with a rather harsh but clever slogan: "It's the economy, stupid!" His point being, what good are we as a country abroad if we are weak at home? Now, one can debate the truthfulness of his assertion, but the fact is his slogan and redirect worked. It would be Clinton, not George H. W. Bush, who would get two terms in the White House.

Where I pastor, there are countless Bible-believing churches within a twenty-mile radius. Occasionally we'll get visitors who come from one of those very churches because they tire of mere moralistic preaching that has more to do with law and less to do with grace. They do preach the Bible. But their preaching is mostly "how to" preaching like "How to have a better marriage, raise godly kids, serve one another, overcome anxiety, get rid of bad habits," etc. They end their messages with an appeal to apply the principles they've learned and, "See you tonight!"

So, to all of you who happen to fit that category, I have a slogan you should think on: It's the gospel, stupid! Moralistic preaching, righteous stands (like boycotting certain businesses), and high standards of godly living will not change the hearts of wicked people. Only Jesus can do that, and He does it through His gospel.

Planting churches has been the greatest ministry joy of my life. But early on in one of those plants we just avoided what could have been a wrong direction in purpose. A godly, well-intentioned woman sent out an e-mail to the entire church, which had a number of new Christians. She urged fellow churchgoers to boycott a certain establishment for its promotion of the homosexual agenda. For sure, this store should be boycotted by Christ followers. But by appealing to this newly formed church to rise up against this establishment, she unwittingly threatened to distort the very purpose of their existence. Our commission is not to change society, but the hearts of individuals, who, by way of their presence and outreach, change environments around them.

I fully realize this is a touchy subject for many. We love the idea of abortion clinics shutting down, strip bars unlicensed, and ungodly companies put out of business by boycotts. We thrill in the idea of electing godly political candidates to office who will uphold our values. Yet issues-oriented, moralistic preaching will never accomplish what Paul described as "the foolishness of preaching." The sad thing is that even to

Bible-believing preachers, God's simple plan to win the lost has become foolish to them as they have largely rejected it for what seems to be a better plan. Resolve to reject this approach to preaching.

I will mentor others to win souls

I'm fortunate to pastor a church with a pastor of evangelism serving under me. Chuck De Cleene is in his sixties and is as effective in winning souls to Jesus as he ever has been. His approach is profoundly simple and even more profoundly effective. He meets people and becomes their genuine friend. He offers a clearly thought-through four-part Bible study that he is in no hurry to get through. The result is a trail of changed lives wherever he goes.

A number of years ago God impressed on him the need to dedicate his life not only to winning people to Jesus but also to mentoring those very converts to do the same. As a result, he began taking individuals out with him on his calls and, by example, showed them how to win souls and influence eternity. To be candid, the process has not exceeded expectations. Yet little by little, and over time, God is steadily raising up a new generation of soul winners—the generation that will take over when we're off the scene. On John Wesley's tombstone are these words: "God buries His workmen, but the work goes on." And the work must go on! Jesus will build His future church to some degree by the mentoring process of this generation.

Resolve, dear brother, to be involved both in the work of evangelism and the mentoring of those who will be left with the baton when we're gone.

The church you pastor, or long to pastor, will be an evangelistic church only if you are. So I charge you before the living God, before Whom we will each stand one day: "Preach the word!" And "do the work of an evangelist, fulfill your ministry" (2 Tim. 4:2, 5, ESV).

Take Action . . .

1. Pray daily for personal opportunities to witness.
2. Schedule opportunities to meet and/or spend time with the lost.
3. Evaluate your preaching and the church's emphases—is either (or both) moralistic?
4. Plan a way to regularly mentor others to win souls.

Discussion

1. Why does everything rise or fall on leadership, not leadership and "followership"?
2. Should you be concerned if you are not regularly baptizing new members?
3. How does a pastor protect his zeal for evangelism after returning from a conference that fired him up? In other words, how does he keep from sliding back into the things that got him to where he was before the conference?

For Further Study

"Bible Truths about Salvation" by Chuck De Cleene. This four-part evangelistic Bible study series is available upon request through Saylorville Church (515-289-2395 or office@saylorvillebaptist.com).

How Good Is Good Enough? by Andy Stanley, Multnomah, 2003.

The Gospel and Personal Evangelism by Mark Dever, Crossway, 2007.

The Master Plan of Evangelism by Robert Coleman, Baker, 1993.

The Prodigal God by Tim Keller, Dutton, 2008.

11

Making Disciples: The Priority and Practice
— Don McCall

I still remember the excitement and anticipation of my first church thirty-eight years ago. There is a certain sweetness in that remembrance, yet there is also the inevitable twinge of frustration. If only I'd known then what I know now. . . . I have to wonder what would have changed. Would my time there have been more productive? more God honoring? Could it at least have been a little smoother? Perhaps. Even so, I still feel a sense of contentment because God has now given me a wonderful opportunity to share what He taught me in the crucible of experience during the twenty-six years I served as a part of that wonderful ministry.

Early in my ministry, Elmer Towns, an author and church consultant, introduced me to the concept of four basic group sizes that are essential to church health. He reminded me that people very naturally interact differently in each context. In fact, the size of each group inherently predetermines the extent and depth of interaction that will occur. The size that I believe is ideal for discipleship will be referenced as the core group or D-Group.

The Core Group

This group's ideal size is three or four individuals who are of the same gender. When this sort of group is established, the prevailing dynamics are a deep level of intimacy, frank openness, and humble transparency. That is an especially significant fact when people grasp this parallel truth as stated by Greg Ogden in *Discipleship Essential*: "Transformation of life occurs when a person grapples with the truth of God's Word in the context of transparent relationships." Other vital aspects in the core group are consistent and genuine encouragement, purposeful accountability, and honest sharing of life experiences at a level far beyond the surface. This is in sharp contrast to the shallow conversations and sharing that often take place in the typical church setting. Interestingly, and inversely, however, if the group comprises only two members, the dynamic is not nearly as effective. In this case, interaction often becomes more "teacher to student" as opposed to the ideal of mutual support and accountability. Furthermore, in a group that is too small, there is a tendency to dismiss the other person's rebuke or observations as merely "his opinion" when there is no one else to confirm the observation. However, it must be noted that if a core group exceeds five members, it will quickly lose the most basic group dynamics as described above.

From a Biblical perspective, it is interesting to observe that when Jesus was developing disciples who would carry out His mission, He used this particular group size to prepare the "prime movers" of the early church. A careful look at the Gospels reveals the numerous times that Jesus took His threesome aside to instruct them. Peter, James, and John—the members of this first-century "core group"—were taken aside at some of the most significant times of Jesus' ministry. We see Jesus intentionally taking only three of the disciples into the room where He healed Jairus's daughter (Mark 5; Luke 8). They were also the only ones with Him at the Mount of Transfiguration (Matt. 17), and just prior to Jesus' arrest, they were the only ones He took with Him to pray (Mark 14). Jesus' strategy for making disciples included an inner circle of three. We would do well to follow the disciple-making strategy of the consummate Disciple Maker and Creator of discipleship, Jesus Christ Himself.

In interviewing over one thousand students in the twelve years I have been teaching in a Bible college, I have found the answer to the following question very disconcerting. When asked, "How many of your churches have intentionally developed anything at a core-group level?" only 3 percent have answered in the affirmative. I am certain this is not because the churches do not see the importance of disciple making, because Christ's mandate in Matthew 28:19 and 20 is quite explicit and is accepted widely as the mission of the local and universal church. Most, if not all, of these churches have made multiple attempts at accomplishing this elusive goal of making disciples. What church has not tried one-on-one discipleship or six-week discipleship classes? Or new convert courses? Or groups studying everything from Scripture or basic doctrine to spiritual formation, as well as Christian-living books, and a plethora of otherwise useful, albeit generally ineffective, material? All of these have implicit value, and I certainly have implemented most of them for a significant period of time throughout my ministry. Yet none of them has demonstrated the ability to sustain the process of disciple making in the long term.

Before reading about the process of discipleship that I believe has demonstrated significant sustainability and effectiveness, take some time to read the following notes that are typical responses from churchgoers following the implementation of the core groups (we identify these groups by the title "D-Groups," which stands for "discipleship groups").

> *Dear Pastor Don,*
>
> The Lord has used you and your preaching and the D-Groups to change our family miraculously. Our relationship has the same consideration and respect that it did when we first started dating. When we met, Trevor was so on fire for the Lord and so strong, which is the main thing that drew me to him; but after years of doing ministry, he just lost his first love and grew weary, which put such a strain on our relationship. I felt we argued about everything (and nothing) and were both doing the "routine" of being a Christian, but our passion for God was gone. But since coming to the church we have been blossoming under your preaching but more than that, each week Trevor learns something new at D-Group. He gets so excited. But it's not just the doctrinal things he is learning. It's so much more. He gets the door again. He holds my hand. He turns off the TV and just sits with me. He plays the guitar for the kids and me and we just sing. He puts the kids to bed WITHOUT complaining. I have my old Trevor back again with his passion for God, life and ME, when I thought he had disappeared for good.
>
> Thank you so much.
>
> *Dear Mr. McCall*
>
> I want to encourage you today to continue on with whatever God is calling you to do presently. Since last fall, our church has been using what you put together as D-Groups material. The groups are growing and multiplying. God is being glorified—we are getting to know Him better. Our lives are changing.

Good Morning Pastor Don,

I've been trying to write this e-mail for quite some time, but never quite get around to it. And, now that I am writing it, I'm not sure what to say, so please forgive any rambling that may go on.

For some time now, it has been clear that without accountability, and mentoring of some kind, I am never going to be the man that God wants me to be. I haven't quite figured out what that man looks like, either, though I have a good idea.

At any rate, I'm losing the battle. I'm losing the battle to be a leader in my home; the battle of showing love to my wife instead of anger; the battle of showing God to those I work with; the battle of being close to God in my own life. I know that I asked God into my life. I remember the night well. I remember the feeling of elation. I remember the burden gone. But since then, I have felt nothing but endless guilt for my lack of participation in God's plan.

This lack of commitment to my spiritual life has carried over into my personal life. I have not been "purposeful" in either area. I have simply let the world take me where it wills.

So here is the question: Do you think that you could find time in your business to help me exit this shell of guilt, take on the mantle of leadership that is waiting for me, and hold me accountable for what I am doing wrong, and help me know what I am doing right?

Thank you very much for what you are doing for our church!

God has proven faithful to change hearts and lives through this method, and my heartbeat is to share the particulars of this process with others. While I was reluctant to accept the challenge of writing this chapter due to the wealth of excellent material on the subject, the last letter came on the day the decision needed to be made. God used it to motivate me to put my pen to paper. So here it is: this is the process that I used for the final seven years at the church I pastored, and that I presently use when God provides the opportunity for me to be an intentional interim pastor. There are seven separate components to the D-Groups that must be understood and implemented for sustainability: God sightings, truth sharing, accountability questions, prayer, growth plans, reproducing reproducers, and leader reflection. Please note that the first four components all take place during the weekly meeting. The last three are critical to the process, and without them, D-Groups will falter.

Seven Components
1. God Sightings

Each weekly session begins with the same basic question: where have you seen God at work in your life this week? It is important for each person to become increasingly aware that God is not simply the God Who is there, but He is the God Who is actively involved in orchestrating the affairs of his life. These events have become known as God sightings, God moments, or hugs from God. The rationale behind this particular element of the Core group is both faith building and pre-evangelistic in nature.

The sharing of God sightings has the profound effect of encouraging and strengthening each group member's faith. When individuals share their sightings, others become more conscious of God's involvement in their daily existence. Excitement and faith sharing become a natural outworking of this exercise.

2. Truth Sharing

Each week's lesson includes a segment of material for interaction: Scripture, book studies, material on doctrine, spiritual formation, prayer, etc. Learners not only read the material, but each individual is to highlight any particularly significant statement. When the group meets, each person has an opportunity to share two insights that were of special interest to him. It is crucial to understand the rationale for this. Most Christians' daily conversations do not include insights or sharing of a spiritual nature. Christians tend to talk about anything and everything but spiritual truth. This segment of the core group is intended to develop both ability and comfort in sharing spiritual insights with each other. Christians can move beyond the surface level of relationships, and that will become a reality as they become accustomed to sharing Biblical truth and insights both inside and outside the group.

3. Accountability

I will not spend much time building a case for accountability. Much has already been written on this topic. Each week, learners are asked certain questions. That these questions are asked on a weekly basis has the effect of fulfilling the injunction of Hebrews 3:13, "Exhort one another daily, while it is called 'Today,' lest any of you be hardened through the deceitfulness of sin" (NKJV); Hebrews 10:24, "Let us consider one another in order to stir up love and good works" (NKJV); and 2 Timothy 2:22, "Flee also youthful lusts; but pursue righteousness, faith, love, peace with those who call on the Lord out of a pure heart" (NKJV). Each individual often comments how the realization that he is going to meet and tell of his actions has deterred him from acting unbiblically as well as encouraged him to action that is appropriate for his life as a Christ-one.

4. Prayer

Prayer is the spiritual discipline mentioned the most times in Scripture, either explicitly or implicitly. Yet this relational discipline is often the weakest area of a Christian's life. Before I developed the D-Group material, I interviewed fifty pastors and fifty laymen and made two amazing and disheartening discoveries: Of the fifty laymen interviewed, only three had ever experienced being discipled, and they spent about ten minutes a day in focused prayer. The fifty pastors interviewed did not do much better. Only three others had experienced being developed in a relational context in the areas of personal Bible study, evangelism, personal holiness, prayer, and ministry. They spent about twenty minutes a day in focused prayer. The D-Group material begins by developing the participant's intimacy with God. It is hoped that a person's love for God and his awareness of God's love for him will be the fruit of the first months in the D-Group.

5. Growth Plans

It is appalling that people have business plans, financial plans, retirement plans, lesson plans, weight-loss plans, education plans, and medical treatment plans, but that churches have no intentional plan for growing spiritually. The second week the D-Group meets, each person is assigned to describe his present practice regarding spiritual disciplines. John Jelinek's diagnostic tool is used to help each participant evaluate his spiritual condition. The last step is to devise a plan for spiritual growth using the spiritual inventory and diagnostic tool. This plan is copied and given to each person in the group as the basis for the first accountability question. This practice is repeated every six months to ensure and track the spiritual progress of all the participants. Apart from this type of structure, spiritual growth tends to be relatively slow and uncertain. An appropriate first accountability question is, "Have you fulfilled your weekly growth plan objectives for this week?" The growth plan is what helps keep a D-Group's ongoing life and vitality over the years.

6. Reproducing Reproducers

It is critical to develop a culture of multiplication within the D-Group strategy. If discipleship is going to happen, individuals cannot remain indefinitely in a group. For multiplication to take place, there must be a strategy for preparing leaders. The process of group multiplication and leadership development is built into the plan for each D-Group. After the initial group has been developed, each group should comprise one leader, one apprentice, and two new recruits.

Our groups multiplied in October and April. The month prior to their multiplication, the leader and apprentice (who becomes a leader) determine which one of their group will become the new apprentice. Each leader then begins to enlist two new recruits for his group. Groups tend to connect best when both the leader and the new apprentice have consensus on who will be invited to join them. Though the group repeats the same material every six months, the group's vibrancy and freshness is maintained through the development of new growth plans and the excitement of developing the new recruits.

7. Leader Reflection

It is important to gather all the leaders together approximately every six weeks to two months to review and reflect on what is happening in the D-Group ministry. This venue provides a time of personal refreshment, testimonials of victories, evaluation of materials, and problem solving. Each leader has the opportunity to share any ideas he has found that will enhance the group's effectiveness. This element cannot be bypassed. When leaders do not have the opportunity to share in this way, the D-Group ministry will begin to lose its momentum.

Mentoring

Effective mentoring narrows the focus to one-on-one, or more accurately, "life on life" relationships. Second Timothy 2:2 certainly emphasizes the priority of this type of relationship: "The things that you have heard from me among many witnesses, commit these to faithful men who will be able to teach others also" (NKJV). I would like to add a few observations to this conversation.

Servanthood

The development of leaders through a mentoring process is modeled throughout Scripture. I have found that mentoring through serving the mentor has been sadly overlooked. Note the following pairs—Aaron/Moses, David/King Saul, Elisha/Elijah, Timothy/Paul. You will see a number of common factors:

- They experienced life together.
- Their development was not done at a distance.
- The person being mentored served the leader.

As a mentor, you might find this difficult, even resisting the thought of someone serving you. Yet this appears to be a significant part of the growth process. Seldom will a person become an effective leader apart from learning first to humbly serve others.

Enlistment

We seldom see volunteerism found in Scripture. Instead, we see enlistment, as with the pairs mentioned above. This, too, is an element we must embrace in the mentoring process. Pray prior to enlisting individuals for mentoring. This is certainly what Christ modeled for us prior to enlisting His disciples. The right people at the right time will result in relationships that will continue the process mentioned in 2 Timothy 2:2.

Modeling

Doing life together is the essence of mentoring. It is in this context that a person begins to grasp what it is you are teaching and living. Some would say that character development and skills development are more caught than taught. Modeling in a life-on-life context will have a profound impact. It will necessitate creating space in your life. It will mean living transparently before the one being mentored. Consider the many opportunities that you have on a weekly basis. Why not involve your "mentoree" in meals, visitation, family outings, sermon preparation, counseling sessions, board meetings, staff meetings, recreation, and the like. Each of these situations can provide a venue for personal and ministry development.

Making disciples is not an optional activity for anyone who takes seriously the command of Christ and the mission of the church. There are many approaches to this objective. The core-group approach is one I have experience in. The result has been hundreds of individuals entering full-time vocational ministry and thousands growing in Christ. May God's great grace be upon you as you apply yourself to this endeavor in your context and culture.

Take Action . . .
1. Evaluate your church's discipleship program. Does it include core groups?
2. Evaluate various discipleship programs and choose one to be used in your church.
3. Introduce a core-group type discipleship ministry to your church.

Discussion
1. Why should discipleship groups be of the same gender?
2. What will "transparent relationships" in a core group look like?
3. Does your church disciple at a core-group level? What are the benefits if it does? What could be the benefits if it did?
4. How could you motivate new believers to meet weekly for discipleship (before they become committed to the group)?
5. Why don't "most Christians' daily conversations . . . include insights or sharing of a spiritual nature"?
6. What are the strengths and weaknesses of accountability relationships?
7. Why is it critical to develop a culture of multiplication within a core group?

For Further Study
The Disciple-Making Pastor (2007) and *The Disciple-Making Church* (2010) by Bill Hull, Baker.
"What Is Intentional Ministry?" at texasbaptists.org.

12

Visioneering
— Stephen Viars

The trinitarian God of Scripture is the consummate planner. The Bible opens with the picture of the Holy Spirit moving over the surface of the waters. Why? Because He was planning to do something. At a critical juncture in Jesus' ministry, the Lord announced to His disciples that "I will build My church; and the gates of Hades will not overpower it" (Matt. 16:18, NASB). Nearly two thousand years later, men and women around the world are involved daily in the accomplishment of that strategic plan. God the Father chose to reveal His mercy and grace through His breathtakingly beautiful plan of redemption. "And we know that God causes all things to work together for good to those who love God, to those who are called according to His purpose. For those whom He foreknew, He also predestined to become conformed to the image of His Son, so that He would be the firstborn among many brethren" (Rom. 8:28, 29, NASB).

That is why we have gorgeous beaches and towering mountain ranges. That is why my fingers can receive a signal from my brain and move around this keyboard. That is why the Children of Israel offered sacrifices in the wilderness. That is why we have the cross. That is why we have rainbows. That is why we have hope. The list of examples is practically endless. Open your Bible to just about any page and you will see evidence of a God Who plans.

Magnifying God by Planning Well
Because others formulate their view of God by watching us

One amazing aspect of the Lord's design for creation is that human beings are made in His image and likeness (Gen. 1:27). Because of that unique position and calling, we were simultaneously given privileges and responsibilities like no other aspect of God's created world. We could never have achieved what theologians often call the "creation mandate" without the ability and willingness to plan. To the degree to which men and women planned well, we were choosing to be like our God.

In the Sermon on the Mount, Jesus told His followers that they should "let your light shine before men in such a way that they may see your good works, and glorify your Father who is in heaven" (Matt. 5:16, NASB). The entire context revolves around planning and living in such a way that our watching world would have a better understanding of what God is like. Fundamentally that is what it means to glorify God—to give others a better understanding of Him.

Yet consider what would happen if a person walked inside the average church and asked a series of simple questions:

1. What is this church specifically planning to accomplish in the next year, three years, or five years?
2. What are the ten to twenty specific plans that have been accomplished by this body of believers in the last twelve months?
3. If I bring my family and associated resources to this church, what assurance would we have that those gifts, abilities, and treasures would be stewarded well?
4. If God chose to bless this church financially in an unusual way this Sunday, do you have unmet plans and dreams that could be accomplished?

In other words, do people have a better understanding of the nature of God as a result of watching the way the average church functions? Or is it possible that the haphazard and unorganized way we sometimes (frequently?) live and do ministry leads others to the powerful though misguided conclusion that God must not have His act together because His people surely don't?

Because of the principle of stewardship

Please pause for a moment and think about all the resources God has entrusted to your church. You may even want to begin listing them on a sheet of paper. Write down all the people and their experiences and spiritual giftedness. Think about your property and buildings. Consider the financial wealth Americans enjoy. Then look out the nearest window and begin listing all the ministry opportunities. God has entrusted you with all of that.

Allowing that trust to motivate you to action is the essence of the

Biblical principle of stewardship. Undoubtedly you remember Jesus' parable in Matthew 25. "For it is just like a man about to go on a journey, who called his own slaves and entrusted his possessions to them. To one he gave five talents, to another, two, and to another, one, each according to his own ability; and he went on his journey" (Matt. 25:14, 15, NASB).

Consider carefully what the first faithful steward did next. "Immediately the one who had received the five talents went and traded with them, and gained five more talents" (NASB). I absolutely love that guy, don't you? He knew exactly what he would do if he had more resources. And when the trust came, he got after it "immediately." The tense of the verb "traded" also suggests that this was not a onetime windfall, but that the man worked his plan of investment over and over and over. I believe it is impossible to be a faithful steward without a specific and aggressive plan to leverage all the resources God has entrusted to His church.

Because of the principle of accountability

This book is especially directed toward pastors and other church leaders. Regardless of your church's precise organizational and administrative structure, there is no question that the offices of pastor and deacon are emphasized in Scripture as possessing significant influence and authority. Rarely does a day go by when I do not thank the Lord for calling me to be one of His pastors.

However, as is often the case in the economy of God, with authority comes accountability. The writer of Hebrews explained this principle when he said, "Obey your leaders and submit to them, for they keep watch over your souls as those who will give an account" (Heb. 13:17, NASB).

Like every steward, someday God will call his pastors before Him and ask for an accounting of our leadership in Christ's church. I agree with those who say in reference to 1 Corinthians 3:10–15, "As a Christian, I do not fear the fire of Hell, but I certainly fear the fire of Heaven." Wise planning prepares us to honor Christ with a good account of what has been entrusted to us.

What about you?

I would encourage you to evaluate yourself on the issue of how well you have influenced your church to make wise, careful, and aggressive ministry plans. Have you given others the right opinion of God in this matter? Have you been a faithful steward of leading your church family to carefully invest the many resources entrusted to you? If called to do so today, would you be able to give a good account to Christ because you have planned and executed well? If not, why not pause and ask God to forgive you for this oversight. "He who covers his sins will not prosper, but whoever confesses and forsakes them will have mercy" (Prov. 28:13, NKJV). Then ask our merciful God to give you wisdom as you consider what it means to be a visionary leader.

Managing the Church to Accomplish More

Visioneering is the process of leading a church family to accomplish what God desires in specific, measurable, and fulfilling ways. Some pastors might object with excuses like "I'm not a gifted administrator" or "planning doesn't come easy for me" or "I just want to preach and pray."

Good luck with all of that, guys. Scripture makes it clear that pastors, among other things, are "overseers" and "managers." Whatever we think about administration, the plain truth is that certain terms and concepts are used to describe us in ways unlike anyone else in the church. Paul asked young Timothy, "If a man does not know how to manage his own household, how will he take care of the church of God?" (1 Tim. 3:5, NASB). Administration, planning, and vision casting may be very difficult tasks for you. If so, there is nothing wrong with bringing other people in your church family who are skilled in these areas around you to help and assist. But ultimately it is your responsibility to lead and manage the church under your care.

Teach your church the focus of the plan

The first step in anything that will matter in eternity is to be sure that everyone involved is growing in love for Jesus Christ. The sad tale of Mary and Martha is instructive on a daily basis for many of us.

> Now as they were traveling along, He entered a village; and a woman named Martha welcomed Him into her home. She had a sister called Mary, who was seated at the Lord's feet, listening to His word. But Martha was distracted with all her preparations; and she came up to Him and said, "Lord, do You not care that my sister has left me to do all the serving alone? Then tell her to help me." But the Lord answered and said to

her, "Martha, Martha, you are worried and bothered about so many things; but only one thing is necessary, for Mary has chosen the good part, which shall not be taken away from her" (Luke 10:38–42, NASB).

The focus of our entire planning process should be the person and work of our Redeemer. We should contemplate the cross and rejoice in the empty tomb. Our lips should speak in amazement at His grace in calling us to Himself and choosing to use us in ministry.

Write a mission statement together

If your church family has not gone through the process of developing a clear and compelling mission statement, I would encourage you to make that job number one in the planning process. It is impossible to have an effective strategic plan without knowing why you exist and what you believe God wants you to achieve together.

Our church family chose to keep our mission statement very simple: "The mission of Faith Church is to glorify God by winning people to Jesus Christ and equipping them to be more faithful disciples." We encourage every person in our church family to memorize this statement. I jokingly tell our people that if I called them at two o'clock in the morning, even before they could remember their own name, I would hope they would be able to recite our mission statement. We avoid all kinds of opportunities because they simply are not essential to our mission. Conversely, we do many other things tirelessly because we have decided together that a particular activity is central to why we exist.

Establish a futures committee

It is highly likely that many reading this chapter will say that planning and administration do not come naturally. If that is the case, there very well may be some other spiritual men and women in your church family who are quite gifted in these matters.

At Faith we go through a strategic planning process once every five years. At the beginning of the planning cycle, we invite anyone who wants to participate to serve on the futures committee. They are told at the beginning that they are a working committee, not a decision-making body. Their role is to assist the pastors and deacons by providing leadership to the planning process. Ultimately our forty pastors and deacons serve as the decision-making filter because we are the ones our church family has elected to provide leadership to the congregation. However, the futures committee can be a marvelous tool if it comprises visionary men and women who love using their administrative gifts to help the church family plan well.

Launch a church- and community-wide evaluation process

An effective plan has to bubble up from the grass roots. I have always believed that the next best ministry idea may be resting in the heart of someone in the church family or perhaps even in the community. We generally design two surveys, one for the congregation and one for the community.

We make it clear on each survey that we are asking for frank, honest, and direct evaluation. We believe we need others to give us straightforward feedback so we can ascertain exactly where we are as a church ministry at any given place in our history. Some of the questions ask for help in identifying what we are doing well as a church. But we also design many questions to invite people to offer constructive criticism from a variety of perspectives. Those are not always the easiest answers to read, but they often give us profound insight into what we need to work on to be more effective for Christ.

The surveys also ask people to help us identify ministry opportunities in our neighborhood, our community, and our world. I love asking people, "What are the needs that you see in our community that a church like ours might be able to meet?" We also ask men and women to tell us about their ministry dreams with questions like, "If resources were not an issue, what would you love to see us do for God in this place?"

We also ask folks to talk to us about any perceived threats. What do we need to guard against? What do we need to be sure we protect? What is on the horizon that could bring us down?

Congregational surveys are distributed and made available online. Community surveys are mailed to our neighbors, advertised in the local newspaper, and made available online. Some of the questions request numerical evaluation, while others ask for short answers. We generally receive four hundred to five hundred completed surveys.

Collating all the raw data is a significant task. By God's grace we have several widows who spend hours entering all the handwritten answers into a single document. Another team assembles all the numerical data.

This synthesis generally forms a thirty- to forty-page report. All the data, unedited, is then published online. Some of it is not particularly flattering, but if it is part of the way people perceive you or your ministry, you need to know about it. We then encourage our people to carefully and prayerfully read the entire report.

Brainstorm initiatives

In my way of thinking, this is where the fun starts. Now we ask our church family and anyone from the community who wishes to participate to begin suggesting initiatives—specific steps we might take in the upcoming days to either build on one of our strengths, shore up one of our weaknesses, seize one of the opportunities, or fortify ourselves against a threat.

We ask our folks to pray for creativity and passion during this particular phase. We tell them over and over that there are no bad ideas at this point of the process. Our goal is that we might generate five hundred to six hundred possible strategic initiatives. All of these ministry ideas are then printed and distributed to the church family.

Let the best initiatives rise to the top

For Faith, it typically takes us approximately six months to get to this point. All along the way I have been talking in sermons about what's happening, and other church leaders are emphasizing it in their spheres of influence. Updates and discussions would have been given at every monthly pastor and deacons' meeting. Everyone on the team knows that developing the next strategic plan is a major emphasis at the church.

At this point it is important to host a series of congregational meetings. It is critical to try to have as large a percentage of the church family there as possible. I simply tell our folks, "If you're saved, you'll be there." They generally get the point.

Now it is time to determine which ministry ideas are really the best. There is no way that our church in its current configuration could take on six hundred planning initiatives. It would bury us. So we try to let about 110–120 rise to the top.

The discussion can be a great time of equipping for the church family. We ask questions like these:
- Which ten initiatives do you believe are most closely connected to our mission statement and why?

- Which of these initiatives do you believe accomplishes the greatest amount of impact while expending the least amount of resources?
- Which of these initiatives would be the greatest blessing to our community right now?

My observation over the years has been that it is amazing to watch the best ideas rise to the top. When men and women are filled with the Spirit of God and truly desire to be good stewards of what He has entrusted to them, a mission-driven approach to ministry often thinks along similar lines.

Formally adopt the plan

At this point certain strategic decisions need to be made. For example, how many years will your plan address? At Faith, we typically establish a five-year ministry plan, but there is certainly nothing set in stone about that. You also have to decide how many initiatives you will seek to accomplish each year. For us, we generally attempt twenty-two to twenty-four per year. Then a decision also has to be made about the order in which the initiatives will be addressed. In our system, that level of direction is generally left to the pastors.

After all of that is determined, the final plan is discussed and adopted by congregational vote. If the process has truly reflected a grassroots approach, the vote should be strong. At Faith, each of our strategic plans has passed on the strength of at least a 98 percent vote.

Invest in excellent design and printing

We all live with limited budgets. However, this is a place to splurge if at all possible. You want to have a plan document that looks sharp and communicates well. You want your church members to hang on to their plan and review it often. I jokingly tell our folks that we would like them to laminate it and put it under their pillows.

Celebrate and commit to accomplish the plan together

It generally takes our church family nearly a year to complete this process. It requires a ton of work, but there is great excitement because of what we are planning to do together with the help of God. We then schedule a stewardship banquet where everyone on our team has the opportunity to commit themselves in writing to working together to achieve what we have set out to do as a church family.

Build in a system of regular accountability

There has to be some mechanism in place to keep the plan before the minds of God's people. We actually frame several copies and hang them in strategic places in the church. I keep a framed copy on a central wall in my office so I see it every day. We also use it as a teaching tool in our prospective members class so those who are thinking about joining our church understand the direction we're heading.

At the beginning of each year we spend the first few Sundays highlighting the initiatives for that particular year. One of our staff members is assigned the responsibility of making sure that any initiatives that fall under his particular area of ministry will be accomplished. Staff members also must give quarterly updates of their progress, along with an explanation of what will be done for the remainder of the year to ensure that the item will be completed on time and within an allotted budget.

As I look back over the twenty-five years the Lord has allowed me to serve at Faith, certain activities rise to the top when it comes to the matter of what really made a difference long term. I think practically everyone in our church would say that strategic planning fits into that category.

Yes, God is the consummate planner. Perhaps it is time for His people to follow His example.

Take Action . . .

1. Summarize your church's plans for the next twelve months; for the next five years.
2. If your church family has not gone through the process of developing a clear and compelling mission statement, put that process into motion.
3. Organize a futures committee if your church does not have one.
4. Create surveys to help your church evaluate itself, its ministries, and its ministry potential.
5. Collect and evaluate ministry ideas.
6. After prayerful consideration, formally adopt the ministry initiatives the Spirit has led you to.

Discussion

1. Do people have a better understanding of God's nature as a result of watching the way your church functions?
2. How would you explain the Biblical principle of stewardship to adults? to youth? to children?

3. If a pastor is not good in administration, how can he find people in his congregation who are?
4. Read your church's mission statement. What are some good activities or ministries that your church might accomplish because of your mission? What good activities or ministries might it decline or avoid because of its mission?
5. Should the church body be as deeply involved in the process of choosing the church's plans for the future, as outlined in this chapter? Explain.

For Further Study

Faith Church, Lafayette, Indiana, has sample church and community surveys and a plan document at faithlafayette.org.

Primary Competencies

13

Developing a Local Church Educational Strategy
— John Greening

Observing the educational development that shapes a person is a fascinating process. From day one, a newborn emerges from his or her mother's womb and begins to feel, hear, see, smell, and taste things never experienced before. Immediately that baby begins to learn. In the early years of life, a child grows in language and motor skills, gradually learning to read and write. Elementary and adolescent years mark the progression in thinking from literal interpretation to abstract reasoning. Ideally, the early learning that takes place in a child's life equips him or her to be a lifelong learner, able to impart knowledge and expertise to others.

While a portion of foundational learning happens randomly as a person experiences life, much cognitive development occurs through a coordinated and deliberate approach to education. Parents help the child to develop skills. Teachers provide age-appropriate instruction, systematically building from one level of comprehension to the next. This integrated approach typically achieves the desired outcome, producing a knowledgeable and functional member of society.

What is true of general academic education is also true of Christian education within the local church. A believer, having experienced "new birth," is to grow through an educational process in which the Word of God is taught and learned. Each believer has the indwelling Holy Spirit serving as the divine teacher. Ultimately the Holy Spirit is the One Who turns on the light of illumination, enabling the believer to understand the Scriptures. However, the believer also has the responsibility to seek growth through a self-disciplined regimen of Bible reading and study. The Holy Spirit's role and the believer's responsibility in learning God's Word do not preclude the need for serious strategic thought to how people teach and learn the Word within the church's educational environment.

A local church is a complex educational system, encompassing all ages, from the nursery to the elderly. A wide variance of Bible readiness exists within the church—some people are Biblically literate with a good awareness of the Bible story line and doctrine, while others are deficient in their knowledge of the Scriptures. Some may not yet be saved, while others have been believers for years. Adding to the complexity of the age span and Bible readiness is the variety of learning styles among the people in the church. They absorb information and develop understanding through their own combination of hearing, seeing, speaking, and doing learning modes. Added to these factors is the reality that much of the church's teaching staff is composed of volunteers. Some teachers are experienced and capable, while others are novices in need of training. Organizing the church education program also requires determining curriculum, designing classroom and learning settings, and choosing instructional resources. Facilitating effective church education is a challenging task!

Some church administrators attempt to simplify this complexity by maintaining a Sunday School and holding preaching services. By doing so, they may believe that their instructional job is done and then go on to another pressing task. Certainly preaching services are central to a Biblical approach to church. And a Sunday School does provide an excellent structure to coordinate instruction. However, basic questions remain: What is the desired outcome of the instruction? Is the desired outcome being realized? How is learning assessment conducted? Does the whole organization share a common vision and coordinate instruction in working toward common educational goals?

The Desired Outcome

People often paint life with broad brush strokes. If you were to ask a pastor what he hopes to achieve through his teaching, ask parents what they desire their child to become, or ask Sunday School teachers what they want to see happen in the lives of their students, typically they would state their aspirations in general terms. In the same manner as the apostle Peter, a pastor may say, "I want the people in my congregation to grow in the grace and knowledge of Christ" (2 Pet. 3:18). Parents may follow the lead of the apostle John by responding, "We want our children to walk in truth" (3 John 4). Sunday School teachers and youth workers may echo the apostle Paul by expressing, "I desire that my students imitate me, even as I imitate Christ" (1 Cor. 11:1). No one would question the sincerity or validity of these aspirations, which have a Biblical basis. The challenge lies in the disparity between the current level of the learners' spiritual development and the level their instructors desire them to attain. This gap that exists between the present state and the desired level of spiritual development calls for an educational strategy for spiritual formation.

Definite learning objectives

As Paul taught the Word of God, he had in mind a definite learning objective toward which he desired believers in churches to move. Within a context of church education, Paul said to the church in Ephesus, "Till we all come . . . unto a perfect man, unto the measure of the stature of the fulness of Christ" (Eph. 4:13, KJV). He wrote to the church at Colosse, "Him [Christ] we preach, warning every man and teaching every man in all wisdom, that we may present every man perfect in Christ Jesus" (Col. 1:28, NKJV). Paul told Timothy in 2 Timothy 3 that all Scripture appropriately taught and learned would result in the man of God being "complete, thoroughly equipped for every good work" (v. 17, NKJV). Those instructional aspirations assume that the teacher has a clear sense of what the instruction is meant to accomplish in the learner.

Church education does not take place by randomly collecting content and presenting it in a haphazard manner. Rather, church education is a deliberate process by which the Word of God is methodically taught—paving the way for an unbeliever to become a believer by introducing him to Christ and gradually moving him toward spiritual maturity. That process requires thoughtful design.

Intentional design

It is worthwhile to lay out an intentional instructional design for spiritual maturity. In designing your instructional plan, the following questions are important to consider.
- What does spiritual maturity look like?
- What knowledge should a spiritually mature person possess?
- What behaviors should characterize a spiritually mature person?
- What beliefs and values does a spiritually mature person hold?

By investing the time and effort in laying out clear learning objectives, leaders build a greater level of intentionality and order into their church's educational strategy.

Assessment of Desired Outcomes

Take an honest look at your church's educational strategy. After evaluating your answers to the questions on the previous page regarding spiritual maturity, ask these assessment questions:

- Would you say that your church has a coordinated and comprehensive plan in place that introduces people to salvation and develops them toward spiritual maturity?
- Do all of the instructors in the church share a common vision for spiritual maturity?
- Are believers progressing toward spiritual maturity?
- Is their spiritual formation well rounded in all dimensions of spiritual maturity, or lopsided in just a few?
- Is there a procedure in place to evaluate the learning environment of the church?

Strengths and weaknesses

Assessment is a healthy, essential part of ministry. It enables the identifying of when and where effective progress is made, and conversely, when and where improvements are needed. Christ's assessments of the seven churches of Revelation are enlightening to read. Christ noted strengths in the churches but also identified areas that needed work. Based upon His assessments, He proposed remedial steps for correcting the deficiencies.

In reality, each of the New Testament epistles is an assessment of a local church. Each one mentions areas of strength and areas needing improvement, along with steps for making corrections. For example, the writer of Hebrews conducted an assessment of the believers' spiritual progress. He acknowledged having to adjust his teaching downward because the believers had not progressed as far as they should have for the time they had been saved. Those believers should have been teachers; instead they still needed to learn the basics. This assessment enabled the instructional approach to be changed to accommodate the learners.

Learners' spiritual progress

Accurate assessment requires a close, trusting relationship between instructor and learner. How well do you know the spiritual progress of believers in your charge? The better you know your learners, the more effective you can be as an instructor. Your awareness of your learners enables your teaching to be on target for their level of spiritual maturity, rather than shooting too low or too high. You can maximize the effectiveness of your instruction by knowing your learners well and assessing their needs.

Desired Outcomes for Specific Learners

In your mind, glance through the faces of the people whose names are listed in your church directory, or look around the classroom where you teach or the auditorium where you preach. Each of those people is entrusted to your pastoral care. As a shepherd, your primary duty is to teach the Word to those people. Are you certain your teaching is connecting with each individual? When thinking about your learners, ask yourself these questions:

- What are their interests?
- What are their struggles?
- How will a passage of Scripture impact their lives?

In preparing and delivering instruction, a teacher must pay primary attention to the text of Scripture to be taught. However, a good teacher studies not only the text, but also the learners.

Spiritual-formation levels

First John notes what is true in most churches: a range of spiritual maturity exists within a congregation. John framed his instruction to address the unique needs of believers at three levels of spiritual formation: fathers, children, and young men. While universals apply to all of these groups, each of these spiritual-formation levels has distinct abilities—as well as limitations and challenges—in knowledge and behavior.

Readiness for learning

A local church has a range of chronological ages and Bible readiness. Each age level from babies to the elderly has age-appropriate needs, requiring that instruction be framed to suit them. Similarly, a wide range of spiritual maturity is present. A teacher must thoughtfully consider the way in which to communicate instruction. Some people may know with great depth the content of a passage of Scripture. In that same group, other people who have had little exposure to Bible teaching may have difficulty locating the passage of Scripture. The reality of the disparity in levels of spiritual understanding requires that teachers frame their instruction to include all learners.

To address the disparity among learners, some learners may need instruction that readies them for deeper learning. This would include basic instruction on the Bible's structure and story line and the basics of doctrine. Individualized instruction may be arranged to help answer questions and to guide the learning process.

Training teachers

When a teacher is being groomed for service, the preparation should include a progression of teacher training. An effective method of pedagogy is to train teachers through a multistage process: direct instruction, teacher-student shadowing, teacher-student mentoring, and student soloing. The outcome of the time invested in teacher training will produce effective instruction. If a person is thrown into a teaching role for which he or she was not equipped, the result might be uninformed learners who underperform.

Delivery Systems

A delivery system by definition is a means for providing a product or service to the public. In a church education setting, the delivery system would be the means by which Biblical instruction is delivered to church members and attendees. Conventional delivery systems for the church include preaching services, Sunday School or Adult Bible Fellowship classes, youth groups, and children's ministries such as Vacation Bible School or weekday Bible clubs. Additional instructional means—such as church libraries, church radio programs, and recorded messages—can enhance a standard approach to church education.

For a church to expand the influence of its instructional ministry, it must think beyond conventional delivery systems. Jesus was a great model of using a variety of delivery systems to convey instruction. He utilized conventional instructional settings such as the synagogue, the temple, large group outdoor venues, and private homes. The Gospels also contain accounts of Jesus using many nonconventional settings to connect with learners, such as on a boat in a storm, next to a well in Samaria, or at the sickbed of a diseased person. Consider these possibilities for today:

- Include remote locations, such as wilderness camping sites and international mission fields. In these settings learners gain fresh insight through on-site experiences in which the instructional lessons are being lived out in real time.
- Through home-based growth groups, learners can further their understanding of how Sunday pastoral messages apply to their lives. The intended learning objectives of the conventional preaching message are enhanced as facilitators ask thoughtful application questions.
- Small-group settings that focus on specialty topics can augment learning. Interaction among small-group members who have a special interest in topics such as Biblical parenting, Biblical financial management, overcoming grief, or conquering addiction can be an effective means of learning.
- Smartphone apps open new possibilities and can bring Bible studies to groups such as businesspeople who have full schedules on weekdays.
- Church-based online groups can utilize the distance learning environment provided by the Internet to greatly expand the possibilities for instruction.

Content

The Bible is the singular authority for local church instruction, but most churches use instructional resources to aid teachers in effectively teaching the Word. This means that careful consideration must be given to ensure that teachers use only high-quality, doctrinally consistent resources. Many duties will fill your schedule as pastor, but make it a priority to establish a screening process for instructional resources. This will ensure that what is being communicated from the resources matches your church's beliefs and values.

Other criteria to consider for choosing educational resources include age appropriateness, creativity of presentation, clarity of instruction, and appropriateness of application. Remember that, ultimately, learners in the local church need to be exposed to the whole counsel of God to grow toward full spiritual maturity. Some publishers, due to their desire to appeal to a broad audience, will omit distinctive teachings to avoid offending the users. Make sure all the Bible is being taught in your educational strategy. Well-chosen resources can help you achieve that goal.

Conclusion

Paul in 1 Corinthians 3:9–17 described a future day when the Lord will assess the instructional approach that has been implemented in a local church. Paul recognized his own accountability in instructional strategies and the accountability of others who would come after him. Only strategies consistently built according to the standard of Scripture will be rewarded. A strategy that does not meet the Scriptural standard will result in loss for the builder. Building lives God's way is the only right way to do the job!

Take Action . . .

1. Define a spiritual maturity profile.
2. Design a spiritual maturity assessment tool to gauge the spiritual development level of the learners in your church.
3. Read through the Gospels and list the different delivery systems Jesus used in His teaching. You will be amazed at the creativity of Christ, the Master Teacher! Follow His lead and consider the possibilities as you build the instructional strategy for your church.

Discussion

1. Does your church have an intentional spiritual formation strategy in place?
2. Are all of your church instructors coordinated in executing a common spiritual formation strategy?
3. What problems occur when a common spiritual formation strategy is not in place?
4. What are the benefits of a common spiritual formation strategy?
5. Where do you need to make improvements in your overall church education approach?

For Further Study

Blueprint for Spiritual Maturity by John and Daria Greening, Regular Baptist Press, 2005.

Impact Teaching by John and Daria Greening, Regular Baptist Press, 2000.

Jesus, the Teacher by J. M. Price, vol. 7 of Southwestern Library of Centennial Classics, Southwestern Baptist Theological Seminary, 2008.

14
Working with Deacons
— Will Hatfield

We're looking for a few good men." With this phrase the U.S. Marines recruited men of courage, endurance, and mental toughness. Their role: to get jobs done no one else could do. My grandfather fought on Iwo Jima in WWII as a marine. He was with a unit that went onto the beaches that first afternoon. Knifed in the hand, he returned to the landing ship to get medical attention and then fought back to his unit. Unfortunately he was shot, taking him out of the battle. After the war, he was very proud of what the marines accomplished together. They were given a commission and they accomplished it.

In Matthew 28:19 and 20 the church is commissioned to make disciples of all nations. We as churches are called to preach the gospel and teach those who believe how to follow Christ. Since God includes deacons as part of a healthy church, they are vital to the church's effectiveness to fulfill this commission. The gospel is the message and the heart of church. Deacons enable the church to live out the gospel in practical ways.

There is a debate as to what exactly it means to be an effective deacon. Nowhere in Scripture are we given a specific list of duties or a job description for a deacon. In recent years, deacons have often operated like the board of directors of a church—very similar to many corporations. The pastor is the one who preaches, teaches, and "does the work of the ministry." The deacons are the ones who handle the business of the church, set policies, and generally handle the direction of the church. Some, as they observe this in action, question how faithful this is to the Biblical model. Alexander Strauch in his book *Minister of Mercy* argues that using deacons as a board of directors is contrary to Biblical direction. Because the root word for *deacons* (*diakonos*) basically means "waiting on tables," deacons should lead the compassion ministry of the church—meeting physical needs. Strauch writes,

> While some churches wrongly elevate deacons to the position of executive board members, others mistakenly reduce deacons to building managers, glorified church janitors, or sanctified grounds-keepers. This view (and a similar view that turns deacons into church financial officers) seriously demeans the office of deacon and denies the local church the necessary ministry God designed the diaconate to provide for His people. In response to this position, we must ask ourselves why God would demand that deacons meet specific moral and spiritual qualifications and undergo public examination, like the pastors of the church (1 Tim. 3:10), if all deacons do is wax floors or mow lawns. . . . My heartfelt burden is to help deacons get out of the boardroom or the building-maintenance mentality and into the people-serving mentality. Deacons . . . are to be involved in a compassionate ministry of caring for the poor and needy. The deacons' ministry, therefore, is one that no Christ-centered, New Testament church can ever afford to neglect. Christians today must understand the absolute necessity for and vital importance of New Testament deacons to the local church so that the needy, poor and suffering of our churches are cared for in a thoroughly Christian manner. This is a matter dear to the heart of God.

Strauch makes a compelling case for reexamining the role of a deacon while overstating the case for deacons solely working in compassion ministries. For instance, consider the situation in Acts 6 as a church of ten thousand: widows may have been 6 percent of the congregation (the current percentage in the U.S., so a very conservative estimate). Seven deacons would not have been enough to handle the task of caring for six hundred women without involving others in it and administrating it. To understand how deacons can be most effective, it is important to examine the goal that good deacons will achieve.

The Goal

In 1 Timothy 3:13, Paul gave a clear idea of what the result of an effective deacon ministry will look like: "For those who serve well as deacons gain a good standing for themselves and also great confidence in the faith that is in Christ Jesus" (ESV). The goal for an effective deacon is twofold: respect within the church and great boldness in the gospel.

The phrase "good standing" includes the ideas of status and platform. When a deacon serves well, he gains respect within the church. People look up to deacons as role models. They achieve a certain status, but they also gain a platform. The deacon possesses a greater ability to send a message on the importance or vitality of the reasons for his service. Politically, a platform is all about clear communication. Serving well as a deacon enables better communication of something. That "something" is found in the next phrase—"great confidence in the faith that is in Christ Jesus." Kevin Bauder explains in *Baptist Distinctives,* "Deacons who spend hours helping people with their needs will certainly develop spiritual influence within the church."

Deacons will gain great confidence in the faith in Christ Jesus. But what does this mean? Does this mean great boldness in faith? That is, will their faith be much stronger or bolder in the face of adversity? Will they live by faith more consistently in the midst of trials? Or does it mean that they have great confidence in the doctrines of the faith? Will they hold to the doctrines of the gospel more closely and teach them more passionately? Actually, the phrase includes both ideas. If pastors are to defend the message of the gospel (1 Tim. 1:18), then deacons have a platform to boldly defend the lived-out gospel: enabling and encouraging the church to live it out, helping the congregation to see it in action.

Deacons, when they serve well, have great confidence in the gospel. They believe in its message and power more strongly. This is the goal pastors should have for their deacons.

Pastor, consider these questions:

- Do you take time every year to teach how the gospel is connected to physical needs?
- Do you help deacons process how the gospel will meet the needs they can't meet physically/emotionally and how to help people draw strength from Christ?
- Do you take time to talk about the town/area you live in and how the message of the gospel needs to impact the preconceptions of people living in your area? how it will benefit those in your area to believe in Christ in specific ways? how it will challenge those people?
- Do you take time to help each deacon focus his spiritual gifts on the

tasks he's been given—how he can motivate the people he serves alongside, with how the gospel is impacting the people they serve?

The Qualifications

Not only does the goal of being a deacon reflect the priority of the gospel, but the qualifications do as well. Deacons' qualifications are listed in 1 Timothy 3:8–13. We can look at this list both for individuals and for a common theme. First, notice that the deacons' qualifications are following the pastor's qualifications and that they are connected by the word "likewise" or "in the same way." Deacons are not spiritually immature men; they have the same sin nature as pastors, but they are mature in their obedience to the gospel. They have equivalent qualifications—just different roles. Note the list of qualifications:

- *Honorable or dignified.* They are committed to proper relationships or seeking to conduct themselves in a way that brings honor to Christ. The next three qualifications are negative and probably spell out the opposite of what "honorable" means.
- *Not double-tongued.* They are committed to honest communication. The deacon does not speak out of two sides of his mouth. He seeks honesty and openness in all his relationships. He is not using relationships to get what he wants by manipulation or deceit. Nor is his idol one of pleasing people by telling them what they want to hear.
- *Not addicted to much wine.* They are committed to self-control. In a world where pleasure and license promise joy, the deacon has learned that joy comes through sacrifice and doing good to others. Honor demands that he live in such a way as not to be out of control especially by mind-controlling substances. He takes to heart the admonition in Proverbs 31 that, like a king, he needs to be wise at all times to make wise decisions in serving people.
- *Not greedy.* They are committed to higher values than mere profit. In a world where money is power, the deacon serves and lives not for the bottom line but for the blessings he can bestow on others.
- *Holding the mystery of the faith with a clear conscience.* They are committed to personal integrity. This phrase means two things—both important: (1) The deacon understands that though not everything in Scripture is easily understood, he holds firmly with confidence to what God has revealed, and (2) he seeks to live in public and in private based on what he believes. He does not have a conscience that

is accusing him of living two lives. He is not concerned about being observed and tested by the congregation.
- *The husband of one wife.* Each deacon is committed to his wife and to her alone. This is the same as for pastors (see chapter 3 for a fuller discussion) and mimics the qualification for widows on the "list" in 1 Timothy 5:9.
- *Managing their households and children well.* The deacon knows how to "shepherd a child's heart." He also knows that things run decently and orderly to bless those around him and more easily point their hearts to Christ. He uses his authority in the home to encourage and nurture—not to dominate and control, nor to check out and be passive.

The passage also talks about qualifications for "women" or "wives." The purpose of this chapter is not to solve this debate. Kevin Bauder comments, "The notion of women as deacons would probably seem less jarring if the office of deacon were properly understood in terms of service rather than leadership." However, the word "wives" seems to be preferred over "women" because of context. Wives of deacons, then, are evaluated along similar qualifications: they are honorable, not slanderers (very similar to not double-tongued but more focused on personal relationships), sober-minded (understanding the need for wise living), faithful in all things. Wives must be real partners with their husbands in defending the gospel by living it out.

Just as the qualifications for a pastor have a common theme of blamelessness, so the qualifications for a deacon have a common theme of honor or dignity; that is, commitment. Commitment to Christ is the air he breathes, even before he becomes a deacon. A deacon understands that his committed action makes God's world known. David Brooks in *The Social Animal* remarks,

> In 1997 Gary McPherson studied 157 randomly selected children as they picked out and learned a musical instrument. Some went on to become fine musicians and some faltered. McPherson searched for the traits that separated those who progressed from those who did not. IQ was not a good predictor. Neither were aural sensitivity, math skills, income, or a sense of rhythm. The best single predictor was a question McPherson asked the students before they even selected their

instruments: How long do you think you will play? The students who planned to play for a short time did not become very proficient. The students who planned to play for a few years had modest success. But there were some children who said, in effect: "I want to be a musician. I'm going to play my whole life." Those children soared.

Deacons understand the value of commitment, that knowing God takes more than a year or two. They know that the New Testament points to the commitment of faith in order to know God well (Col. 1:21–23; 1 Peter 1:7–9; Jude 20, 21).

The Duties

Finally, the duties of a deacon focus on helping the church live out the implications of the gospel. The word "deacon" means "servant" or "waiter." It follows the Biblical pattern for leadership that is focused on serving more than on authority and glory (Luke 22:25, 26). Servant leadership is the paradigm for how all leaders in the church should serve: seeking to bless those under them and looking out for their needs and interests (Phil. 2:4, 5). The concept itself doesn't give us clear ideas for what deacons are to do, however.

Acts 6:1–7 is usually treated as the prototype for deacons. If we don't use this passage, there is very little in Scripture to guide us in what deacons are to be doing. Acts is descriptive in its theology rather than prescriptive, so we must be careful in how we apply it.

One interesting qualification was that the deacons be Spirit-filled, wise men of good reputation. Most likely these qualifications actually came from the Pentateuch, which describes the kind of men Moses chose as leaders to help him with the burden and responsibility of leading God's people: from Exodus 18—wise men chosen as leaders, and from Numbers 1—men given the Holy Spirit.

There are differences between the New Testament account and the Old Testament accounts: (1) the person/persons choosing the men (which is an argument in itself for congregational polity) and (2) the result of the process. The New Testament story demonstrates the purpose of the church and the spread of the gospel by creating unity between different cultures, where the Old Testament accounts point toward preserving the unity of one nation.

The similarities are more profound:
- Choosing leaders resulted from complaints by the people because of physical needs.
- Choosing leaders resulted from having too many people to deal with effectively at one time.
- Choosing leaders resulted from the priority of the leaders' responsibilities.
- The solution helped relieve burdens on the leadership.
- The solution also illustrated the power of God before the people.

Therefore, the men chosen as deacons protected the pastors' priorities not only by allowing them to focus their time and energy on certain tasks, but also by helping the church live out the teaching of the apostles in everyday ways. Because the deacons were wise and filled with the Holy Spirit, they could effectively live out what they believed in front of and with the congregation without being micromanaged by the apostles.

This suggests some key ideas for the duties of deacons:
- They are to bring unity by dealing with problems.
- They are to help the church live out its purpose of spreading the gospel by being at the front lines of the cultural transformation the gospel brings.
- They are to help protect the pastor's priorities.
- They are to meet practical needs for spiritual purposes.

Take Action . . .

Depending on which end of the continuum the deacons are operating from (more administrative or more of compassion ministries), deacons should be aware of what their role should be and cooperate with what God is seeking to do in their lives and churches.

1. For deacons on the administrative side of the spectrum, be wary of the weakness inherent in setting policy and rules. Understand the purpose of the law (1 Tim. 1:8, 9). Avoid using policy to manufacture spirituality, but instead serve those who are struggling in sin with grace and personal accountability. Deacons should seek a Biblical unity, not a political unity. Deacons in this type of area need accountability in living out the gospel themselves. Remember that adopting a "board" mentality is very easy and actually negates the gospel the church is preaching by passively promoting a "'more spiritual' leadership vs. 'less spiritual' congregation" division within the church.

2. For deacons on the compassion side of the spectrum, be wary of easily sliding into a "social gospel" type of ministry. Being often at the front lines of where the gospel is profitably changing people's lives, do not forget the vital truth that the church is united first by "being" and then by "doing." Overcome conflict instead of trying to avoid it. Getting the Hellenistic and the Hebrew Christians together wasn't easy. Therefore, doctrine matters. We are in Christ as God's sons and daughters, brothers and sisters, disciples together first. Only then can we do ministry together. Therefore, we must prioritize the proclamation of the gospel through various means in everything the church does.
3. Review regularly together as pastors and deacons the pastors' priorities. Review how the deacons are helping protect those priorities: not only the pastors' time and energy, but also the pastors' message and vision. The pastors and deacons should be united in how they are trying, not only to preach the gospel, but also to exemplify the gospel in their community. Deacons should be on the front lines of whatever that looks like.
4. Finally, train deacons and their wives (or deaconesses) in how to meet physical needs and how to point to Christ while doing so. From helping people move, to hospital visits, to caring for widows, make deacons wise in how to encourage faith in the midst of trial, joy in the midst of pain, and compassion in the midst of suffering. Train wives, especially, in caring for the basics of the myriad women's issues that can arise in ministering to hurting people. Study and make available some good Biblical counseling resources.

With this type of ministry, deacons will see the gospel in action and proclaim it with joy. Remember Paul's model and memory of a good deacon is most likely Stephen, who went from deacon to evangelist because of the confidence he had in the gospel. The commitment that he gave to the gospel of Christ resulted in Paul's salvation.

We are looking for a few good men—to do different things than the marines—but with the same commitment and for something much more eternally significant: enabling the church by example and guidance to live out the gospel of Christ for all to see.

Discussion

1. Why does God demand that deacons meet specific moral and spiritual qualifications and undergo public examination, like the pastors of the church (1 Tim. 3:10)?

2. How can deacons demonstrate their confidence in the gospel?
3. How can deacons demonstrate their obedience to the gospel?
4. What are the implications of the gospel for everyday life? In what concrete ways can deacons help believers in their church live out the implications of the gospel?

For Further Study

Baptist Distinctives by Kevin Bauder, Regular Baptist Books, 2012.

CrossTalk: Where Life and Scripture Meet by Michael R. Emlet, New Growth Press, 2009.

Deacon Training Teacher's Manual by Robert Smith, M.D., Resources of Faith, 2003.

Minister of Mercy: The New Testament Deacon by Alexander Strauch, Lewis and Roth Publishers, 1992.

The Ministry of a Baptist Deacon: A Handbook for Local Church Leaders by Paul Chappell, Striving Together Publications, 2010.

When Helping Hurts: How to Alleviate Poverty without Hurting the Poor . . . and Yourself by Steve Corbett and Brian Fikkert, Moody, 2014.

15

Guiding the Staff
— Don Shirk

A guide is "one who shows the way by leading, directing or advising," according to the American Heritage dictionary. Whether it is in the wilderness of some remote area or the complexity of a big city, what makes a guide is familiarity with the terrain. A good guide not only enables those being guided to get from point "A" to point "B" safely and in one piece, but also, along the way, informs, educates, and even equips with needed skills those they guide.

When it comes to guiding a pastoral staff, many of us find ourselves on the short end of training. Perhaps I was asleep that day, but I do not recall a class in Bible college or seminary that taught how to guide a staff! Yet many men in ministry can relate stories of how they became familiar with the rugged terrain of pastoral ministry. Learning how to guide a staff is much more than scheduling staff meetings and assigning tasks. For many senior or lead pastors, it was unanticipated wilderness seasons in *their* previous subordinate ministry positions that equipped them with a philosophy of how one day they would develop and maintain staff relationships.

Early Lessons from Lumpville

I recall a prominent ministry friend sharing the advice he gave a young man who asked how he could be like him someday in an exciting public ministry position. His counsel went something like this: "Get your Bible education and then take an assistant pastor position in an insignificant place in the middle of nowhere and let them beat the snot out of you for a couple of years. After that you'll be ready for ministry."

While that counsel was rather raw, it also rings the memory of a lot of men in ministry. Many lead or senior pastors can relate to their early days in ministry as the equivalent to pastoral hazing. Difficulties of all shapes and sizes that they never signed up for hit them like grenades coming from all sides. Some young men are able to handle the depth of hurt and disappointment experienced in those contexts, but unfortunately many drop out and no longer pursue the pastorate. It can be easy to smugly conclude, "Well, it's obvious they didn't have what it takes; otherwise, they would have stuck it out."

I was two years out of seminary and thoroughly enjoying my first position as an assistant pastor. A new senior pastor was called to the church, and I began serving under his leadership. Prior to his arrival, I had begun a young-marrieds Sunday School class that met in the gymnasium. The class took off and went from around ten attendees to nearly forty in a short time. Those were exciting days of purposeful ministry. Couples were growing in their walk with the Lord and being strengthened in their marriages. Meaningful, caring relationships were being developed.

One day the senior pastor called me into his office and said, "I want you to split your class." He mentioned something about us becoming "a church within a church" and instructed me to find another teacher to take the other half of my class. More than a little puzzled by his assessment of our class, I found another teacher and two available classrooms for the two classes to meet. After several Sundays of having two classes, it was obvious my classroom was too small for my new class, as people were even sitting outside in the hall. I approached the senior pastor and asked him if my class could go back into the empty gymnasium. My classroom was just too small. I will never forget his response: "No, you either split your class, or you have your walking papers."

Nothing could have prepared me for that answer. I was devastated. There I was, sincerely trying to serve the Lord and help that church become spiritually healthy and grow, and, because of that, I was threatened with the loss of my job!

With a wife and two small children to provide for, that hill was not worth dying on. So for the next two years I had to "eat" submitting to and serving under a pastoral staff philosophy that I could not buy into. In those early days of ministry, this became the most difficult spiritual wilderness experience I had ever been through. This issue became compounded by other issues. I was numb. My drive and motivation were gone. I could not process the "why" of what I was going through when all I wanted to do was serve the Lord.

Little did I realize how the Lord was using that season to humble me and teach me the terrain of what should and should not characterize pastoral staff relationships. That season formed and shaped my philosophy of how I would one day guide a staff, should the Lord ever give me that opportunity.

The Vision for Raw Material

In 1 Timothy 4, Paul directed Timothy in pivotal truths for a pastor to both know and exemplify. Paul impressed on the younger Timothy the critical necessity for being an example of spiritual maturity even though he was young. In verse 15 Paul wrote, "Meditate on these things; give yourself entirely to them, that your progress may be evident to all" (NKJV). I love that word "progress." In essence it means "to make pioneer advance." Specifically, Paul spoke to Timothy about his need to move forward in uncharted aspects of various disciplines, like proficiency in the Word, spiritual giftedness, and compelling, godly character.

What strikes me in this text is that Paul wanted Timothy to stand out in the crowd as a model of spiritual maturity. I'm not talking about a prideful display of "look-at-me-ism." I'm talking about the critical need for God's people to see spiritual "real deals" in ministry-minded men.

Why is this so important? Because this kind of appropriate self-attention is a primary means God sovereignly uses to create spiritual buy-in for people trying to figure out this God-thing. In verse 16 Paul stated, "For in doing this you will save both yourself and those who hear you" (NKJV). Frankly, everybody's from Missouri—"show me."

Where am I headed with all this? When it comes to guiding a pastoral staff and effective staff relationships, senior or lead pastors need to own the responsibility of the intentional mentorship of young pastors. It's understood that sometimes age is hazy in this equation. I'm simply talking about the principle of doing with our staff what we seek to do with our people—take them from the raw material of what they currently are to where they spiritually need to be. This is what Paul did with Timothy.

When I had the opportunity to candidate at Grace Baptist Church, Batavia, New York, over twenty-five years ago, I was asked about my philosophy of working with people. I was thirty years old and fresh out of my spiritual wilderness. In brief, I recall sharing that my heartbeat was to focus on working with men, seeing them saved, and growing them to the point of (and these are my words) "working myself out of a job." By that I meant that I wanted to multiply myself in preparing men for ministry.

I wanted to do all I could to encourage men to flourish in their faith even to the point of seeing some become pastors.

Consider Growing Your Own

After fifteen years of pastoring Grace, I had to bring our congregation through a major paradigm shift. Specifically, it was to consider calling to our staff our own men that we were mentoring for ministry. For our situation, this was a stretch, because traditionally when a church looks for needed staff, they look outside their own walls. While there is nothing intrinsically wrong with this, I have found it comes with subtle shortcomings.

The "Messiah mind-set" is a mode of thinking that marks many when looking for staff. They want a highly gifted person who will solve their ministry problems or meet needs in a particular area like youth, education, counseling, music, or missions.

Over time, I had to ask myself the hard question, "What is my life producing? Who is experiencing a God-initiated desire for ministry under my leadership?" God was at work, and we were helping several men get their theological training for ministry. Yes, they were active and growing. Yes, they were Biblically qualified and no longer spiritual novices; and, yes, some people had a tough time accepting the serious consideration of these men to become our pastors.

Why was this? I believe the answer is subtly seen in a mind-set captured in Matthew 13:57 when Jesus said, "A prophet is not without honor except in his own country and in his own house" (NKJV). Frankly, Jesus was rejected by His own people in His own city because He looked too normal. He was too much like them. He was just "the carpenter's son" (v. 55, NKJV). They couldn't handle the evidence of His giftedness. Their main mistake was to limit Jesus because of His familiarity. Evidently Jesus' day was much like ours—when it comes to staff selection, people can give more credence to those they don't know well than to those they do know well.

My point is this: local churches ought to be places where people get saved and grow spiritually through learning and ministry. In time, men gifted for and called to ministry begin to surface. It is the local church's responsibility to note this giftedness and foster it. The tough thing is this: in the course of time, will the church be willing to take the risk and call one of their own "known commodities"?

While it took some time and much teaching, the church now views this method of adding to our staff as a tremendous asset. Our two associate pastors came on board with a true passion for their local church. This is the place where God got a hold of their lives, and this is the place where they want to make a difference. No learning curve is needed for adjusting to the area and ministry. It is home. A network of meaningful relationships and contacts is already in place. Plus, as pastors, we are already on board with a working relationship and understood philosophy of ministry. There are no surprises. We work together like peanut butter and jelly.

Calling our own staff from within has also resulted in a long tenure of service for each staff member. Why? Again, it is home. Family and friends are here. What they are doing matters in the community that matters to them.

I fully understand that this scenario is not the only right way to bring on staff. There are times when a staff position requires a specific area of giftedness that must be found outside the church's four walls. However, I do believe getting your staff from within is Biblical; and for our church family, it has been an exciting modeling experience. Our congregation is not just hearing the stories of what God did yesterday; they are seeing what God is doing today.

Staff-Guiding Is More than Being Large and in Charge

When the rubber meets the road in pastoral staff relationships, many don't last long. Slow leaks develop and relationships that started well not only can go flat, but they can turn toxic. What are some attributes a senior or lead pastor needs to have in place in order to foster a positive and effective ministry environment?

Here are fifteen aspects of a senior or lead pastor's leadership style that I believe strengthen and encourage staff relationships:

1. *Challenge the staff's personal spiritual vitality.* Godliness is perceived. People have an innate radar for sincerity. Authentic godliness has a pervasive aroma about it that compellingly captures both attention and desire. It causes people to conclude, "I want that. I need that!" Sincerely desire to cultivate a genuine walk with God and talk about it. Share victories and defeats with staff—mountaintop moments and time in the darkness of the valley.
2. *Speak transparently where and when you fall short or make mistakes.* Don't be blind to your faults. Embrace brokenness. Apologize. Some men in leadership seem incapable of admitting wrongdoing.

3. *Be personal.* You can spend oodles of time with some leaders and never really feel like you know them or connect with them. Take extra relational measures, like writing notes of encouragement or following up with a matter of prayer or something that you sensed was important to a staff member.
4. *Be gracious.* Seek to minimize differences and offenses. Accept the tension that staff will make their fair share of mistakes, blunders, and ignorant, shortsighted, and sometimes selfish decisions that might force you into a position of having to respond. Let your response be patient, kind, and gracious. Even when mistakes are made or disagreements surface and you may be upset or even hurt, never give yourself the deluded luxury of losing your cool or belittling a staff member. This does not mean that you turn a blind eye to faults or allow yourself to be a pushover or a doormat. Not at all. Be secure in who you are, but don't thump your chest like King Kong.
5. *Sensitively and wisely address areas of weakness and needed development with your staff.* Do it winsomely, positively, and constructively. Also, tell them when they've excelled and ministered wisely. Don't be so insecure that you cannot utter a compliment. Be liberal with encouragement. This alone empowers and feeds the ox (see 1 Corinthians 9:8–10).
6. *Be flexible.* Work to understand the unique demands of ministry on family life, and accommodate the needs of staff members. While you rightly expect them to carry out their responsibilities—and you give real ownership of the ministry—keep the doors of communication open for occasional times of needed flexibility and freedom with schedules and time management. Try to say yes as much as possible when staff have legitimate needs to change a normal work schedule. This can be life-giving to a staff member's family.
7. *Recognize that as pastors, you are each a workhorse in your own right.* Workhorses wear blinders and set themselves to pulling the plow until the job is finished. It's very easy in times of busyness to allow room for relational distance and gaps in communication. At some point this lack of communication leads to awkward circumstances. Take the initiative to just simply touch base with staff relationally. Don't allow long periods of distance or relational silence to create awkward moments later.
8. *Persevere in the trenches of making vision reality.* Do not allow your own insecurities to dictate decisions and direction in ministry. Recognize when there is a need to advance in an area that may be stretching to

you personally. Things like new ministry initiatives, capital campaigns, and building projects can fall into this category. Model to your staff what it looks like to take defining steps of faith, just as you preach to your people. Encourage your staff to help the church make these advances regardless of your comfort level.

9. *Respect the staff.* Affirm staff from the pulpit. Give staff the respect of a fellow pastor. Do not treat them or speak of them as though they are less than a real pastor. This has a profound impact on the perception of the congregation. They will not be left wondering how your relationship works, or if it does. Most congregations won't even realize the degree of comfort and freedom they have when they don't have to worship and serve in their church under the distraction of pastoral staff drama.

10. *Take a personal interest in the lives of your staff and their families.* Recognize that pastors and their families need pastors too.

11. *Celebrate staff "wins."* Whether these are personal or ministry, celebrate them—not just on a personal basis, but when appropriate, publicly.

12. *Encourage personal and professional development.* This can come through conferences, training, and continuing education opportunities. Don't be intimidated by gifted people, especially those who have strengths where you may be weak. Rather, embrace and empower them. Do not be so insecure that you keep them at arm's length and keep the lid on their ministry opportunities and potential. You want them to succeed (1 Tim. 4:15).

13. *Choke pride when it rears its head in your heart.* Work hard at diminishing selfish ambition, and do not allow ego or self-exaltation to hinder the ministry or negatively impact those around you. Hate and fear pride because you are vulnerable to its compelling lie, "You need to be a somebody." Pride is not the problem of just novices.

14. *Ask yourself the hard question, "Would I follow myself?"* Strive to be prepared and organized in all you do, from meetings to messages. Answer e-mails and be on time. Why? Because that kind of courtesy builds credibility and creates buy-in as to what a godly leader looks like. The job of a leader is to define reality. People who want to be real will follow you if you are real, and few things reveal that quality of character like sensitivity to common courtesy. Failure to believe these issues are important flushes your credibility with your staff.

15. *Make time to pray and plan with your staff regularly.* Foster constant

communication that results in an open-book approach among the staff. When everyone knows what is going on in their co-laborers' ministries, the problems of private agendas and a multitude of misunderstandings are minimized.

A Word to Those Guided

Remember, it takes two to tango. The flip side of pastoral staff relationships is the associate or assistant pastor's responsibilities for a successful working relationship. Here are a few items that work well in any context:

1. *Know your parameters.* Understand your role and the margins in that capacity. Don't usurp responsibility that is not yours.
2. *Seek clarification.* When there is a need to talk things through, don't sulk or brood. Rather, take the initiative to address a misunderstanding or an expectation. Be loyal and work hard at giving the benefit of the doubt when it comes to resolving issues. Be solution oriented.
3. *Respect preferences.* Respect the senior or lead pastor's leadership and ministry preferences without making him feel he has to defend why he does what he does. Be supportive even though you might do things differently if you were responsible.
4. *Don't die on molehills.* Have a mature capacity to let go of the nonessentials. It's not about your way, but about what is wisest and best for the church in your quest for more and better disciples.
5. *Know that God understands.* Your lead or senior pastor is not the fourth person of the Trinity. Realize he will have foibles and won't bat one thousand every day, just as you won't. Work hard at choosing to let "love . . . cover a multitude of sins" (1 Pet. 4:8, NKJV). Most importantly, know that if you have something on your plate that is very uncomfortable—from a task you don't like, to the heartache of an injustice—know that God is in it and has yet to say, "Oops." He has something valuable for you to learn and grow from; He divinely permitted your current circumstance. Your ultimate goal is "to be well pleasing to Him" in all things (2 Cor. 5:9, NKJV).

Take Action . . .

1. Evaluate your attitude toward your staff. Is it godly?
2. Consider the "raw material" of each staff member. Decide what you can do to help guide each one to spiritual maturity. Begin to do so.

3. Identify the young men in your church that God might be leading into pastoral ministry roles.
4. Prayerfully consider filling ministry openings with men from your church. Are there potential staff members already trained and ready? Would your church body be open to calling one of its own? Plan how to help men prepare for ministry and your church body prepare for the possibility of calling one of its own to a staff position.
5. Write out your answers to Discussion question 3. Ask these same questions of yourself to some trusted leaders in your church.
6. If you are a senior or lead pastor, evaluate yourself regarding the fifteen aspects of leadership style listed on pages 156–159.
7. If you are an associate or assistant pastor, evaluate yourself regarding the five features for staff members listed on page 159.

Discussion

1. Can you relate to the author's difficult experience in a subordinate staff position? If so, in what ways? How did that experience shape your philosophy regarding pastor-staff relationships?
2. What are the pros and cons of hiring staff from your own church? What would this do for your people? What obstacles or objections would this pose for some? How might you address them Biblically? Would your church consider financial assistance for the theological education of those in your church who have ministry potential, particularly if they might return to your church on staff?
3. If you are looking to add a staff position in your church for the first time, what are your strengths in working with people? How would you utilize your strengths in fostering a positive working relationship with a staff member? What are some potential areas of need in your leadership style?

For Further Study

Becoming a Healthy Team by Stephen Macchia, Baker, 2005.
Church Staff Handbook: How to Build an Effective Ministry Team by Harold J. Westing, Kregel, 2012.
The Leadership Baton by Rowland Forman, Jeff Jones, and Bruce Miller, Zondervan, 2007.
Leading from the Second Chair by Mike Bonem and Roger Patterson, Jossey-Bass, 2005.

Leading Leaders by Aubrey Malphurs, Baker, 2005.
"Tending the Weeds in Your Ministry Relationships" by Paul Tripp, available at thegospelcoalition.org.
"Two Common Church Hiring Mistakes" by Eric Geiger, available at thegospelcoalition.org.

16

Working with Volunteers
— Jon Jenks

Behind every volunteer is a story. The context of church does not change these stories. Each story contains failure, success, sorrow, hope, torment, encouragement, godlessness, and revival. In each ministry team, these stories merge so that the farmer whose father told him he was "stupid" every day of his childhood serves next to a district manager who has known only success. They are joined by a divorced lady who escaped an abusive husband, and the team is completed by her friend who grew up in the church with standards as her guide. These pictures of their lives in the past tell you nothing of today's pressures that change and shape them in an ongoing way. The shepherd's task is daunting. Can such diversity be harmonized into a unified, productive ministry force?

Ultimately, if we are to work alongside one another with joy, our stories must merge before the cross. Before the light of the cross we are revealed as slaves of sin, producing shameful fruit unto death. But in the sacrifice of the cross, Christ set us free from sin. We become slaves of God, which produces holiness and everlasting life, as Paul wrote in Romans 6:20–22. As believers, we must share this common ground of salvation in Christ, and we must embrace this position as slaves together. In our culture, the concept of slavery is fraught with bad imagery and context, but in the New Testament Paul embraced believers' position as slaves. Spiritual slavery is different, for we have chosen it. As pastors, we prepare volunteers to serve by helping them understand and embrace their position in Christ. As this identity takes shape in them, they begin to serve with a Christlike passion and commitment. At this juncture, we must link them organizationally and then be ready organizationally to launch, support, and adjust their service.

Preparing the Volunteer to Serve
The pastor

This war for the volunteer's soul must begin in the prayer closet. The pastor must pray, and he must drink in God's Word that it might guide his very soul. He must beg understanding from God, and through Him gain insight into the fears and pride that block his fellow slaves from embracing the Master's call. The pastor must drink deeply from His well of satisfaction so that no plan, pretense, or part of him creates a wall between the Master and him. Ultimately, this preparation is about his heart being renewed, humbled, and submitted to Christ. This keeps his speech gentle and his encouragement genuine. From God's Word the pastor becomes wiser than his teachers as the Spirit guides and as He guides the pastor out of the prayer communion of his study.

No other foundation but this truth-filled, Spirit-altered, constantly nurtured relationship with Christ can be firm and spacious for God's plan. God uses this foundation lived openly with fellow slaves to shape and protect His vessels. This must be the pastor's ultimate start and constant power source. He will know if this is occurring, first, by what fruit is being produced in the lives of volunteers and, second, by what they value. What they value, they build into the ministry before them. Do they build fellowship in Christ together with other believers and long for it? Do they pray together and admonish one another?

Often I have observed volunteers committed and working with me but lacking power and a Christ-centered perspective. When I see this, I know I have failed and that I have raised them up on a man-powered platform that left them powerless and subject to storms they cannot withstand. Their very faith and families risk being damaged, and Christ's reputation will be questioned. We must build from a right foundation. Although building ministry may start more slowly in such an endeavor, the outflow will be massive victory.

A focus on God's grace

To begin laying this foundation, we must define who and why we serve. Each slave grasps this from the Master's gracious hand. As believers experience the truth of His grace in His forgiveness, guidance, patience—and so many other abundant blessings directly from His hand and from the hands and lips of His other slaves—they will be overwhelmed. This produces a holy desire to be committed to Him and His plan. We do love because

He first loved us. A church must plan to have places where this awakening can take place and be fostered, or the new believer or fallowed (inactive) believer may never blossom.

Believers need to hear of this grace and have it ministered to them. Fostering these relationships in today's busy culture requires intentionality and the involvement of many, not just hired staff. Some churches use a Sunday School hour to form small groups, Adult Bible Fellowships, or care groups to accomplish this goal. This needs to be planned as a normal guided step for all people in the Body, making it part of the culture. Having couples together in these groups, along with a mix of ages and maturity, seems to foster this grace-giving best. This focus on God's grace keeps the service for Him, not for the church or the pastor.

Leaders' example

New believers and longtime servants must see their leaders as rejoicing slaves of Christ. Love for Christ and of Christ must radiate out of leaders. This does not mean they must be flawless, but rather striving, enjoying the grace of God that covers sin and strengthens areas of weakness. They should see leaders giving thanks always in all things, desiring Christ and every assignment that He sends their way. Leaders should obey Christ's assigned rest and relish His protection. Christ lived openly as a slave among men, so leaders' slavery must be lived among men as well.

A slave mentality

Some may question the use of the word *slave* over *volunteer* to this point, but God's Word is replete with this image for His children. While most translations soften the image with the word *servant*, the word that would normally be translated *servant* rarely occurs in the original language. Several books communicating this point have recently been published, and each notes that the slave of a prominent owner had more freedom, prestige, and delights than the average freedman. These owners at their death often gave complete freedom, position, and finances to their slave. Often slaves were offered freedom at some point, but chose slavery instead. They trusted their owners, who were required to provide for them. Similarly, believers were purchased out of slavery to sin and Satan and given freedom in Christ, which causes them to be His slave because He purchased them, and He will provide for believers forever. The label *volunteer* seems weak and man centered when compared with the Bible's teaching of the

Master-slave. The pastor strengthens volunteers to serve by helping them understand and embrace this truth. As their identity in Christ takes shape in them, the pastor and leaders must reveal how they can serve in the local body of Christ.

A culture of service

All of this teaching and shared experience creates a "serve" culture at church. All that the church does throughout the year and in each area of ministry should emphasize this culture of service. The pastor's preaching should have application in this direction; the church's worship should celebrate the fruit that God is producing; and the focus should remain on Christ as the Body watches His work in others. The pastor must shepherd with this as his goal. All new members should know that the expectation is loving Christ, Who loves them, and that His plan is for believers to love others by serving them and by serving alongside them. As a shepherd, the pastor must check the flock and be sure that each spiritually healthy member is fellowshipping in a small group and is either serving or being trained for service, unless God has given them some unique assignment outside the church, such as caring for a parent in hospice. Members outside these parameters should be pursued by healthy members or pastors to show them God's love and to invite them to serve. This perspective and expectation are key for a church to be healthy. Age does not stop the servant, although adjustments may need to be made to fit his capacity to serve.

Evaluation for placement

The last step toward preparing and keeping a volunteer productive is evaluation and placement. Church leadership must evaluate a volunteer's skills, spiritual giftedness, schedule, competency, experience, and aptitude as a spiritual servant. For example, a highly skilled person lacking humility may need to be harnessed to a more spiritually guided partner. In contrast, a humble person lacking skills will need a trainer or guide who knows how to develop competencies in this area. Some ministry opportunities in your church may need to be designed around the type of schedules your people have, which may vary depending on the time of year. A person desiring to serve may fail if his chosen ministry lines up poorly with life demands such as work or family. People may also need coaching in how to control the demands of work or family. Hobbies should be used for God's glory and balanced by God's values. How does your church specifically respond to and disciple according to these evaluation areas? Evaluation efforts and the right response to them are a part of helping a volunteer to succeed in ministry. This requires a lot of organizational effort by the leadership.

Preparing the Church for Volunteers
Organization

In addition to preparing volunteers for ministry, the church's leaders must prepare ministry for volunteers, and this begins by defining each ministry. (1) Begin by evaluating each ministry's purpose, value, and goals, and its connectedness to the other ministries and the church's God-given purpose. (2) Then compose a general task list and a list of competencies and giftedness that will enable success for each role in each ministry area. Good evaluation requires both of these steps. Working at these steps as a ministry team helps to remove competition for resources and helps to forge a balance in the church's energy output in areas such as evangelism, worship, care, and education. As leaders work through this evaluation, they may realize that some ministries are duplicating each other and that other ministries should remain but should change their focus. The streamlining of efforts helps each volunteer see the need for his work as well as how it connects to the whole as God desires. A clear reporting and authority structure should be a part of this organization.

Training

After the leadership has defined these roles, organize a training program for each ministry position. General skills should be covered in general leadership or teacher training, with specialized training coming from the ministry leader to whom volunteers report. Some positions should have a mandatory training proficiency. Whenever our church has ignored these guidelines, we have paid with a job done poorly or one that produces more work for the ministry leader. Each leader should know who he is responsible to train, and the trainees should know as well.

Ongoing management

Organization and training do not complete the process. The process will fail without ongoing management. This means the trainee and leader are reporting to one another and requiring reports and accountability. They are working together to constantly keep a pulse on the ministry and the people it impacts. They are making adjustments and allowing the Spirit of God to Biblically guide their steps.

Submission and celebration

The last step in this process is conducting a thoroughly systematic ministry evaluation on a yearly or quarterly basis, depending on the ministry need. This evaluation measures the ministry against its purpose, goals, and God's direction. Often a ministry may hit its goals but not fit into the church properly, or it may miss its goals but have been used by God in an unforeseen way. This step might best be called submission and celebration. Leaders and volunteers submit to God and how He may reveal their deficiencies. Then they celebrate what He has done and how He is growing them. Goals for the next stage of ministry, as well as budget planning, will come out of this evaluation.

Individual ministry structure

When a volunteer desires to go from casual serving to the slave level, the church must be ready. If a church desires to bring people purposefully to this level (which is God's commission), it must prepare some structure. Beneath the overarching structure, or culture, of service, the pastor must craft a proper structure for each area of ministry. This structure provides clarity for recruitment, action, and evaluation, and defines the roles needed in each ministry. These roles and their accompanying responsibilities should tie directly to each ministry's purpose, plan, and goals. This may seem like a lot of planning, but it communicates clearly for the pastor when he is not present. As you design each of these individual ministry structures, ask yourself, Would this give my fellow workers the information they need to run the ministry if I were gone for a year? You might think your ministry is too small for this, but the smaller a ministry, the clearer things need to be so that each person can work with maximum effort in the right way on his own, as well as in training others.

Meetings

The clearer your plans, the easier it is to see who fits where in ministry, as well as your objectives for training. Each season should begin with each ministry team reviewing its ministry's purpose and goals, as well as each position and how all the positions connect. Consider the following dynamics for profitable meetings:

- *Make time for prayer and spiritual encouragement.* These should dominate these kickoff meetings.
- *Focus on ministry skills and dependence on God's grace.* After covering details in a meeting, focus on a capability or skill needed for that ministry, as well as on continued dependence on God's grace.
- *Meet frequently.* Generally, the more people that your individual leaders lead, the more often you must meet with these leaders. For instance, if a ministry leader leads ten to fifteen leaders who lead thirty to fifty people, a weekly meeting would be normal. While that may add up to a lot of meetings, keep in mind that these ministry leaders are enabling you as pastor to lead fifty people with a couple of hours' investment a week.
- *Welcome guest trainers.* Having guest trainers is a great change-up to use with your ministry leaders. Also, training a combined group of leaders from various ministries can be effective. If your budget is small, an article, online message, or book that your team shares together could be considered a guest trainer.
- *Expect a complete picture, and report/communicate what is happening.* These meetings are a key time for ongoing communication and reporting. Each leader should come ready to report on his tasks, heart pursuits, budget, calendar, problems solved, needs, and prayer focus. Each leader should know who he is responsible for, and those serving under his leadership should have communicated to him so he has a complete picture. As a pastor, you should know your leaders' passions and what each leader plans to do with the leaders under him and with his area of ministry.
- *Carry on evaluation.* In a sense, each meeting should have a level of ongoing ministry evaluation that helps in making needed adjustments.

Evaluations

After each big event or season, each leader and the leaders under him should conduct an evaluation.

- As a pastor, I like to have leaders in the various ministry areas do their own evaluation, then I can save my efforts for hearing about their work and considering how it fits in an evaluation of the entire church ministry each year. This way I am able to see patterns of weakness, discouragement, or God's leading.

- Don't forget to give your leaders a way to evaluate your impact as well. Work to develop a relationship where they may freely and kindly do this.
- The clearer each area's purpose, plan, and goals for ministry are—along with its tie to the whole church—the more helpful the evaluation of each ministry and its leaders will be.
- Evaluation should be a time of celebration, renewed dependence upon God, and dependence upon His grace. Your church's goals, structure, personnel changes, and prayer focus should come out of this work.

Patience and love for one another prove that "we are His slaves." When my church began this overhaul, it took four years just to get the basics up and running together. Changing a ministry structure and goals is easy; changing a culture takes personal heart change in the pastor and his team. Pastors must first preach the ministry mind-set and shepherd it with expectation. Intentional discipleship comes next, and then people begin to launch.

As you seek to build your volunteer ministry, be prepared for setbacks, but always keep God's plan in mind. In the first three years after I initiated training for teachers, five of the seven moved away. But God's church was served and His purpose fulfilled. Now fifteen years into the process, twelve people are in full-time ministry, and scores have been trained so that they lead ministry areas and train others regularly in a multiplying fashion. This story happens everywhere that Christ's slaves do His work in His way. Just follow His plan; He will do exceedingly beyond what you can imagine.

Take Action . . .

1. All of this information may sound good on paper but seem overwhelming to implement. If much of this is new for your church, make a list of the cultural adjustments needed; then choose one and begin to implement the change.
2. Make a list of your church's ministries, their leaders, and the leaders whom they lead.
3. See if any of the ministries have good structure or leadership in place that already reports to or serves with you, and refine the structure and evaluation in this area this year.
4. Pray and seek some accountability from your leadership team as you begin to work in these two areas. Set small goals and take your time,

but set time aside each week to focus on these change areas. As things go well, prepare the paperwork structure change for a second ministry area.

Discussion

1. How does your church intentionally prepare volunteers to serve as slaves of Christ? What might be missing or need strengthening in the areas of intentional evaluation, prayer, discipleship, or slave mind-set?
2. With whom should you read this chapter and begin to work through some improvements in working with volunteers?
3. In which of your church's ministries are things most organized? What small structure and evaluation additions will be needed to get started well in this area?
4. List your church ministry areas and connect them to the Biblical commands for the church, then add the leaders, sub leaders, and number of people being led by them.

For Further Study

A Better Freedom by Michael Card, InterVarsity Press, 2009.
Biblical Slave Leadership: A Stewardship from Above to Lead from Below by Daniel L. Anderson, Regular Baptist Books, 2013.
The Disciple-Making Church by Bill Hull, Revell, 1990.
The Disciple-Making Pastor by Bill Hull, Revell, 1988.
Me to We by Alan Nelson, Group, 2007.
My Life Is Not My Own by Bill Bright, Regal, 2010.
Personal Disciple-Making by Christopher B. Adsit, Here's Life, 1988.
Slave by John MacArthur, Thomas Nelson, 2010.

17

Planting Daughter Churches
— Ken Davis

America has an estimated 200 million lost and unchurched people, more than the entire populations of all but four other nations. Yet today there are far fewer churches per capita than a hundred years ago. Because church planting is "the most effective evangelistic methodology under heaven," writes C. Peter Wagner, intentionally parenting a daughter church is one of the best ways to reach the unchurched.

Biblical Foundation for Reproduction
The creation mandate

From the beginning, the Creator designed all healthy organisms with the capacity and desire to reproduce. God's purpose for all living creatures was clear: "Be fruitful and multiply" (Gen. 1:22, 28, KJV). Multiplication was the sign and substance of God's blessing. Each group was commanded to "bring forth" (reproduce) "after their kind," and that is exactly what they did (1:11, 12, 21, 24, 25, KJV). This principle of reproduction marks all of life. Whether cells, plants, animals, or humans, each species has "seed . . . in itself" (1:11, KJV) to give birth to the next generation. Since the church is a living organism, God's creative plan requires that the church, too, continually reproduce itself. Thus church parenting is natural.

The commission of Christ

The Great Commission strategy of Christ is actually a spiritual multiplication mandate. He expects His followers to make and multiply disciples (Matt. 28:19, 20). Christ's disciple-making plan is to be carried out through the agency of the local church. Thus, to obey His mandate, if a nearby community has no congregation, we must start one. That's the story of the book of Acts: when people were saved, they were added to the church (2:42–47). Christ's call is for both individual and corporate reproduction. Thus church parenting is Biblical.

The pattern of the early church

The book of Acts shows how the apostles and first Christians carried out the last command of Christ. When God's people obeyed their marching orders, three things are said to have "multiplied": the Word of God (Acts 6:7), the number of disciples (6:1), and the number of churches (9:31). Throughout Acts, the spread of the gospel and the expansion of the church are intertwined. Acts 16:5 summarizes the church's rapid expansion: "So were the churches established in the faith, and increased in number daily" (KJV). They started with one church in Jerusalem; they became many through multiplication. Thus in Acts, church parenting is seen as normal—not the exception.

Intentional church reproduction is seen most clearly in the example of the church at Ephesus. Using the school of Tyrannus as his regional training base, Paul evidently mentored about fifteen leaders, sending them out in teams to plant at least six daughter churches in Asia Minor so that the entire region "heard the word of the Lord" (Acts 19; 20; Rev. 2; 3, KJV). Epaphras, one of his disciples, started the church at Colosse. Ephesus became the mother church of all the churches of Asia Minor.

The Process of Reproduction

Birthing a daughter church follows certain logical and sequential steps. The following overview is adapted from Dan Maxton and provides basic procedures involved in reproducing a daughter church.

1. Learn about the unchurched through solid research

Find out who the unchurched are in your community and where they are located. In obedience to Acts 1:8, look beyond your own "Jerusalem" to nearby unreached towns and cities (your "Judea") as well as to unreached ethnic and immigrant populations (your "Samaria"). Ask the Lord of the Harvest to open your eyes to the growing cultural, economic, ethnic, and generational diversity in your nearby mission fields. Realize that it will take all kinds of churches to effectively reach all the different kinds of people. No one church can realistically disciple everyone.

Take action . . .
- Do a thorough demographic study using the latest U.S. census data (census.gov) or order a ministry area profile (perceptgroup.com). These will help you understand the need and potential for new churches in your area.
- Go to peoplegroups.info to discover more about your region's ethnic, language, and immigrant peoples.
- Get a vision for the lost and unchurched people in your community.

2. Mobilize intercessory prayer

Starting a new church shouldn't be undertaken without considerable forethought, planning, and prayer. Prayer must permeate the entire process, starting with the pastor and leaders and flowing down throughout the congregation. Birthing a church is a spiritual process that requires God's leadership and blessing (see John 15:5).

Take action . . .
- Identify people of prayer in your church body and ask them to intercede for the Lord's direction as to when, where, how, and with whom the new church should be started.
- Encourage teams of prayer warriors to begin interceding for God to raise up new churches to reach your entire region with the gospel. Furnish these groups with resources that enhance prayer: appropriate Scriptures, books and videos on intercession, demographics, and testimonies from the front lines.
- Train your teams to do prayer walking in potential target communities.

3. Creatively cultivate parenting vision

Building a corporate parenting vision is best done by the lead pastor. Create a mentality for multiplication and church planting through your public preaching, private conversations, and leadership networking. Expect at least six to twelve months for your people to catch the vision and commit to parenting. Let your passion for the lost be first seen, heard, and felt by your people before asking for a response. To build shared vision, leaders must be willing to continually share their personal visions and then ask, "Will you follow me?"

Take action . . .

Dan Maxton suggests eight creative ways to generate a congregational vision for parenting:
- Flesh out the vision personally by building relationships with lost people so your people can see how you invest your time and energy.
- Share stories of other parenting churches and people being reached in new churches.
- Interview successful church planters with passion and vision.
- Host a "local missions" conference focusing on your own Jerusalem, Judea, and Samaria.
- Recruit your artists and media experts to create videos, PowerPoint presentations, and other visuals that communicate the need for more churches.
- Use your church newsletter, website, Facebook, and other social media to create interest in regional planting.
- Write challenging Bible lessons on church multiplication for your Sunday School classes and/or weekly small groups.
- Send your adults and teens on short-term missions trips to assist new churches.

Your objective through all this vision casting is to sow the seed for corporate reproduction and to get it down deep into the very DNA of your church.

4. Seek support of key ministry leaders

There is a big difference between compliance and commitment to parenting. You'll need your key ministry leaders on board. Seek to move them from a spirit of fear to faith, from complacency to compassion, and from safety to sacrifice. Realize that with some of them, a values shift may take time, so be patient and prayerful. To build consensus, be open to examine your assumptions Biblically and to listen to others.

Take action . . .
- Create a list of opinion leaders (those to whom people look for direction) and ensure that it includes both formal and informal leaders.
- Meet with each one to share your passion for planting.
- Anticipate possible responses to the parenting vision and come prepared to address questions, objections, and fears. Here are four potential dialogue questions:

(1) What are our congregational strengths?

(2) What church needs should we address in the next two or three years?

(3) What community needs should we be addressing?

(4) What issues do we need to address before we begin implementing our church parenting strategy?

5. Develop corporate ownership

Avoid the pitfall of moving ahead with parenting before gaining congregational support and commitment. Here are five signs that the congregation has owned the vision for parenting a daughter church:
- Supportive congregational leadership
- Greater involvement in prayer for the lost and new churches
- Growing excitement and momentum
- People's actions validating their deepening compassion for the nearby lost
- People committing to become a part of the new church or launch team

Take action . . .
- Freely acknowledging the challenges that will be encountered, seek to provide helpful and Biblically based answers to honest questions and objections.
- Help members see the benefits of starting a daughter church, but don't force a decision before people are ready.

6. Determine the best parenting model

There is more than one way to parent a new church. Here are nine.
- *Commission a launch team.* The church sends out a small pioneering team of leaders to reach a different focus group or nearby community. To be successful, the team needs those with a unified vision and outreach focus and complementary gifts.
- *Release a core group.* Here a significant group of "seed families" is recruited, prepared, and sent out to be a stabilizing core. In this case, 10 percent or more of the parenting congregation is often released for the branch church.
- *Send your pastor.* As in the Antioch model (Acts 13:1–3), sometimes

the Spirit leads a healthy church to give up one of its senior pastoral leaders. Sometimes seed families are sent to help.
- *Partner with other churches.* When financial and people resources are limited, several area churches may cooperate to extend the gospel to their region. Sometimes a state or regional association of Bible-believing churches may take the lead.
- *Go multisite.* Some fast-growing churches in heavily populated areas are becoming "one church in different locations," providing worship teams and staffing for each site. Though there is often no original intention that the campuses become autonomous, in God's providence, some do later become independent.
- *Restart.* A stalled church plant, prematurely launched, is relaunched by a healthy congregation, this time utilizing proven missiological principles. A new church is birthed, often with a complete change of leadership and location.
- *Adopt.* Sometimes a declining, dysfunctional, or recently disbanded older church requests help. A healthy congregation comes alongside to rescue, refocus, and revitalize the unhealthy body that still has potential.
- *Allow death with dignity.* A dying or closing congregation sells its property and assets, giving the funds to an association, mission agency, or new planting project. The goal is to pass on to future generations its values and beliefs so that the Great Commission is carried forward into another community.
- *Avoid an unplanned pregnancy.* In the sovereignty of God, two churches survive and thrive out of a heartbreaking church split. This is "accidental parenthood" as opposed to "planned parenthood," which is far more preferable.

Each of these models has its own strengths and weaknesses. The wise parenting church will seek to evaluate these various approaches. Which of these models best fits your parenting vision and church resources? Which will be more effective in reaching the ministry focus group of the future church?

7. Locate adequate funding

Parenting churches need to make three key decisions about funding support.

First, to what extent will your church invest financially in this project?

How much your church invests depends on whether it will cover any or all of these four options:
- planter support,
- start-up costs,
- facility rental, and
- a monthly subsidy for the baby church's ministry expenses.

Whatever you decide, short-term financial assistance is recommended. To avoid dependency and not weaken the new church's growing participation in stewardship, rarely should outside support be extended beyond three years.

Second, where will your church find the resources? For most potential parents, there are at least five funding options from within the congregation to consider:
- the missions budget,
- harvest offerings,
- not replacing a recently departed staff person,
- undesignated funds (from a departed member's will or living trust), and
- profits from the sale of assets.

Church leaders may want to brainstorm other creative ways to participate in the financial support of the new church.

Third, are outside sources of funding available? Consider these:
- state or local associations,
- other area churches of like faith,
- individual donors outside your church,
- Christian foundations,
- bivocational church planters, and
- a working spouse.

Explore all options and expect God to wonderfully supply.

In God's "glocal" stewardship plan, all the resources for the harvest are normally found in the harvest. As the new church grows and disciples are made, it should have increasing people and financial resources to do what God is calling it to do in the target community.

8. Select a suitable target community and ministry focus group

Use your previous demographic study to identify, describe, and prioritize nearby communities that need a gospel witness. Is a new housing development being built a few miles away? Are there economic, ethnic, or lifestyle groups you need to reach? What people groups are yet unreached? Is there a nearby town with insufficient gospel witness? Do you have people coming from one of these areas who are willing to help start a church in their community?

Take action . . .
- Do on-site field research by walking the streets of potential communities and talking to people.
- Discern each community's spiritual climate and receptivity to the gospel. What is God already doing in these places? What kind of church is needed in each setting?

It may be wise to start your first daughter church among a familiar group before seeking to parent in a more challenging context.

9. Recruit people to send and equip

The number of people sent from the parenting church varies with the parenting model chosen. Normally, the more people recruited and trained, the stronger the new church is likely to be. Aim for giving twenty-five to fifty people or more, if possible. Are there other churches in the area that would be willing to give or loan two to five families to the new project?

Providing sufficient people resources has greater impact than just pouring money into a planting project. Supplying short-term outreach and ministry teams, staff mentoring and expertise, and ongoing training for the launch team really makes a difference.

10. Enlist an entrepreneurial church planter

Look for a person with a proven track record who can cast vision and gather and motivate people. Because everything rises or falls on the right leader, it's best to consider at least three viable candidates before making your final decision. All potential candidates should be thoroughly investigated. Look at calling, character, competency, and chemistry.

Take action . . .
- Consider utilizing a planter assessment center that uses multiple tools and trained observers or a behavioral interview process with online assessment. ELI's Planter Profiles, churchplanterprofiles.com, and LifeWay's Church Planter Candidate Assessment, churchplanter.lifeway.com, are helpful tools for assessing potential church planters.

- Develop a written job description outlining expectations, responsibilities, and the accountability structure to share with potential candidates.
- Seek to match your lead planter to your targeted community and primary ministry-focus group. Most effective planters tend to reach people most like themselves.
- Once you have identified your chosen planter, ask him to prepare and submit a written planting proposal before he plants.

11. Help the planter bond with the parenting church

Bring the prospective church planter onto your staff for a period of three to six months before launching the new church. This allows him to build relationships with the mother church and with members of his launch team. It also provides time for him to become familiar with and begin working in the target community. Provide him with lots of visibility by scheduling him to preach periodically and to participate in your services. Many parenting pastors give their planter a "fishing license" to freely recruit key leaders and givers for his launch team.

Plan a commissioning and prayer service for the planter and his team before sending them out. Give your planter access to the parenting church's office equipment, files, worship slides, and ministry systems (financial, guest follow-up, assimilation, etc.). Encourage your planter to borrow and adapt lots of ideas. Give your people a list of needed start-up equipment/supplies and consider holding a "baby shower" for the new church.

12. Identify a coach for the planter and a mentor for the pastor

A qualified coach will help your planter succeed by listening, encouraging, giving wise counsel, and celebrating wins. A coach meets with the planter regularly, often holding him accountable to a prepared checklist. Ideally, the coach should be a veteran planter; it is best if the parenting pastor not be the planter's coach. The mentor performs a similar service for the pastor of the parent church. The best mentor is another pastor whose church has successfully parented before; his experience will be invaluable when questions and concerns arise.

13. Embrace your changing parenting role

It is essential that church leaders understand four developmental stages in the life cycle of a new church. Each stage requires the parent church to assume a critical role and focus upon key tasks.

- *Reproduction stage.* Congregational support is sought, target communities are selected, a parenting model is chosen, and funding sources are identified. The parenting church casts vision and encourages commitment.
- *Conception stage.* Everything that needs to be done before the lead planter moves on-site is completed. The parent church assesses and selects the best-qualified lead planter and approves of his written proposal.
- *Prenatal stage.* Essential outreach and ministry systems are developed before the new church goes public. The parent church holds the planter accountable and provides the necessary people and financial resources.
- *Birth and growth stage.* Public worship services begin, and essential ministry systems are implemented. The parent gets out of the way and releases control.

The leadership of the parenting church is most needed during the two early stages because it sets the crucial DNA code for the new church. After this, the parenting church's impact and role decrease over time. Healthy parents don't smother! They don't expect an exact replica, but allow the daughter to be unique and have her own personality (ministry philosophy). Over-control can lead to resentment and dependency upon the parenting church. Allow your offspring the joy of following the Lord's leading without interference. Begin viewing them as an adult sister church rather than as a daughter.

14. Plan for the release and recovery

The "cutting of the apron strings" comes much earlier in the church-planting life cycle than it does with humans. While the parenting church may still require reports and provide some funding for up to two or three years, the tie binding the daughter church to its mother should be cut within three to twelve months after the start of the new church. Let the new congregation learn to trust God and stand on their own two feet.

After giving birth, parent churches need adequate time for rest and recovery in several key areas. Most churches will need three to six months for restoring finances, regaining attendance, and replacing key leaders. The rate of recovery will largely depend on the health of the church before parenting. If you have effective outreach and assimilation systems, the rebuilding stage may be shortened. Remember that it is impossible to out-give the Lord! Expect Him to bless your obedience, creatively restore your energy and resources, and renew your vision.

When the time is right, your congregation will need a new focus. Be prepared to lead them by pointing them to the harvest and a new God-given vision for church multiplication. Dream about reproducing many children and grandchildren to impact your entire region for Christ!

Discussion

1. What is the Biblical rationale for churches intentionally planting daughter churches?
2. How would a senior pastor go about cultivating vision and support for parenting?
3. Discuss some of the many ways, or models, an established church could actually get involved in birthing a planting project.
4. Where could prospective parenting churches look to find adequate funding sources for a new church plant?
5. Using the life cycle model of parenting, how does the parenting church's role change over time?

For Further Study

Be Fruitful and Multiply by Robert Logan, ChurchSmart Resources, 2006.
Church Planting for a Greater Harvest by C. Peter Wagner, Regal, 1990.
Church Planting Is for Wimps by Mike McKinley, Crossway, 2010.
Churches Planting Churches: A Comprehensive Guide for Multiplying New Congregations by Robert E. Logan and Steven L. Ogne, ChurchSmart, 1995.
Churches That Multiply by Elmer Towns and Douglas Porter, Beacon Hill, 2003.
The Dynamic Daughter Church Planting Handbook by Paul Becker and Mark Williams, DCPI, 1999.
Exponential by Dave Ferguson and Jon Ferguson, Zondervan, 2010.
How to Multiply Your Church by Ralph Moore, Regal, 2009.
Legacy Churches by Stephen Gray and Franklin Dumond, ChurchSmart Resources, 2009.
"Mentoring Church Planters" by Ken Davis, *The Journal of Ministry and Theology,* Fall 2010, vol. 14, no. 2, 47–61.
Multi-Site Churches by Scott McConnell, Broadman and Holman, 2009.

A Multi-Site Church Road Trip by Geoff Surratt, Greg Lignon, and Warren Bird, Zondervan, 2009.

The Multiplying Church by Bob Roberts Jr., Zondervan, 2008.

The Nuts and Bolts of Church Planting by Aubrey Malphurs, Baker, 2011.

Parent Church Landmines by Ben Ingebretson and Tom Nebel, ChurchSmart Resources, 2009.

Planting Churches: A Framework for Practitioners by Stuart Murray, Paternoster, 2008.

Planting Fast-growing Churches by Stephen Gray, ChurchSmart Resources, 2007.

The Ripple Church by Phil Stevenson, Wesleyan Publishing House, 2004.

Spin-Off Churches by Rodney Harrison, Tom Cheyney, and Don Overstreet, Broadman and Holman, 2008.

"Twelve Steps to Parenting a New Church" by Dan Maxton, available at convergeworldwide.org.

Viral Churches by Ed Stetzer and Warren Bird, Jossey-Bass, 2010.

Winning the World for Christ: The Untapped Potential of Daughter Church Planting by Mark Alan Williams, DCPI.

The YBH (Yes, But How?) Handbook of Church Planting by Roger N. McNamara and Ken Davis, Xulon Press, 2005.

18

Guiding the Local Outreach Program
— Jim Vogel

I think you need to go too," my young associate pastor, Brian, declared. He was referring to a weeklong evangelism conference in another part of the country that I had encouraged him to attend—by himself. Brian was a pastoral colleague in my first ministry, tasked with leading our church in more effective outreach.

"We both need to go," he repeated. "Our people need to know you are committed too. And I'm sure you will learn something."

"But I already know how to witness," I countered. "Can't I be committed from here?" But he persisted, and I reluctantly went.

I still look back on that conversation and the resulting outreach training as transformational in my pastoral ministry. Brian was right to insist I go, and I have never been the same since. I not only learned a great deal about being a more effective witness personally, but I also caught a vision of the kind of impact an evangelistically focused church can have. That conference launched me on an outreach ministry journey—one that continues to this day. And it is this journey and the things I've learned along the way that are this chapter's emphasis.

Due to limited space, I'll be summarizing. I'll begin with five core outreach convictions I believe should drive pastoral leaders in developing effective outreach ministries. Then I'll suggest ten areas of specific outreach strategy with suggestions for strategic action.

Five Foundational Convictions
Churches and evangelization

Churches remain at the center of God's plan for local and global evangelization. The New Testament is clear about the centrality of the church in God's outreach purposes in this age. The church is the primary training center for believers, fostering their spiritual growth and equipping them for outreach. It is crucial to the discipling mission that new believers are grounded within the context of a community of faith. While other ministries outside the local church can provide assistance and motivation in its task, the church is still the "hub of the wheel" of outreach.

Disciple-making

Christ's disciple-making mandate is at the heart of every local church's mission. His words in His commissions in the Gospels (Matt. 28:16–20; Mark 16:14–18; Luke 24:44–49; John 20:19–23) and Acts (1:8) must be understood in the context of what God was doing in those transitional days after Christ's resurrection and ascension in anticipation of the birth of the church as described in Acts 2. Can there be any doubt that He knew that those timid followers He met with in Galilee and Jerusalem would form the leadership nucleus of this new entity, the church? Surely He did. In His commissions He was giving missional instruction for the church. The connection is hard to miss in Christ's words in Luke, where He emphasized His followers' responsibility to proclaim, and witness to, the gospel message (note the reference to Jerusalem; cf. parallel wording in Acts 1:8) and connected this instruction with the Day of Pentecost and the birth of the church. He declared, "Behold, I am sending forth the promise of My Father upon you; but you are to stay in the city until you are clothed with power from on high" (Luke 24:49, NASB). Clearly our Lord's outreach mandate to be witnesses and make disciples is normative for the church. It is her central mission.

Pastoral example

Pastoral example is crucial in the church's outreach ministry. God has given pastors the responsibility to provide loving, balanced leadership to local churches, and our example is our most powerful leadership tool. The people we serve take note of those things we both preach and practice. When it comes to outreach, pastors cannot coach from the sidelines. It's my conviction that pastoral example is one key to outreach effectiveness in any church. We can set this example by committing to faithfulness in our own personal witness, participating directly and visibly in church outreach events, evidencing our commitment to outreach in our congregational prayer times, being "out front" in motivating everyone to stay committed to the church's outreach mission, building relationships with local community leaders, and giving passionate overall leadership to the outreach strategy of the church. The bottom line: when it comes to outreach, pastors are "player-coaches."

Church health

Church health is foundational to outreach success. No church is perfect, for obvious reasons: every church has "stuff" to work on. Nonetheless, even churches "in process" can be healthy—when they are marked by unity, Biblical leadership perspectives, true caring concern for one another, changeable methodology, solid Biblical teaching and preaching, meaningful worship, and the like. Ensuring church health is critically important, because the church, by God's design, is the primary "incubator" for newborn believers (not to mention older believers). Healthy churches produce healthy believers, who in turn reproduce themselves.

Intentional strategic effort

Intentional strategic effort is necessary for effective outreach. Long gone are the days when we could expect the lost in our communities to come to us. We are no longer living in a churchgoing culture. Interest in spiritual things is waning. People stay away in droves. Such realities demand a new focus for churches that desire to impact their communities in obedience to Christ's commission—an outward focus. This new focus recognizes the importance of intentional strategic effort in reaching out to those without Christ. Toward this goal, consider the following suggested outreach initiatives as a starting point in the development of an individual church's outreach priorities.

Ten Strategic Outreach Initiatives
1. Make outreach-focused prayer a high priority

Somehow we've missed the connection between prayer and outreach. Consider the New Testament pattern (e.g., Paul's prayer request for the Colossians in 4:1–4 or his request of the Ephesians in 6:18–20) and start here with a twofold emphasis: your own pastoral example of prayer both privately and publicly, and your need to mobilize your people to be outreach focused in their praying.

Take action . . .
- Start with a private commitment to pray every day for the salvation of your own friends, family, and acquaintances.
- Commit to regular prayer for the church's corporate outreach ministries.
- In public prayer times, consciously include the outreach ministries of the church and their leaders.
- Enlist a team of people who will join in praying for the church's outreach ministries. Keep them informed of specific people who have responded to the gospel or those who are close to a salvation decision.
- Ask the team to come together for special prayer on the days specific outreach events are taking place. Or ask them to meet following the event to seek God's continuing work in the lives of those who attended.
- Affirm the efforts of all those who pray, specifically by regularly talking about the fruit of their efforts.

2. Increase ministry visibility

For a church to have a spiritual impact, people in the community need to know the church exists—where it meets, what its basic ministries are, and that its members genuinely care about them. They need to know how to contact the church when they need help. A church needs to be visible in its community.

Even if a congregation is not large and the church building is not located on a busy street, the church can have good visibility, because visibility is not related to facilities alone; it also relates to the influence of the church people who live and work in the community and make others aware of their church and its ministry.

And remember that as pastors, we are often the point persons in this visibility effort. Especially in small towns, we can become well known and highly regarded in our communities, and thus bring visibility to the churches we serve.

Take action . . .
- Make your website attractive, informative, and outreach sensitive.
- Consider direct mail contact with community newcomers.
- Use social media.
- Take part in community events, such as parades, fairs, holiday celebrations, and community projects.
- Attend the local schools' drama productions.
- Volunteer at community fund-raising events.
- Serve as a chaplain for the local police or fire department.
- Join Kiwanis.
- Sponsor an open house for the community, inviting everyone to the church for free food, games, and recreational activities.

3. Establish a reputation for compassion in the community

One of the best ways to become more visible in the community is to demonstrate God's love in practical ways—with no strings attached. It can be costly and time consuming and even uncomfortable at times, but it brings rich dividends. Churches that become known in their communities for caring for others open doors for the gospel.

Take action . . .
- Establish a food pantry or clothing distribution ministry.
- Provide a free Thanksgiving Day dinner at the church.
- Consider simple acts of kindness, like raking the leaves of homes near the church in the fall or distributing free bottles of water at a local park on hot summer days.
- Offer your building for use by the local city council or for neighborhood meetings.
- Provide an after-school program for neighborhood children.
- Host a free appreciation dinner for public and private school teachers.
- Clean up a local park.
- Provide free school supplies to needy children.
- Participate in your state's Adopt-a-Highway program.
- Offer your building as a polling place or a blood-drive center.
- Hold a health fair in your gym or foyer.
- Recruit tutors for a nearby school.
- Provide employment counseling and training.
- Offer to teach parenting classes at a local school.

4. Train everyone in lifestyle evangelism

Not everyone has the giftedness and calling to become an evangelist, but every believer is tasked with the responsibility to be a witness. When we, as pastors, strategize and implement a plan to provide congregation-wide training in everyday witnessing, the church's outreach potential is multiplied exponentially. An army of knowledgeable and confident believers who are passionate about sharing their faith with friends and coworkers will fuel all the church's other outreach efforts.

Take action . . .
- Set a goal of church-wide witnessing training.
- Teach and preach on the "every believer" responsibility to witness.
- Select a training curriculum, or write your own, on how to share one's faith in the context of daily living. Plan for a series of six to eight sessions.
- Choose a training venue that best fits your people's availability: Friday–Saturday meetings, Sunday School classes, small groups, Sunday night meetings, or online training approaches. Recognize that it will require time and an ongoing commitment.
- Regularly communicate the goal of 100 percent participation.
- As new members join the church, remind them of the goal of full participation in this training.
- Stick with it. This ministry is accomplished over time.

5. Build church-wide guest sensitivity

Churches that effectively reach out to the lost in their communities often have pastors who have fostered a culture of congregational outreach. Their people are focused outward, toward the lost. They expect to see guests regularly at services and events, and are sensitive to the first impressions those guests have. Recognizing that many of these guests may be unbelievers, they are thrilled to greet and welcome them. They realize that these guests may be reached with the gospel through the church's ministries. Unfortunately, however, such perspectives are not the norm in many churches. Rather than an outward focus, there is often an inward one protective of long-standing norms and insensitive to guests. Encouraging the former perspective and fostering a church-wide outreach passion is crucial in effective outreach.

Take action . . .
- Teach the congregation the importance of being aware of and sensitive to guests.
- Enlist and train a "first impressions team" of leaders who will help strategize ways to welcome guests without embarrassing them.
- Ensure adequate outside and inside signage that makes clear to guests the locations of parking spaces, church entrances, restrooms, nurseries, the worship center, etc.
- Enlist and train a "welcome team" of parking attendants, greeters, and ushers to assist guests without ignoring regular attenders. Train them to prioritize their ministry to newcomers.
- Build and staff an accessible welcome center in a visible location near the church's main entrance to provide helpful information for guests and assistance with ministry questions.
- Consider establishing a post-service event or newcomers' reception where you can meet guests, answer questions, and determine spiritual needs.
- Train church members to be aware of guests and greet them warmly as a first priority.
- Ensure that classes and small groups are guest friendly and that corporate worship is alive, relevant, and comprehensible by unbelievers.

6. Mobilize the Sunday School for outreach

Sunday Schools may be on the decline in churches these days, but I'm convinced that it's still the best tool for teaching our people the basics of Bible content and doctrine. I also believe that the Sunday School can effectively include an outreach component. Its structure and approach are conducive to both the training of believers and outreach to unbelievers. Pastors who retool the Sunday School to include this focus will reap the benefits of added outreach potential.

Take action . . .
- Train teachers to be sensitive to guests who may not know Christ.
- Ensure that all teachers know how to share the basic plan of salvation.
- Seek to connect guests who attended worship services or events to an appropriate Sunday School class as an initial follow-up priority.

- Encourage the ongoing connection of these Sunday School guests to a class (enrollment) as soon as possible.
- Establish a guest follow-up plan in each class that recognizes potential spiritual needs, provides caring contact outside of class, and seeks opportunities to share the gospel.

7. Discover your unique "target group" outreach opportunities

Every church is uniquely positioned to reach segments of its community using some connection (or potential connection) between the two in order to share the gospel. For example, churches in college towns have targeted students. Those near a jail or prison may reach out to inmates. Churches located near major sports venues might target athletes. Many churches in urban settings (rural ones too) have reached out to the homeless or the poor. Others, depending on their locations and resources, may target immigrants, orphans, those with addictions, latchkey kids, single moms, military families, unwed mothers, those with broken marriages, police officers, firefighters, cancer patients, hunters, the deaf community, or business professionals.

Take action . . .

- Prayerfully consider what opportunities exist for outreach to specific groups of people to whom you can naturally reach out. Gather information; view demographic data; seek input from the congregation; brainstorm with other leaders.
- Make a decision, perhaps starting with just one target group of people, and develop a specific step-by-step strategy for reaching out to them. Consider available resources, and plan for any funding needs.
- Be sure to include plans for specific events/activities where the gospel can be shared clearly and tactfully.
- Enlist and train those who will direct and serve in the ministry.
- Implement the plans; enlist church-wide support; be committed over time.

8. Establish an evangelistic events calendar

Every church can increase its outreach effectiveness through scheduling events that are specifically focused on outreach beyond the church's regular services and ministries. These events provide a more focused opportunity to reach the lost in what is often a more informal or welcoming atmosphere. They can also provide an additional avenue for presenting the gospel for those in the congregation who are witnessing to friends, family, or coworkers. Most will be onetime events, but some may be recurring ones, depending on goals and methodology. Outreach events might include fall carnivals, Easter egg hunts, holiday dinner theaters, sportsmen's dinners, ladies' luncheons, Christmas pageants, sports clinics, marriage seminars, Valentine's Day banquets, Easter passion plays, program alternatives to Halloween, golf tournaments, back-to-church Sundays, summer ice cream socials, Christmas Eve services, musical concerts, Fourth of July extravaganzas, and the like.

Take action . . .
- Consider a basic annual calendar of outreach events. Start small—perhaps one or two a year at first. A natural place to begin is with holiday-themed events, such as Easter and Christmas programs.
- Be sure to keep the focus evangelistic. It may be necessary to retool events that have been part of the church's calendar in the past to ensure they will be devoted to outreach and not merely include an outreach component. Unless this emphasis is maintained, events often revert over time to a focus on believers, and their outreach effectiveness can be lost. Keep the outreach focus a priority.
- Plan thoroughly, with a timetable for completed preparations.
- Recruit and train volunteer leaders to administer each event. Determine the provisions for funding and lines of accountability.
- Advertise and promote events in the church and community. Emphasize the importance of personal invitations of friends, family, and neighbors.
- Think through how to follow up on guests; for example, provide response cards, which might include an invitation to receive information about how to have a relationship with God or to participate in a Bible study. Promptly follow up on these responses.
- Consider scheduling recurring outreach events, such as quarterly women's outreach luncheons, children's sports camps, and evangelistic Bible studies.

9. Follow up promptly on guests, especially those who may not know Christ

Those who come to an event or worship service—either at the invitation of another attender or due to the church's visibility—are a top priority in outreach. They have taken a step toward the church and are more likely to be willing to respond to another contact. When we as pastors sense that a guest may not be a believer, prompt follow-up on that person is critical.

Take action . . .
- Unfortunately, since many guests prefer anonymity, receiving basic information such as names and addresses can at times be difficult. Strategize ways to receive this information without offense, through guest cards in worship services, registrations in Sunday School, guest registries in the lobby, contacts in the welcome center, contacts made during newcomer receptions, and the like.
- Establish a plan for the initial follow-up of worship-service guests, which might include the delivery of a note of thanks and a small gift basket to the home within a day or two, a handwritten note from the pastor within the week, or a contact and invitation from a small group or Sunday School class leader within the week.
- Consider using an online feedback survey from guests when contact information is available.
- When guests are probably not believers, prioritize additional follow-up, seeking a personal appointment with a pastoral staff member or trained outreach volunteer when the time is right but without unnecessary delay. Meet the unbelievers at a restaurant or in their home to get to know them. When it is deemed appropriate, ask permission to share the basics of how one can be sure of salvation. If the response is positive, set up another time to share the gospel. Be proactive but wise, prayerful, and noncoercive.
- Monitor the ongoing attendance of guests and establish a plan for the follow-up of repeat attenders, incorporating some activities similar to the initial contacts.

10. Make a plan for discipling new believers and connecting them to the church

Surprisingly, most churches don't have a strategic approach to working with those who make salvation decisions. We're thrilled they're in the family, but we seem to feel that the regular church services and groups will be sufficient. In most cases they're not. We might have been able to get away with this approach when there was greater Biblical literacy and spiritual awareness in the culture. But not today. A specific strategy is needed that incorporates both individual and group initiatives.

Take action . . .
- First, ask those who lead someone to Christ to do initial follow-up. Show them how to discern between a true and false decision and how to affirm the new convert's assurance of salvation. Find helpful printed materials or write your own.
- Next, enlist and train a group of committed disciplers who know how to explain the five basic areas of growth for new believers: Bible study, prayer, church involvement (baptism, membership, fellowship, service, etc.), overcoming temptation, and witnessing. Find curriculum that covers these basics or write it yourself.
- Then connect these disciplers with new believers. Hold them accountable to meet at least biweekly to discuss the above topics and report on the progress of those they are discipling.
- Following the one-on-one meetings with disciplers, bring new believers together with other new believers in an eight- to ten-week series of classes (Sunday School or small groups seem best) to review and expand on areas of growth.
- Finally, enlist and train a group of mentors who can follow up on the work of the disciplers and provide another level of friendship and guidance. Mentors should walk new believers through the membership process and the discovery of their gifts and places of service.

Discussion
1. If a person were to look at your church budget, could he immediately discern that evangelism and discipleship are a priority?
2. Does church outreach depend on highly social extroverts? What suggestions could you give to church members who want to be involved in outreach but consider themselves shy?
3. Should follow-up and discipleship efforts use a standard printed curriculum?

For Further Study
Becoming a Contagious Church by Mark Mittelberg, Zondervan, 2007.
Beyond the First Visit by Gary L. McIntosh, Baker, 2006.

The Complete Evangelism Guidebook edited by Scott Dawson, Baker, 2008.
A Heart for the Community edited by John Fuder and Noel Castellanos, Moody, 2011.
Surprising Insights from the Unchurched and Proven Ways to Reach Them by Thom S. Rainer, Zondervan, 2008.
Telling the Truth edited by D. A. Carson, Zondervan, 2002.

19

Leading in Finances and Facilities
— George Prinzing

My father said that a good indication that God has a hold of a man's heart is if He has a hold of that man's wallet. Matthew 6:21 bears this out: "For where your treasure is, there your heart will be also" (ESV). This principle extends to the local church too. Its giving is a strong indicator of its heart. In a world where people naturally love, trust, and hoard money, finding an individual (or congregation) who loves and trusts God and is generous with his resources is evidence of heart change. God is a giver (Matt. 5:45; John 3:16), and His children are expected to have His traits (Luke 6:38; 2 Cor. 8:7). So a church's finances say a lot about its status. If offerings are strong and increasing, usually the church is. But generally, if the finances are plateauing or declining, so is the church.

Avenging Angel of Finance

A pastor must not be a lover of money, yet the church's finances often do have a great impact on his happiness. If the offerings are good, he can breathe easy. If they are low, he too will be. After all, salaries and bills must be paid, missionaries need their support, and perhaps the giving (or lack thereof) is a referendum on the pastor's performance! Add to this the suggestions of some well-meaning members recommending strategies and cuts to keep the church afloat—some of which are agenda-based and contradict Scripture. In a business meeting at my first church, a man stood up and said, "This monthly budget report doesn't add up, and I'm an avenging angel sent to keep an eye on things!" I gulped. Our treasurer tried to explain that indeed it did add up, but it was to little avail. He would not be convinced, and sometime afterward he quit attending.

These are the burdens a pastor carries—trying to preach the Word, care for the flock, and reach the lost—and on top of this see to it that the offerings are good and that all finances are handled and spent properly. So when the finances get tight and the criticisms and suggestions begin to mount, what's a pastor to do?

Teaching Biblical Giving
1. Teach stewardship
Giving in the offering plate should be taught in the context of stewardship. Believers need to be taught and reminded that they are not their own, but have been bought with a price and are to glorify God in all they do, which includes giving (1 Cor. 6:19, 20) and that they will give account to Christ for how they stewarded/managed their lives and resources (2 Cor. 5:10). Further, God wants His children to experience the blessedness of giving (Acts 20:35; 2 Cor. 9:7).

2. Teach stewardship at the beginning of the year
I used to avoid this because I didn't want to be labeled a "money preacher," but I have since changed my mind. People need to be taught this regularly. If your church is growing, there are many who have no idea that God expects them to honor Him with their firstfruits and to live on a budget (Prov. 3:9, 10). And don't limit this to just one message—probably two or more are needed for it to really sink in. Combine it with having your small groups or Sunday School classes teach it for that same time period. It will help greatly if you tie this to your Strategic Ministry Budget (discussed later), because people give better to a bold vision than they do to an appeal based on duty. As a pastor, you should be calling them to devote their lives, fortunes, and sacred honor for the great cause of Christ in your community.

3. Teach tithing
Though it may not be the letter of the law, the tithing principle (giving 10 percent of one's gross income) is healthy for the believer and the local church for several reasons:
- *It is fair.* With few exceptions, 10 percent is something everyone can do.
- *It is significant.* For those who have never tithed, this will be a momentous (and blessed) decision.

- *It is continual.* Salaries, bills, and missionary support are continual—so, too, does the income need to be.
- *It is Scriptural.* John Piper convincingly shows that Paul taught the tithing principle. The apostle reasoned that since the tabernacle/temple work was supported by the tithe (Num. 18:20, 21), so should the church. "Do you not know that those who are employed in the temple service get their food from the temple, and those who serve at the altar share in the sacrificial offerings? In the same way, the Lord commanded that those who proclaim the gospel should get their living by the gospel" (1 Cor. 9:13, 14, ESV, emphasis added).

Where Is Your Church on the Giving Scale?

In 2002 the per capita giving in the United States for a growing church was $767. The rule of thumb is that the typical attendee gives about $1,000 per year. So a church with an average attendance of 100 would have an annual income of $100,000. Now by Biblical standards this may be low, but this is the norm nonetheless and will give a local church a sense of where they are or could be.

The Strategic Ministry Budget

Too often the annual church budget is viewed as pure drudgery. But it should not be this way. The pastor must strive to set the tone that putting together the annual budget and the congregation's voting on it is the people of God declaring, "This is what we want to do for God in the coming year!" Sadly, many church budgets reflect that a church is planning only to maintain the status quo. This is why each church needs a Strategic Ministry Budget, because the goal is not just paying bills, but strategically engaging in the unique ministry of that unique church.

Admittedly, it takes prayerful diligence to produce a church budget that truly reflects a church's commitment to the Great Commission, but it is a worthy endeavor for the pastor and his leaders. First, the church must decide what its mission is and how it plans to accomplish it. A mission statement is helpful here (e.g., The mission of First Baptist Church is to glorify God by edifying the saints and evangelizing the lost). Obviously, this mission will require funding and a church budget that supports it. This statement will be helpful in determining which items need to be included, eliminated, or scaled back. James D. Berkley comments, "Prepared thoughtlessly and used slavishly, a budget can be a moronic master, mindlessly hindering ministry, squelching spontaneity, and engulfing leaders in dreary busywork. . . . A budget that remains suspiciously like that of the previous year will most likely drag down a ministry into a static status quo. Instead, a proper church budget ought to stretch imaginations, cause a slight gasp, expand vision, and enable ministry."

Once the mission statement is in place, the second exercise would be to put together the Strategic Ministry Budget. This begins with estimating what the coming year's income will be. You must track at least your church's last three years of giving and look for a trend. Then base your budget on these real numbers. In the excellent book *Money Matters in Church,* the authors recommend that a budget be broken down into these four fundamentals:

1. Missions (10 percent)—foreign missions and local evangelism (Matt. 28:18–20).
2. Personnel (50–55 percent smaller church; 45–50 percent larger church)—salaries and benefits for pastors and staff (1 Tim. 5:17, 18).
3. Programming (20 percent)—Sunday School, small groups, worship-preaching services, Vacation Bible School, as well as copiers and office supplies.
4. Facilities (20–25 percent)—mortgage payment, insurance, and utilities. Once a mortgage is paid off, a church should save money for future facility needs rather than divert all the extra funds to other areas.

It would be helpful for you to take a look at your church's current mission statement, its budget, and these percentages and see where it stands. Pastors should not be afraid to challenge the status quo and cut what is ineffective or unhelpful. People may not agree, but it is the pastor's duty to lead the church to effective ministry.

The Safe

A pastor friend told me that back in the 1970s when he or the youth pastor needed funds for a church project the senior pastor would instruct them to take cash from the church safe! Oh, the good old days! Obviously this practice honored neither Paul's example (2 Cor. 8:16–24) nor his instruction that "all things should be done decently and in order" (1 Cor. 14:40, ESV).

Guidelines for Handling Church Finances

1. Offerings should be collected by a group.

2. Offerings should be counted by a group.
3. Offerings should be deposited by two.
4. A system must be in place to receipt those who desire a giving statement.
5. Checks may have one signature up to a certain amount; then two signatures should be required.
6. Use purchase orders for non-staff.
7. Receipts for all purchases must be required.
8. Pastors should not be involved in collecting, counting, or depositing funds or signing checks.
9. The church should be incorporated.
10. The church should have liability insurance.

Subtotal

It is crucial that a pastor grasp and confidently communicate to his leaders and members the strategic mission of his unique local church. According to Berkley, "People don't get excited about the mundane. They do, however, flock to persons and ideas that are compelling, bold, and full of vision. They will dust off their checkbooks to support what stirs and inspires them." When you combine a Biblical, bold vision with a Strategic Ministry Budget to support it and the wise handling of funds, you will create an atmosphere of trust and confidence. Conversely, when there is little direction and a status quo budget, even if money is well cared for, the church will likely struggle. So ask God to help you understand His unique mission for your church. Discuss it with your leaders. Pray with them regarding it. Then seek their help and others in coming up with a Strategic Ministry Budget that supports it. When your congregation hears how it ties in to the Great Commission, they are likely to support it generously.

To Build or Not to Build

The belief that a new building will lead to dynamic church growth can be enticing. But be careful. I know personally that this is not always the case. The church where I am pastor relocated to a new site and new facilities and experienced only modest growth (about 10 percent). I was told that explosive growth would occur, but it didn't. True growth did not occur until about a year later—and that was due to a renewed sense of mission on the part of the congregation. While it is true that the right building at the right time can greatly enhance ministry and allow for healthy growth, too often pastors and leaders in an effort to jump-start growth lead their churches into detrimental building projects.

It is imperative that the pastor and leadership of the local church answer the right questions before entering any kind of new facility plan. In *When Not to Build*, Ray Bowman and Eddy Hall advise that fifteen questions be answered before initiating a building program:

_____ Do you expect a new building to attract new people to the church?
_____ Is it your goal to design a building that will inspire people to worship?
_____ Do you expect your members to be more motivated to reach out to others once you have a new building?
_____ Do you think a building program will motivate your people to give more generously to the work of the church?
_____ Do you expect the building program to unify your people behind a significant challenge?
_____ Do you hope that a building program will involve more people in the work of the church?
_____ Do you see the building as a way to make a statement to the community about the church's importance?
_____ Do you hope that a new building will help your people take more pride in their church?
_____ Do you need a larger sanctuary so the entire congregation can worship together at one time?
_____ Do you need to add more educational space so all your classes can meet at once?
_____ Is it possible that your space needs could be met through more creative use of your present facilities, such as converting space to multiple use, changing furnishings, scheduling ministries at alternate times, or using off-campus meeting space?
_____ Are you still paying off debt on your last building?
_____ Would you have to borrow a major part of the finances for a building program?
_____ Would payment for the project depend on the church's future growth?
_____ To help pay for the building, would you explore ways to cut spending on your present ministry programs and staffing?

Every yes response is a possible reason "not to build, to delay building, or to seek another appropriate solution through prayer, research, and reevaluation."

Basically, do not assume that when your worship attendance reaches 80 percent of the sanctuary space and/or all Sunday School rooms are completely occupied that it is obviously time to build. While this is a good kind of problem to have, and a solution is needed, it would be a better use of God-given resources to open a second worship service and Sunday School, thereby immediately doubling your square footage! This would allow the church to focus attention and resources on ministry (and more money can be saved for a future, truly needed building project). So before you build, be honest with these questions and be creative in your solutions.

That being said, there comes a time when a major building project is the only remedy for space problems. Keep these basics in mind:

1. Appoint building committee leaders who understand the church's mission and who are already serving. Members who are contractors, plumbers, etc., rarely make good leaders of church building projects (though their expertise is valuable and should be consulted throughout).
2. The church's unique ministry mission must drive what kind of facility is needed.
3. Generally, a church's mortgage should not exceed 25 percent of its income.
4. Though there are exceptions, it is advisable and beneficial to utilize the services of an outside Christian professional to help raise funds.

Total

My advice is that in the areas of giving, budgets, and buildings, a pastor should speak early and consistently about Biblical priorities—and likewise he must listen carefully and make needed adjustments. Great patience is needed in this process. Leading in the area of finances and facilities can be overwhelming, risky, and wearisome. But if done right, it can foster honest, helpful relationships within the leadership and create an atmosphere of trust, stability, and healthy growth.

Take Action . . .

1. Summarize what you as a pastor are doing on a yearly basis to help your congregation understand Biblical stewardship.
2. Compare your annual church budget with the percentages listed in the "Strategic Ministry Budget" section on page 198. What does the comparison reveal about your ministry priorities?

3. Outline your church's policy regarding the receiving, accounting, and spending of church funds and compare it to the "Guidelines for Handling Church Finances" section beginning on page 198.
4. Is a new building project truly the answer to your ministry needs, or would a creative look at your current facilities prove wise? Invite a few trusted members who can think outside the box to think through this with you, using the questions in the "To Build or Not to Build" section on page 200.

Discussion

1. Why would God's hold on a man's wallet indicate God's hold on that man's heart?
2. What are the reasons for and benefits of teaching/preaching on stewardship?
3. What are the reasons for and benefits of teaching/preaching on financial stewardship in the first month(s) of a year?
4. What are the reasons for and benefits of teaching/preaching on tithing?
5. How do a mission statement and a budget relate to each other?
6. What might happen if a church neglects budgeting for missions, personnel, programming, or facilities?
7. How could having a strategic ministry budget excite a congregation?
8. Should a church go into any debt to build, or should it wait until it has saved the needed funds?
9. Does a church require professional help to raise funds to build or expand its physical structure?

For Further Study

The Business Side of Ministry by Michael Nolan, Regular Baptist Press, 2011.
The Dynamics of Church Finance by James D. Berkley, Baker, 2000.
LifeWay Architecture provides pamphlets and publications at no or low cost to churches on a variety of building and planning subjects. Visit their site at lifeway.com/Article/composite-services-architecture-Resources.
Money Matters in Church by Aubrey M. Malphurs and Steve Stroope, Baker, 2007.
Planning and Building Church Facilities by Gwenn E. McCormick, Broadman Press, 1992.
When Not to Build by Ray Bowman and Eddy Hall, Baker, 2000.

20

Overseeing the Church's Corporate Worship Gathering
— Ken Pyne

The Scriptures are clear that God's people are called to gather together to worship God. This gathering for corporate worship is the most public activity of the church; therefore, proper attention must be given to its form and function. Pastors should not be guilty of what William H. Willimon describes as a "casualness with the Holy" or "sloppiness with the liturgy." Though the pastor seldom leads every part of the corporate gathering, he must accept responsibility for it to be conducted decently and in order for God's glory (1 Cor. 14:40).

Thinking Theologically about Worship

Thinking pragmatically about corporate worship instead of theologically is dangerous. Franklin Segler and Randall Bradley state, "Worship—not church growth—must be the church's priority. . . . Worship used for any purpose other than God's glory is not true worship." Worshiping God is the highest goal; it is not secondary to anything else.

Sometimes church leaders try to fix the symptoms of what is deficient in a worship gathering without first addressing the foundational Scriptural necessities that must be present for "true worship." Consider this definition and summation of theological principles for corporate worship.

A definition of corporate worship

In obedience to God's call to come, and in anticipation of when we will be with God eternally, believers in Jesus Christ come together to actively participate in honoring and interacting with God and in celebrating their life in Christ, resulting in transformation of character and lifestyle and an intensified desire to serve the Lord, as well as the salvation of unbelievers who are also in attendance.

Theological principles: The God we worship

God has called us to worship (Heb. 10:19–25). He is seeking people to be worshipers (John 4:23). Worship is His idea, and we respond to His call.

God is to be the subject and object of our worship. Worship is directed to God and focused on God. God is the only One Who is to receive our worship (Exod. 20:3, 4; Ps. 29:1, 2; 116:17–19). Theology (focus on God) should not become anthropology (focus on humans). Under the guise of worshiping God, people too often get the attention.

God should be seen as actively present, desiring to have communion with us. When we realize that God intends to commune with people and transform lives, we then understand the power of God that is resident in a corporate worship gathering (Ps. 139:7–12; Jer. 32:17).

God is a transcendent God Whose greatness and majesty must be proclaimed (Isa. 40:12ff.). He is also an immanent God Who desires to have a relationship with us (Exod. 25:8; Matt. 1:23; Heb. 10:19). Maintaining a balance or "healthy tension" between acknowledging God's transcendence and His immanence is critical. Marva J. Dawn states, "Worship that focuses on God's transcendence without God's immanence becomes austere and inaccessible; worship that stresses God's immanence without God's transcendence leads to irreverent coziness."

God should be understood as Father, Son, and Holy Spirit. The Trinity is a unique feature of Christianity; therefore, worship services should reference all three members of the Godhead.

Ultimately, worship should be Christ centered. Worshipers remember and celebrate the gospel of Jesus Christ and the salvation He has provided in anticipation of when they will be with Him for eternity.

Theological principles: The people who worship God

True worshipers worship God in spirit (internal, not just outward acts) and in truth (with integrity and in light of God's revealed truth) (John 4:23, 24). They recognize that access to God is only through Christ (Heb. 10:19–25; John 14:6; Acts 4:12), not through any human merit. True worship and fellowship with Christ requires repentance of sin and approaching God in humility (Ps. 15; 1 John 1:5–10; 1 Pet. 5:6). True worshipers understand that corporate worship is "liturgical," meaning that it is something we actively participate in together (Ps. 100; Heb. 10:25; 13:15). As Robert Webber says, "Worship is a verb. It is not something done to us or for us, but by us."

People who come to worship God often come needing to get their focus back on God and to correct their perspective that has become skewed during the week (Ps. 73). I like to think of a worship service in this way: worship takes me in my dislocations and relocates me in God.

Spending time worshiping God should make an impact. Believers should draw closer to the Lord and be edified (Heb. 10:19–23). The corporate worship of God's people empowered by the convicting work of the Holy Spirit will also result in unbelievers coming to salvation (1 Cor. 14:23, 24; Ps. 40:1–3).

Putting a Worship Service Together

Worshipers appreciate a service that makes sense. There should be a cohesiveness of the parts. To accomplish this, the pastor or worship leader has to know what he is aiming for and be intentional about getting there. Here are some suggestions on how to do it.

1. Pray! Never underestimate the need to seek God's help in planning a service intended to bring Him glory and focus attention on Him.
2. Remember your theology of worship. Make sure what you plan fits within that theology.
3. Consider your frameworks. As I plan a worship service, I keep two frameworks in mind. First is the framework that a service should be viewed as a time of communion or interaction between God and His people (Isa. 6). Truth about God and from God is being given through songs that are sung, words that are said, and Scripture that is read or preached. Then, through music, prayer, and other means, worshipers respond to that truth. I want to plan a service that keeps the focus on this interaction.

The second framework is an adaptation of what Robert Webber called a fourfold pattern of worship.

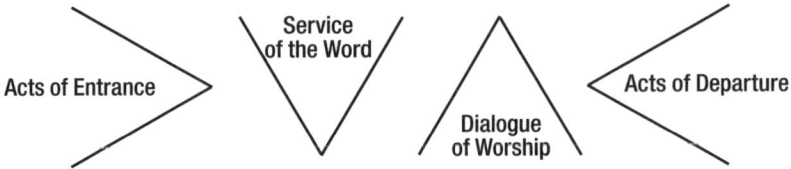

The first arrow pointing in symbolizes "acts of entrance." A recorded or instrumental prelude may help to establish an atmosphere for worship. People can be welcomed and reminded that they are gathered to corporately worship God. The theme of the service can be mentioned. A Scriptural "call to worship" can acknowledge God's character or express our desire to be in God's presence and to praise Him. Songs that express the worshipers' desire to come and worship are appropriate here.

In my planning, the next two arrows symbolize the dialogue that occurs between God and the worshipers. The downward arrow symbolizes the "service of the Word," which I understand to include any time in a service that the truth of the Word is given, as in that way God "speaks" to us. The upward arrow symbolizes the worshipers' responses to God in light of truth given. This "dialogue of worship" stresses the need to have both declaration of truth and response to truth as part of the service. Music used, therefore, should have a healthy balance of declaring truth and responding to truth, both hearing from God and responding to God.

The final arrow fans outward and symbolizes "acts of departure." Here worshipers transition from the corporate gathering to going out into the world to "be the church." Worshipers should be reminded through songs and spoken benedictions that God goes with them (He doesn't stay in the "sanctuary"), and that the truth that has been proclaimed should now be applied in everyday life. Here is an appropriate time for announcements that promote opportunities to serve God and make disciples.

4. Be mindful of any themes already determined for the service (e.g., missionary speaker, baptism, Communion). Pastors can assist musicians and others involved by communicating sermon texts and themes as far ahead of time as possible.

5. Include the nonnegotiables or "ordinary elements" that must be a part of the service (e.g., a sermon, singing, prayer, an offering).

6. Consider the negotiables or "propers" that could but don't have to be a part of every service (e.g., a testimony, a media presentation).
7. Remember the time frame for the worship gathering. We will have to wait until we are in Heaven for endless corporate worship! Here on earth, there are normally time parameters for the worship service. A pastor should communicate with others planning the service how much time he needs for preaching and for any other parts of the service he is leading. Then the other ordinary elements and propers can be included in proportion to the time available.
8. Contemplate the possibilities. Dream a bit. As time allows—which is why it is good to plan weeks ahead—be creative.
9. Compile all the elements of the service together in a way that makes sense and is not disjointed. I always ask how I am focusing the worshiper's attention on God. Remember content and flow. Is the service designed so the people can readily hear from God and respond to Him? Are God's transcendence and immanence apparent? Is the service Christ centered? Does the service encourage the people to participate?
10. Now that there is a tentative plan for the service, think about the logistics of the service. Can the ones leading the service get to where they need to be without distraction or waste of time? Can videos, music recordings, or media presentations planned for the service happen seamlessly as much as possible so there isn't dead time? Are some verbal bridges needed to help with the logistics of the service or to transition from one worship element to the next? The more these things are anticipated, the less likely that issues will come up that interrupt a worshiper's focus on interacting with God.
11. What about the announcements? Church bulletins, websites, social media, e-mails, and media projection before and after a worship gathering are some ways that pertinent information may be communicated. Any announcements given during the worship service should be appropriately placed and communicated; otherwise, they can easily disrupt the worship flow of a service.
12. Be intentional about how the worship service concludes. The ending of the service should encourage appropriate final responses for the worshipers. Sometimes because the timing of a service has gone awry or has not been adequately planned, it can end suddenly or awkwardly. If the corporate gathering is viewed as a dialogue with God, there needs to be an appropriate conclusion where worshipers sense finality.

13. Keep records. As one who has planned years of worship services, I find it very helpful to keep records of the order of worship services; the congregational songs we sing; the music used for offertories, choirs, or vocal solos; and the Scripture readings. This keeps me from overusing certain songs or Scriptures. It also helps me when I am struggling to plan a service. I can look back and remember what I did before. Other church musicians also appreciate having access to these records.

The Preacher and His Worship

When worship is understood as a time of dialogue between God and His people, there is no better time in a corporate gathering for God's people to hear from Him than during the sermon. The sermon, therefore, should be viewed as an integral part of worship. Herbert Carson writes, "The sermon is not a mere postscript to a service, nor is it to be seen as distinct from the service. It is itself part of the worship." What happens before the sermon should never be considered "preliminaries," and what happens after the sermon should not be considered a tacked-on "appendix." Each part of a corporate worship service should be viewed as important in its own right for contributing to one's worship of God, but without the regular presentation of God's truth in preaching, a church's opportunity for true worship is weakened.

A preacher should see himself first as a worshiper, and then see what he does as vitally connected to the other parts of the worship service. He should model appropriate worship participation during the times when he is not leading or preaching. It is helpful when he conscientiously makes bridges from the other parts of the service to the truth he is sharing in his message.

Observance of the "Church Year"

Every church, even non-liturgical ones, follows its own "church year" calendar, where certain observances are traditionally emphasized in the worship gathering. Without needing to observe the entire "Christian church year" calendar, non-liturgical churches should give consideration to which Biblical events are important markers for telling the story of Christ and the church. Webber observes that churches have "allowed a secular view of time to permeate the worship of the church." Instead of celebrating events that lead us to worship God, we celebrate events that potentially may divert our attention to humans.

Christmas and Easter are Biblical events that churches choose to observe each year. Expanding Christmas to include the observance of Advent during the Sundays in December adds further opportunity to celebrate and reflect on Christ's incarnation. Expanding Easter to include Palm Sunday and Good Friday allows for additional attention on Christ's passion.

Another Biblical event to observe is Pentecost. In the early church, Pentecost observance was second only to Easter in its importance. Pentecost Sunday allows a church to regularly remember the "rest of the story" already started at Christmas and Easter. Christ came to the earth (Christmas), He died and rose again (Easter), and He gave to us the Holy Spirit as the One Who indwells and empowers individual believers and the church (Pentecost). We celebrate the birthday of the church while reflecting upon God's gracious gift of His Spirit and His importance to the church's ministry.

Use of the Arts in Worship

We live in an age of media explosion. People have access to all types of information that communicates to their senses. For the church to be effective in aiding people in worshiping God, the use of the arts in worship must be considered.

Art may be understood as the "expression of truth through beauty." In a church context, the arts may be understood as the expression of truth through beauty with the intent to inform, assist, or inspire worship. The following list is a sampling of "art" used in the Bible.

- Congregational singing
- Choirs
- Musical instruments
- Drama, symbolic action
- Preaching and storytelling
- Banners
- Architecture and design
- Textile arts, symbolic art
- Gestures and movement

God is a creative God. Created in the image of God (Gen. 1:26, 27), believers in Christ reflect that image as they cultivate the stewardship of the arts. Hill states, "Aesthetic appreciation was part of the endowment given to humanity created in the image of God." Believers should purpose to reflect God's character by offering artistic expressions to Him with excellence, thoughtfulness, and sacrifice (Ps. 33:3; 47:7; 2 Sam. 24:24). Bob Kauflin states, "Skill matters to God. It should matter to us too."

Music in Worship

Until the Lord returns, there will be tension over what are appropriate and inappropriate musical expressions of worship to God in a corporate setting. Here are some guidelines to consider.

- Music is an emotional language. Expect people to express their emotions.
- Music should accomplish the purposes God established for it: to glorify God, to teach, to admonish, to evangelize.
- Music should function to communicate accurate Biblical teaching.
- People leading music should portray an inner attitude of humility and gratefulness to God and exemplify a proper relationship to God.
- Musicians should practice for excellence in all music expressions.
- The Bible endorses and encourages the use of instruments in worship.
- Realize that musical styles will continue to develop and change. This is a helpful observation: "History indicates that the body which canonizes musical form and style begins to 'fossilize' right there. The very nature of music which has brought the church much good, demands that it will continue to develop and change."
- Follow the example of the Levites. Have leaders who are appointed to oversee deciding what is acceptable and appropriate for your worshiping congregation. Avoid the trap of doing what everyone else is doing. Every church has its own "worship voice." Determine what that "worship voice" is, and do not be concerned if it is not the same as other churches in your area.

Technology in Worship

The importance of technology in worship cannot be ignored. Technology develops quickly and can easily stress out a church's budget, making it difficult to stay up to date with what is available. Hopefully a pastor can have assistance in this area from an associate pastor or a tech-savvy individual. He should learn all he can about the proper use of sound, video, lights, and projection and utilize them in a way that enhances people's ability to worship.

Questions to Ask When Evaluating a Worship Service

In conclusion, here are some questions for evaluating a worship service.
- Was God the subject and object of our worship?
- Was both God's transcendence and immanence acknowledged?
- Was God worshiped as Father, Son, and Holy Spirit?
- Was there a focus on Christ and the gospel?
- Was God's active presence anticipated?
- Was interaction with God encouraged?
- Did the people actively participate?
- Was transformation of lives expected, and did it occur?
- Was the preaching integrated with the other parts of the worship service?
- Were worship leaders careful not to be a distraction?
- Was the use of technology and the arts appropriate and helpful?
- While focusing on believers worshiping, was the corporate gathering welcoming to unbelievers?
- Was there adequate planning and communication ahead of time?

Take Action . . .

1. Write out your philosophy of corporate worship.
2. Adopt frameworks for planning a worship service.
3. Connect all the parts of the worship time by theme, transitions/segues, etc.
4. Outline the logistics of each service.
5. Keep records.
6. Consider adding Pentecost Sunday to your church calendar if you are not already celebrating it.
7. Evaluate your church's use of art forms used in Biblical worship.
8. Find your church's "worship voice."
9. Using the questions in this chapter, evaluate your church's worship services.

Discussion

1. What is your church's corporate worship theology and how does it influence the worship services you plan?
2. What additional steps should you take in planning so that the parts of the worship services are more cohesive?

3. What are ways a preacher can integrate his sermon with the other parts of the corporate gathering?
4. Do you think it would be helpful for your church to observe Christmas, Easter, and Pentecost each year?
5. How can your church's use of the arts in worship assist in communicating to people's senses so that their worship is enhanced?
6. How can you make sure that your church's use of technology serves to help people focus on God without becoming an idol in itself?
7. Which areas suggested by the evaluation questions does your church need to give attention to?

For Further Study

Christ-Centered Worship by Bryan Chapell, Baker Academic, 2009.
Christian Worship, 3rd ed., by Franklin M. Segler and revised by Randall Bradley, Broadman and Holman, 2006.
The New Worship: Straight Talk on Music and the Church by Barry Liesch, Baker, 2001.
Perspectives on Christian Worship edited by J. Matthew Pinson, Broadman and Holman, 2009.
Real Worship, 2nd ed., by Warren Wiersbe, Baker, 2000.
Who Stole My Church? by Gordon MacDonald, Thomas Nelson, 2007.
The Worship Architect: A Blueprint for Designing Culturally Relevant and Biblically Faithful Services by Constance M. Cherry, Baker Academic, 2010.
Worship as Pastoral Care by William H. Willimon, Abingdon, 1979.
Worship Matters by Bob Kauflin, Crossway, 2008.

21

Ministering Effectively to Marriages and Families
— Scott Poling

Everyone in ministry is in the "family business." Whether realized or not, a calling into ministry automatically includes a call to minister to marriages and families—to strengthen, help, and protect any and all relationships within the home.

It is important to recognize and acknowledge marriage and the family as God's idea. The family unit is God's ordained foundation of society as well as the backbone of the local church.

It is God Who created and brought the man and woman together: "God made them male and female. For this reason a man shall leave his father and mother, and the two shall become one flesh; so they are no longer two, but one flesh" (Mark 10:6–8; Gen. 2:22–24, NASB).

It is God Who gave marriage as a beautiful, living illustration of His love for the church: "This mystery is great; but I am speaking with reference to Christ and the church" (Eph. 5:22–33, NASB).

It is God Who desires marriage to last a lifetime: "What therefore God has joined together, let no man separate" (Mark 10:9, NASB). "For I hate divorce, says the LORD the God of Israel" (Mal. 2:16, NASB).

It is God Who blesses a man and woman with children: "Behold, children are a gift of the LORD, the fruit of the womb is a reward" (Ps. 127:3, NASB).

It is God Who desires parents and children to be drawn closer together: "He will restore the hearts of the fathers to their children and the hearts of the children to their fathers" (Mal. 4:6, NASB).

It is God Who delights the hearts of grandparents with grandchildren: "Grandchildren are the crown of old men" (Prov. 17:6, NASB).

The Epidemic

Marriage and family are of utmost importance to God, and they are under attack in unprecedented ways. Divorce continues to rip countless homes apart every year at nearly a 50 percent rate. Cohabitation of couples before marriage has grown from 450,000 in 1960 to 7.6 million in 2011 and is wrongly seen as preparation for marriage. Homosexuality and same-sex marriage are becoming the cultural norm supported by much of the press, Hollywood, and even our government. Sexual immorality among teenagers is a continual concern, with 47.4 percent of students having sexual intercourse by the time they graduate high school. Struggling single parents and blended families, who are raising 29 percent of American children (up from 6 percent in 1960), are desperate for answers and help. The family unit has become more and more dysfunctional and disconnected with its frantic, dizzying pace, desperately trying to keep up with busy schedules and unhealthy choices. Many American homes are in a state of crisis and in desperate need of spiritual physicians who will

- practice preventive medicine by boldly prescribing and encouraging healthy family choices,
- accurately diagnose the problems among individual relationships,
- gently comfort the hurting with God's grace by refusing to judge them, choosing rather to nurse them back to spiritual health, and
- confront the wrong and prescribe the right course of action that needs to be taken for full restoration of healthy relationships.

Our Diagnostic Handbook

The spiritual doctors who make ministry their livelihood must never underestimate the power of God's Word to transform lives, save marriages, and restore families to optimum health. The Creator of marriage and the family knows how best to make it work, and He has given proven eternal instructions in His Word. Ministering effectively to marriages and families will mean pointing people back to this Biblical foundation, encouraging them to do marriage and the family God's way, not the politically correct, cultural way. People must be taught the plain, straightforward, perfect Word of God when it comes to healthy homes.

- *Husbands need to lead and love their wives selflessly, sacrificially, and sensitively.* "Husbands, love your wives, just as Christ also loved the church and gave Himself up for her" (Eph. 5:25, NASB). "Husbands, love your wives and do not be embittered against them" (Col. 3:19,

NASB). "You husbands in the same way, live with your wives in an understanding way, as with someone weaker, since she is a woman; and show her honor as a fellow heir of the grace of life, so that your prayers will not be hindered" (1 Pet. 3:7, NASB).
- *Wives need to respectfully submit to their husbands.* "Wives, be subject to your own husbands, as to the Lord" (Eph. 5:22, NASB). "Wives, be subject to your husbands, as is fitting in the Lord" (Col. 3:18, NASB). "In the same way, you wives, be submissive to your own husbands so that even if any of them are disobedient to the word, they may be won without a word by the behavior of their wives, as they observe your chaste and respectful behavior" (1 Pet. 3:1, 2, NASB).
- *Men need to carefully, gently, and spiritually lead their children.* "Fathers, do not provoke your children to anger, but bring them up in the discipline and instruction of the Lord" (Eph. 6:4, NASB). "These words, which I am commanding you today, shall be on your heart. You shall teach them diligently to your sons and shall talk of them when you sit in your house and when you walk by the way and when you lie down and when you rise up" (Deut. 6:6, 7, NASB).
- *Women need to prioritize their relationships at home.* "So that they may encourage the young women to love their husbands, to love their children, to be sensible, pure, workers at home, kind, being subject to their own husbands, so that the word of God will not be dishonored" (Titus 2:4, 5, NASB). "Therefore, I want younger widows to get married, bear children, keep house, and give the enemy no occasion for reproach" (1 Tim. 5:14, NASB).
- *Children need to obey their parents.* "Children, obey your parents in the Lord, for this is right. Honor your father and mother (which is the first commandment with a promise), so that it may be well with you, and that you may live long on the earth" (Eph. 6:1–3; Exod. 20:12, NASB). "Children, be obedient to your parents in all things, for this is well-pleasing to the Lord" (Col. 3:20, NASB).
- *Parents need to practice discipline, modeling it after God's purpose of holiness and righteousness.* "But He disciplines us for our good, so that we may share His holiness. All discipline for the moment seems not to be joyful, but sorrowful; yet to those who have been trained by it, afterwards it yields the peaceful fruit of righteousness" (Heb. 12:10b, 11, NASB). "He who withholds his rod hates his son, but he who loves him disciplines him diligently" (Prov. 13:24, NASB). "The rod

and reproof give wisdom, but a child who gets his own way brings shame to his mother" (Prov. 29:15, NASB; see also Prov. 3:11, 12; 13:1 3; 15:5; 19:18; 20:30; 22:15; 23:13, 14; 29:17).

Practical Prescriptions

Having God's "diagnostic handbook" for marriages and families, we ask two questions: (1) How can we minister most effectively to marriages and families? and (2) How can these important Biblical principles be implemented in a practical manner within the context of the local church and the culture at large? This daunting and, at times, seemingly overwhelming task will be accomplished only through much prayer, personal care, bold proclamation, and wise church programming.

Much prayer

We must pray continually, seeking God's help and guidance. Pastors need the wisdom of Solomon to help people navigate the troubled waters in which they find themselves. How do you counsel a couple who are separated and heading for divorce whose problems started on the night of their wedding when the husband informed his new bride, "I just made the worst decision of my life"? How do you minister to families in the church who are heartbroken, devastated, and angry when one child has sexually abused another child? What do you do for a mother and her grown daughter who attend the same worship service and are fighting in court for custody of the same grandson/son, whom they both love?

Today's families are attempting to cope with physical abuse, sexual abuse, marital unfaithfulness, marital separation, divorce, addictions, homosexuality, pregnancies out of wedlock, rebellious children, and the list goes on with multiple combinations and variations. These are waters well over our heads to successfully handle alone.

The people of God will be looking to the leaders of God to help them untangle their lives. Our only help is full reliance upon the Holy Spirit with a humble, sensitive, dependent heart. "But if any of you lacks wisdom, let him ask of God, who gives to all generously and without reproach, and it will be given to him" (James 1:5, NASB).

Personal care

We must commit personal care and time to help the hurting. Church leaders are in the people business and must set aside time to spend with others. Many phone calls will need to be made. Counseling appointments will need to be scheduled. Visits to homes will need to take place. Sincere care must be shown to effectively minister to marriages and families. The apostle Paul gave us a good reminder in Philippians 2:3 and 4: "Do nothing from selfishness or empty conceit, but with humility of mind regard one another as more important than yourselves; do not merely look out for your own personal interests, but also for the interests of others" (NASB). We must invest time and energy into the lives of the hurting in order to reap changed lives and restored families. As many have said, "People may not remember your sermons, but they will remember the time you took to be with them at their moment of need."

Bold proclamation

The proclamation of the Word of God through preaching and teaching represents the first line of Biblical counseling and encouragement. Whether a couple is simply considering marriage, is already engaged, or has been married for decades, the spoken Word of God is foundational to the success of that union. Marriage is more than warm, fuzzy feelings; it is a living model to the world around us of Christ's love for His church (Eph. 5:22–33). Couples must be taught the seriousness of this sacred union. Both young and established families will benefit from and be protected by the truth of God's Word.

Consider planning a special preaching or teaching series on marriage, the family, or parenting as works best in a comprehensive ministry plan, or select curriculum for Sunday morning classes geared toward strengthening the home. It is also important to remember when you are preaching or teaching to model your own family life with an appropriate degree of transparency. This will help others understand that their pastor is not perfect and is able to relate to the everyday struggles of marriage and parenting.

Wise church programming

When programming church ministries, it is imperative to consider the entire family and evaluate the effectiveness of the various ministries to the different individuals and groups within the church. Consider what is currently being done to minister to marriages, divorcées, widows/widowers, parents, single parents, men, women, youth, and children. It is important to realistically assess the strengths and weaknesses of these ministries and then prioritize what can and should be done for any or all of them. It is just as important to assess the leadership potential, resources available, and calendar feasibility to pull off quality, effective ministry.

Pray and plan, thinking in terms of cohesive goals for strengthening the entire family. Choosing a strong Bible-based curriculum that promotes cross-generational discussion among all age groups will develop healthier homes. As Titus 2:3–5 clearly exhorts, "Older women likewise are to . . . encourage the young women to love their husbands, to love their children, to be sensible, pure, workers at home, kind, being subject to their own husbands, so that the word of God will not be dishonored" (NASB). Prayerfully consider how to encourage and recruit the older generation in the church to be a powerful force of ministry to the next generation.

Simplify and Unify

When it comes to programming the church calendar with its various ministries, we must think in terms of simplifying and unifying. We need to ask, How do our ministries and church events help to both simplify and unify family life? There is nothing necessarily wrong with separate Bible studies for men, women, youth, etc., but at the same time, it is important to be intentional about drawing families together. Unifying the family may include any of the following:

- Canceling Sunday night services on Father's Day, Mother's Day, and other holidays to promote family time
- Incorporating service projects that include the entire family's involvement
- Planning outreach ministries that include the entire family reaching out to the lost
- Promoting and encouraging participation in Screen-Free Week with the goal of spending more time during the week playing games, going for walks, and interacting with one another
- Special events for parents and children, such as a mother/daughter tea and father/son campout or canoe trip
- Youth-sponsored and hosted dinner with babysitting at the church to provide husbands and wives a date night
- One night of the week that is totally ministry free

Continually seek to utilize the church calendar and ministries as an encouragement for families to spend more time together, building strong, lasting relationships.

Learn to partner with strong marriage- and family-based ministries. Many churches do not have the time, staff, or resources to handle the challenges that are encountered when ministering to the home. Partnering can include using well-written Biblical materials or a video series, outside counseling services, Biblically based recovery programs, or bringing in speakers for a weekend conference. Never shy away from utilizing the "experts." There are wonderful organizations and ministries that would love to come alongside the local church to help it be more effective in ministering to marriages and families.

Never forget that marriage and family problems give way to great ministry potential! God's people are surrounded by broken relationships in their neighborhoods, workplaces, and schools, and among their relatives. Many people are hungry for help as they watch spouses leave, children rebel, and families fall apart. Reaching out to the hurting with the Word of God, the only lasting solution to their problems, needs to be the priority. Outreach can include an intentional special preaching series on marriage, the family, or parenting; Bible studies geared toward blended families or single adults raising children; divorce recovery workshops; or even financial studies based on God's Word.

The weakness and disintegration of the home make for great outreach opportunities that should be used for the glory of God. Pray and assess the needs of your community and the best possible avenues for your individual church to reach out and impact marriages and families with the gospel of Jesus Christ.

Take Action . . .

1. Pray. Fully rely on the Lord, remembering you are not able to minister to marriages and families without His wisdom and guidance.
2. Personal care. We've all heard it said, "People don't care how much you know until they know how much you care." Prioritize people and their needs by making phone calls, personal visits, and counseling appointments with married couples and families.
3. Proclaim the Word. Plan a special preaching series on marriage, the family, or parenting. Consider curriculum for Sunday morning classes geared toward the topics of marriage and the family.
4. Programming ministries. Be intentional about encouraging families to spend time interacting and building relationships in the home while

also providing fellowship and service opportunities for families to share in the church.
5. Partner. Reach out to marriage- and family-based ministries that can provide resources and encouragement not otherwise available.
6. Potential. Utilize people's problems, seeing them as great opportunities to reach your community. Thank the Lord for the needs around you that will draw people to Him.

Discussion
1. What is the strongest marriage and family ministry in your church? What has made it successful?
2. What is the greatest marriage and family need in your church and what is a practical, realistic way to minister to that need?
3. What are some obvious needs in your community that can be taken advantage of for outreach to marriage and the family?
4. What are the local resources available to assist you in ministry (e.g., counselors, youth centers, crisis pregnancy centers, mental health facilities, recovery programs)?
5. How does God want to develop your own family life?

For Further Study
Books on Marriage
The Act of Marriage by Tim and Beverly LaHaye, Zondervan, 1976.
Before You Remarry by H. Norman Wright, Harvest House, 1999.
Before You Say I Do by H. Norman Wright and Wes Roberts, Harvest House, 1997.
The Five Love Languages by Gary Chapman, Northfield Publishing, 1992.
For Better, For Worse, For Keeps by Bob and Cheryl Moeller, WaterBrook Press, 1994.
Hope for the Separated by Gary Chapman, Moody, 1982.
Love and Respect by Emerson Eggerichs, Thomas Nelson, 2004.
The Ring Makes All the Difference by Glenn Stanton, Moody, 2011.

Books on Parenting
Bringing Up Boys by James Dobson, Tyndale House, 2001.
Bringing Up Girls by James Dobson, Tyndale House, 2010.
On Parenting by James Dobson, Thomas Nelson, 2004.

Parenting Is Heart Work by Scott Turansky and Joanne Miller, David C. Cook, 2005.
Raising a Modern-Day Joseph by Larry Fowler, David C. Cook, 2009.
The Smart Stepfamily by Ron L. Deal, Bethany House, 2006.

Organizations
Awana (awana.org)
Crown Financial Ministries (crown.org)
Family Life (familylife.com)
Financial Peace University (daveramsey.com)
Focus on the Family (focusonthefamily.com)
For Better, For Worse, For Keeps Ministries (forkeepsministries.com)
National Center for Biblical Parenting (biblicalparenting.org)
Visionary Family Ministries (visionaryfam.com)

22

Leading Effectively through Change
— Mike Augsburger

I'll never forget a certain saying. Not because I heard it on a single, memorable occasion, but because I heard it often, and I heard it casually—off the cuff. The saying goes, "People hate two things: change and surprises." At the time, I was a young associate pastor in my first ministry, and the person who said that is the person who taught me most about change in local churches. This person was not a nationally recognized author; he was an eighty-year-old guy named Ray. Generally speaking, senior citizens are not the people giving a pastor advice on how to effect change in the local church! However, Ray was an interesting character. He succeeded as a busy layman in his church because he understood people and could adapt his methodology to meet the specific cultural contours of his congregation. Ray would frequently stop by my office, and I can still see him sitting in my office chair uttering those words: "People hate two things: change and surprises."

Ray has since moved on to Heaven, and I moved on to a lead pastor position; but I continue to implement Ray's principles of change in my congregation. Some might think that a chapter on change will simply be a stab at traditionalism in favor of new methods and contemporary music. That will not be the tone of this chapter. In my first few years of being the lead pastor, we have changed virtually everything about our ministry . . . except the music. And, to the glory of God, our church unity has never been compromised amidst all the changes.

In this chapter, I seek to communicate the basic anatomy of change: what change is, why change happens, and why people are resistant to change. Second, I want to show a Biblical example of handling change in the early church. Third, I will discuss the necessary steps for producing an environment for change in a church.

The Anatomy of Change

Recently I was talking to another pastor and his wife about change. They related a story about moving a piece of furniture in the foyer of their church. Sunday arrived, and they held their breaths. As expected, "that one lady" came into the church and immediately complained about the change. They asked her to explain her objections, but the only reasoning she gave was, "I just don't like change . . . of any kind!"

Change happens . . . like it or not

The story above illustrates an important concept: aversion to change is a human problem, not just a Christian problem, as Larry Osborne points out in *Sticky Teams*. The natural course of life creates cultural change, and we can do nothing about it! Since 1900, the world has endured more change than in all the previous centuries combined. If ever there was a season when people would be reticent to change, this would be the time. The reason people resist change is because a person's culture often represents both his security and his identity. As that culture changes, it causes a person to feel lost, lacking purpose and identity. As an illustration, think about the guy who still sports bushy lamb chop sideburns and dons polyester leisure suits. He dresses like this because he thinks it looks good! Why has he failed to adapt to changing styles? Most likely this look represents a time in his life when he was significant, accepted, and felt a sense of meaning and purpose. Change will happen. The question is, Can we adapt to it when it happens?

Churches must change and adapt to change

The church is not insulated from the inevitability of change. Jim Mellado wisely stated it like this in *How to Change Your Church (without Killing It)*: "Change is not an option for churches. All churches either change to continue prevailing or they change by becoming irrelevant to people and eventually disappear." People often bristle at this concept and would say in rebuttal, "Yes, but aren't we supposed to be sharing the unchangeable Word of God? Culture changes, but the message of the gospel stays the same!" I agree with that statement. However, our modes of communicating God's unchangeable message are, in and of themselves, cultural expressions. A local church from the farming community of Table Rock,

Nebraska, will look different from a local church in Paris, France. Each church possesses the same unchangeable message, yet they express that message differently.

Missionaries face this exact issue. They must learn the language and the culture of their field in order to minister effectively. How does this relate to the need for churches to change in America? Considering the rapid change in our culture, I believe it is imperative that we treat pastoring in America in a similar fashion to pastoring in a foreign culture. The methodology to effectively reach people sixty years ago is no longer suitable for reaching the culture of today. Therefore, churches must change and adapt to the natural change in culture.

Resistance to change is often idolatry

Even though change is a human problem and not just a Christian problem, Christians have a way of exacerbating the universal change problem! The explanation for this is fairly simple. Christians often base their resistance to change on a misapplication of black-and-white Biblical truth, which results in an illogical and unreasonable stubbornness. I'm reminded of King Hezekiah in the Old Testament. Second Kings 18:3 and 4 detail his vigorous campaign to abolish idolatry from Judah. He started in obvious places by removing pagan worship sites and destroying idolatrous symbols. However, verse 4 tells us that he took things even a step further. It says, "He broke in pieces the bronze serpent Moses had made, for until those days the people of Israel had made offerings to it" (ESV).

Can you imagine the outcry from the people? The bronze serpent was a critical part of Israel's national history. It served a helpful purpose, it taught the people a valuable lesson, it produced effective results, and most of all, it was commanded and blessed by God. Unfortunately, by Hezekiah's day, the people had lost sight of its original purpose and instead were using it as an object of worship.

This happens in churches today. As I stated earlier, methodology should change as culture changes. Idolatry happens when people value ministry methodology as much as or more than they value fulfilling the Great Commission. The mission given to us by Jesus should always remain central, and methodology should be the cultural means by which we accomplish our mission. Rick Warren wisely said, "Growing, healthy churches have a clear-cut identity. They understand their reason for being; they are precise in their purpose. They know exactly what God has called them to do. They know what their business is, and they know what is none of their business!" Resistance to change stems from losing sight of purpose and mission. How can we avoid this? Let's look at a Biblical example.

A Biblical Pattern for Handling Change

The early church was not immune from change. In fact, the rapid growth rate, racial diversity, immanent persecution, a developing ecclesiology, and many other factors created need for the early church to change and adapt with fluidity. Acts 6 preserves one of these scenarios of change. Verse 1 tells of a rift in the church stemming from cultural differences. This division in the church created the need for change. Things could not continue as they had "always done it" (albeit only a few months!). The apostles devised a solution, and the church adapted to the change. Let's look at some principles from Acts 6 about their process of leading effectively through change.

A sense of mission drove the change

This was no small change in the early church! The apostles handed over a significant ministry to those early deacons. It would be like a pastor handing over hospital visitation to capable laymen. This could be a traumatic change for some people! Acts 6:2 shows us that the apostles did much more than simply announce the change and expect the church to buy it. They announced the change in the context of the church's mission. The apostles' focus needed to be the ministry of Word and prayer in order to equip the believers. This was the first thing they told the congregation. They said, "We are being hindered from accomplishing our mission. Therefore, something needs to change so we can be true to the mission Jesus gave us." People always respond better to change if they can see how it will enhance and enable the mission.

Both the problem and the solution were clearly communicated to the congregation

A change of this magnitude would impact the entire church; therefore, the apostles made it an all-church business item. The first words of Acts 6:2 are, "And the twelve summoned the full number of the disciples and said" (ESV). From beginning to end, the congregation was privy to the change process. Communicating change begins first with communicating the problem, or need for change. Many pastors fail in leading through change because they announce the change without having established the need for change. The apostles came to the meeting having already determined the solution. However, the first thing the congregation heard was the problem and how the problem was negatively impacting the mission of the church. In essence, then, change is really nothing more than creating solutions to mission-hindering problems. Stated in those terms, congregations should not balk at change at all. However, it takes some time, effort, and communication to help a congregation view change in this light.

The apostles formulated and presented a good solution to the congregation

As I mentioned, the apostles had already decided upon a solution for the problem, but they needed to convey the problem before presenting the solution. Once the congregation understood the need (problem), the leadership laid out the predetermined solution. Most congregants can easily understand the need. However, the congregation will tend to voice a variety of opinions about how to meet the need. Deciding solutions in an open-forum, democratic format usually ends in disaster.

For example, if a tornado blows the roof off of a church, the congregation can easily see the need for a new roof. However, the exact brand of shingles and nails for the new roof should not be debated congregationally! The pastor is the shepherd of the flock. He knows the needs of the flock. He should know what's best for the entire group. Therefore, with trusted counsel, he should bring well-planned solutions to meet church needs.

The apostles predetermined the solution, but verse 3 shows us that they gave the congregation an integral role in carrying out the solution. How did this strategy work? Verse 5 tells us that it pleased the whole congregation. So far, the change process in Acts 6 has been flawless. One more important principle remains.

They considered the needs of the minority within the solution

The problem centered around Hellenistic Jews getting overlooked in the charity ministry. At this point, Jewish believers from Israel composed the majority of the church. However, the number of Hellenistic Jewish believers was increasing, which is what created the problem. The apostles presented the solution, and the congregation selected seven men to aid in this ministry. Notice that all seven men had Greek names. I don't believe this is coincidental! If they had chosen seven men with Hebrew names, the

Hellenistic believers would have wondered if anything would really be different. Instead, it seems that the congregation went the extra mile to make sure that the impending change would truly solve the inequity. In many churches, leaders announce change with a take-it-or-leave-it attitude that shows no concern for those who are most impacted by the change. Though change is necessary, and people need to be willing to put mission above methodology, I believe we honor Christ when we are sensitive to those who may be struggling with change. Notice what happened as a result of the change. Verse 7 implies that the problem was solved, and as a result of the change, the ministry of the Word caused exponential growth in the church. Now that is effective change!

Creating the Environment for Change

Acts 6 gives us a great pattern and great principles to follow when implementing change. However, in order to even get to the point of implementing those four steps, several important elements need to be operative in your church. This is what I would call the environment for change. Many church leaders simply try to implement change in a vacuum. If the environment is not right for change, it will fail miserably. What is the proper environment for change? In a word: momentum.

As we discussed earlier, change needs to come as the answer to some problem or issue facing your ministry. In my current ministry, we are running out of classroom space. People will tell me, "That's a good problem to have." I agree! That good "problem," or shall we say, "opportunity," was created by momentum. As our church gained momentum, we grew very quickly and now are facing a shortage of space. This space problem demands change of some kind. I anticipate that the change will be well received because people are excited about our church's momentum and can clearly see the need. However, church leaders commit a grave mistake when they try to use change as a means to create momentum. Change does not create momentum; momentum creates change! Even in Acts 6 the issue facing the apostles came as the result of momentum and growth. So let's look at the process that creates momentum.

A clear view of Christ and the gospel revitalizes a sense of mission

Earlier we talked about idolatry causing resistance to change, and it happens when people display an unhealthy attachment to culture-specific methodology. To solve this, people need to renew their love for Christ and commitment to the gospel. Christ changes people through the power of the gospel, not through methodology. To create momentum, pastors need to display, or model, the power of Christ in the gospel. What does this look like? Several months into my ministry, each one of our staff members had led somebody, or entire families, to Christ. As these new believers shared their testimonies in front of the church, you could see corporate values and paradigms shifting. Not only did people want to see more of this, but they also wanted to be a part of it! Three years into my ministry, our entire church shared a common sense of mission and purpose. We were all moving in the same direction.

A unified mission and purpose create momentum

Leadership guru John Maxwell likens momentum to waterskiing. Getting up on the skis takes tremendous energy and effort, but once you are up, the slightest effort allows you to cruise the lake. In other words, it is easier to manage momentum than it is to create momentum. As the leaders of a church model a commitment to the gospel's power, it will gradually spread to the congregation. It might take a while and take effort, but eventually people will catch the vision. A church should clearly communicate its purpose and mission in sermons and business meetings, on its website, and in other publications. People unreservedly unify around purpose and mission when the gospel bears fruit in people's lives. It is hard to argue with the power of the gospel in corporate church life! When a congregation rallies behind a unified mission, stand back and get ready for the tidal wave of momentum.

Momentum produces fertile ground for change

With a strong tailwind of momentum, change will take place naturally, and almost effortlessly. Changes that once seemed impossible will not only be possible, but actually be desired by the congregation. Why? Because momentum produces problems—the good kind of problems—and problems demand solutions. Those solutions come in the form of change. When change is viewed as a solution to a corporately recognized problem, then change will not be resisted; it will be readily accepted. Once momentum is on your side and problems (opportunities) have presented themselves, you are ready to implement the steps from Acts 6.

Conclusion

Let's go back now and visit my friend Ray. I remember one occasion when our church was renovating a classroom. This was the right decision on many levels. Our church was growing, and we needed more space that could serve a variety of purposes. However, the challenge was convincing a large group of eighty- to ninety-year-olds that the chairs were better than the old pews! Ray volunteered for the job. He spent several days in the chapel, making sure the arrangement was absolutely perfect. One day I came into the room and asked him how things were going. He replied, "I'm just trying to think of every possible comment, complaint, or objection that some of these 'old people' [He wasn't including himself in that term!] might offer when they come on Sunday and see the new chairs for the first time."

Ray had strategically arranged the chairs to meet the unique needs of this group, and he labored over this for a couple of days because he firmly believed that change could happen gracefully. In that instance, I witnessed brilliancy in leading through change. The church's gospel-based, mission-driven momentum created the need for change. Ray overcommunicated both the problem and the solution. He gathered input from the congregation and involved them in the change process, and then he perfected the solution so that the needs of the minority were adequately cared for. The next Sunday came, and the people loved it! Change will happen. The question is whether a leader will take the bull by the horns and lead effectively through change.

Take Action . . .

1. Model in your personal life and ministry the power of Christ in the gospel.
2. Rejoice when momentum produces new problems (opportunities).
3. Gather input from the congregation.
4. Formulate a good solution that considers the needs of the minority.
5. Clearly communicate to the congregation both the problem and the solution. Involve the congregation in the change process.
6. Help your congregation view change as a solution to a recognizable problem.

Discussion

1. Think of several culturally based church methodologies. In what ways

could these be updated? Are there other methodologies that could be more effective in fulfilling the Great Commission in our current culture?
2. As a church leader, in what ways could you begin to model a belief in the power of Christ through the gospel? How can you get others involved in the same?
3. Think of a time as a leader when your ministry possessed positive momentum. What kinds of problems/opportunities came as a result?
4. Think of a current problem/opportunity in your church, and address it using the principles from Acts 6 that were discussed in this chapter.

For Further Study

The 21 Irrefutable Laws of Leadership: Follow Them and People Will Follow You, 1st edition, by John C. Maxwell, Thomas Nelson, 1998.

Feeding and Leading: A Practical Handbook on Administration in Churches and Christian Organizations by Kenneth O. Gangel, Baker, 2000.

How to Change Your Church (without Killing It) by Alan Nelson and Gene Appel, Thomas Nelson, 2008.

Leading and Managing Your Church by Carl F. George and Robert E. Logan, Baker, 1996.

Lessons in Leadership by Randal Roberts, Kregel Academic and Professional, 1999.

Leadership Axioms: Powerful Leadership Proverbs by Bill Hybels, Zondervan, 2012.

The Purpose Driven Church: Every Church Is Big in God's Eyes by Rick Warren, Zondervan, 1995.

Simple Church: Returning to God's Process for Making Disciples, unabridged, by Sam Rainer and Eric Geiger, Hovel Audio, 2008.

Sticky Teams: Keeping Your Leadership Team and Staff on the Same Page by Larry Osborne, Zondervan, 2010.

23

Guiding the Missions Program
— Gary L. Anderson

Revival! Nothing will do for missions what true revival will. Andrew Murray put it this way: "The only way to waken true, deep, spiritual, permanent missionary interest is not to aim at this itself so much as to lead believers to a more complete separation from the world and to an entire consecration of themselves, with all they have, to their Lord and His service." In a day when sin's influence is expanding and faith's influence is diminishing, what a difference could be made by, as Hudson Taylor put it, "the deepening of the spiritual life of the church, so that men should be unable to stay at home"!

The Church and Missions
Prayer

It would be a remarkable missionary presentation that makes no mention of a need for prayer. Some missionaries may think they can do what God called them to do in their power apart from His, but they would be few and probably new. The great missionary to the Gentiles, the apostle Paul, begged the Romans to pray for him (Rom. 15:30). Modern missionaries, like Paul, have taken their place in the arena of the fiercest of all spiritual conflict, battling over territory that has been under Satan's uncontested control for generations. That territory can as easily be the South Bronx as the heart of Africa or the extreme reaches of the Amazon. Pray when missionaries ask you to pray. Pray prayers that can be measured in intensity as readily as in elapsed time. Strive in prayer. Agonize in prayer. Pray earnestly. Pray effectually. Pray as though your missionaries' success depends upon it, for it does.

The pastor

Rare will be the church that gives missions a place of greater priority than the pastor gives it. The pastor must see and believe that the missionary mandate is a thread woven throughout the fabric of both Old and New Testaments. The mandate is explicitly spelled out in the Gospels and emphatically modeled by the apostles in Acts, but it is rooted in the protoevangelium of Genesis 3:15 and God's promise to Abraham in Genesis 12:1–3. God first declared, "You are My witnesses" in Isaiah 43:10 (NASB), and then "You shall be My witnesses" in Acts 1:8 (NASB). As the Scriptures prepare to close, Revelation 5:9 speaks of a yet-future gathering of the redeemed out of every kindred, tongue, nation, and tribe—a gathering we have the grand and noble privilege to help populate. Nothing so pervasive in Scripture as the missionary mandate should be relegated to the status of an addendum, treated as a nonessential matter that can wait until all matters considered essential to the church (staff, buildings, and programs) have been secured. But if the pastor does not see it, teach it, and live it, neither will his congregation.

Missions policy

Every church should have a comprehensive written missions policy. Done properly, writing the policy will require significant time and energy, but it holds the potential of being the most beneficial missions exercise a church will ever undertake. Dealing with each missions-related question as it arises constitutes writing policy on the fly. That will prove inconsistent and divisive, because it is so susceptible to emotion, personal charisma, and special interests. A comprehensive missions policy will anticipate and address questions before they are asked, establishing Biblically balanced principles and practices affirmed by the congregation. Having agreed on how missions will be managed eliminates surprises, builds trust, and provides continuity through changes in personnel and church priorities.

A comprehensive missions policy should begin with a Scriptural definition of missions that will identify what the church will and will not consider missions. The church I pastored just before I became a mission administrator supported Christian educational institutions and social agencies, but not from missions funds. The church understood Matthew 28:18–20, Acts 6:1–7, and Acts 14:21–23 to teach that missionary endeavor will consistently include all three elements of the Great Commission: evangelizing the lost, edifying believers, and multiplying churches. All three had to be within a ministry's focus for that ministry to gain missions support from the church. Not every church will hold that view, but every church should define its view and act accordingly.

The missions policy is likewise the place to spell out the breadth of involvement the church will allow. The law of creation dictates reproduction "after its kind." God's blessing does not rest exclusively on Independent Baptist entities, but it is not unreasonable for a church to limit its involvement to those missionaries and agencies with doctrinal statements, purpose statements, and principles and practices consistent with those of the church. Churches should expect their missionary efforts to produce ministries essentially like the church's ministry at home.

Room here will not allow treatment of every element that a comprehensive missions policy will address. But here are six elements:

1. The policy should state how the missions committee and subcommittees will be chosen, qualifications for members, terms of office, and duties. It will outline how the missions committee relates to men's or ladies' missionary groups and the elected boards of deacons and trustees.
2. The policy will spell out how candidates will be considered for missionary support and specify a starting minimum amount of support.
3. The policy will delineate the distinct manner in which the church will assist and support missionaries commissioned by the church.
4. The policy will establish the manner and frequency with which missionary support will be reviewed and a procedure for increasing, decreasing, or terminating support.
5. The policy will explain the church's response to a missionary changing ministry, field, or agency and what the church will do when a missionary retires.
6. The policy will contain goals for promotion, training, recruitment, and commissioning of missionaries.

Samples of missions policies can be acquired from most mission agencies. Paul Beals's book *A People for His Name* is an excellent guide for establishing a church's missions strategy.

Recruitment

A church that corporately prays for God to call workers from among their members, actively mentors promising young people for service, and openly affirms those who obey God's call will be the church from which God is most likely to draw workers into His harvest fields. But many churches, even the ones that have carefully nurtured their young people up through high school, tend to step back from that role when young people enter college. It is possible for a college student to surrender for missions, choose a field, and apply with a mission agency before the church is brought into the process in a meaningful manner. Since the church, in concert with the Holy Spirit, is the initiating and sending agent (Acts 13:1–4), the church should be involved in evaluating a young person's preparedness for missionary service and in helping the missionary candidate discern God's will for a field of service, a type of ministry, and an agency with which to partner.

The sending church should likewise play the lead role in getting its members to the mission field. Few churches are able to completely underwrite the support of their missionaries, but before a missionary enlists the aid of other churches, the sending church must show confidence in the missionary by assuming a significant portion of the missionary's support. If each new missionary had the promise of 25 percent of his or her support from the sending church, it would send an impressive message to other churches being asked to help. The sending church can signal its confidence in other ways:

- Pledging 50 percent of the missionary's outfit and passage
- Equipping the missionary for pre-field ministry
- Making the first contacts for the missionary in booking meetings
- Keeping the missionary in a reliable car
- Assigning a couple from the church to personally track the missionary to make sure the church is aware of and responsive to special needs

At a time that the church agrees upon, missionary candidates should quit secular employment and do pre-field ministry full-time. The church could assign them to work with the pastoral staff during the week and travel for ministry each weekend.

No church should be asked to be a supporting church for a missionary who lacks the confidence of his or her sending church. No church should commission a missionary in whom it has less than total confidence.

Mission agencies

Mission agencies do not replace or displace the local church. Agencies serve by providing structure, uniformity, and continuity that would be difficult to achieve without them. Nothing in the Bible prevents a single church from serving as a missionary's sponsoring agency. But going it alone is precisely what drove most founders of existing mission agencies to launch collaborative efforts. They became convinced that if they died, their work would die with them.

Today, going it alone leaves new missionaries without organized teams of coworkers to guide them through the red tape specific to their field, to orient them by means of internships with veteran missionaries, to strategize with them to define their part in the bigger picture, and to collaborate with them to produce ministries that a single missionary family will never be able to muster, such as theological training, camps, and compassion ministries.

Without a field team, missionaries will have no one to cover for them if/when they are off the field. They will have limited options for fellowship while on the field. They will have no one to hold them accountable to acquire the language and learn the culture. If new missionaries are left to trial and error, they will have no one with the experience of a seasoned field administrator to come alongside to help make right what went wrong. Without a home office team, they will have no one enlisting, screening, and training recruits who will prove compatible with them and acceptable to their support base. They will forfeit the assistance of colleagues skilled in support estimates, global finance, taxes, communication, information technology, healthcare/medicine, and management of crises. If an emergency evacuation is required due to health, natural disaster, or civil conflict, the capacity of a single church to help will be tested as nothing else will test it.

Nothing in the Bible prevents a single church from serving as a missionary's sponsoring agency. But experience has proved we can do more together.

Funding

Funding of missions within independent Baptist churches generally follows one of three approaches:
1. It can be a line item in the unified budget, which is evaluated and established as part of each year's budget preparation.
2. It may be an established percentage of the total income of the church so that as income to the church increases, there is built-in growth in missions funds available.

3. It may be faith promise that annually enlists pledges from members, and then giving to missions is handled separately from the giving for church operations.

Regardless of the funding approach chosen by the church, missions should be treated with a sense of urgency that reflects the example of the first-century church. The New Testament church was a missionary enterprise, led by missionaries, and entirely committed to expanding gospel witness. That model is intact today in many mission churches. It is not uncommon for those fledgling congregations to make their missionary commitment their first and greatest commitment. They know that apart from missionary effort, they would still be lost in their sins and their church would not exist. They do not want to deprive others for one day longer than necessary the same blessings that have come to them through missions.

The Church and Its Missionaries

As a class of people, missionaries are not cribbers. They are accustomed to dealing with matters beyond their control. They expect life and ministry to be hard, and they don't dwell on sacrifices they are making. It is far more common to hear missionaries praise their sending and supporting churches than criticize them.

But there are indeed a few ways that churches frustrate their missionaries:

1. Pastors failing to respond to mail or phone calls hurt them. They respect pastors as the responsible agent within the seat of authority for all missionary endeavors. If pastors are unreachable or unresponsive, it creates a problem.
2. Missionaries are troubled by long surveys, often driven by agendas not immediately obvious to a missionary who hasn't kept abreast of current issues in the States. They prefer face-to-face exchange. Our digital world has provided inexpensive means of real-time voice and visual communication. And communication is always better when facial expression, body language, and tone of voice are factored in.
3. Missionaries are uncomfortable when told that missions is getting too expensive, even though no expense seems too great for the things congregations desire here.
4. Missionaries prefer a multiday missions conference over having to report on a full term of ministry in a fifteen-minute time slot in a single

service. And missionaries crave opportunities to speak directly with young people, but more and more church programs insulate young people from direct interaction with missionaries.
5. They know there is nothing they can do if a pastor new to a supporting church sweeps the existing missionary program clean. And they have all experienced turnover in supporting congregations sufficient to make the missionaries strangers in the very churches that initially helped get them to the field.
6. Of all the frustrations missionaries endure, the greatest is knowing that what is expected of them in terms of evangelism, discipleship, leadership training, and conflict resolution is so seldom modeled in the very churches that place those expectations on their missionaries. When churches at home largely neglect the things expected of their missionaries, it can be demoralizing. It should not be that way.

Conclusion

May it never be said of us that in response to Christ's last and greatest command, we remained silent and sedentary. That we were content to leave to others the preaching of the gospel to all nations. That we gave assent to Christ's authority to do with our lives what He chose, and then did what we chose. That when He deserved our obedience, we disobeyed.

Take Action . . .

1. Evaluate ways you are leading your church to greater missionary involvement. Determine how you could better lead. Determine how your church could better follow.
2. Explore ways your church can enhance its praying for its missionaries. Identify your church's strengths and weaknesses in this area.
3. Review and revise your church's missions policy. If it is not written, enlist help to write a comprehensive policy.
4. Intentionally nurture a church culture that values full-time Christian service and breeds the confident expectation that God will call missionaries from its members. Dedicate resources (human and financial) to back those who step out for service.
5. Guide those called as they move through decisions concerning a type of ministry, a host country, and a partnering mission agency. Seek guidance and training to play that critical role.

Discussion

1. What are the benefits of a written church missions policy and the risks of operating without one?
2. Where does missions fall in the priorities of your church? Is it properly prioritized?
3. How can a church be motivated to pray effectively for the missionaries it supports?
4. Why should your church consider supporting only missionaries and mission agencies of like faith and practice?
5. What would it require to nurture a church culture that values and promotes full-time Christian service?
6. How can a pastor influence young people to seriously consider missions, and how can the congregation join in the effort?
7. What are the advantages and disadvantages of a church being its missionaries' sponsoring agency?

For Further Study

A Beginner's Guide to Crossing Cultures by Patty Lane, InterVarsity Press, 2002.

Cross-Cultural Connections by Duane Elmer, InterVarsity Press, 2002.

Effective Engagement in Short-term Missions by Robert Priest, William Carey Library, 2008.

Encountering Missionary Life and Work by Tom Steffen and Lois McKinney Douglas, Baker Academic, 2008.

Final Analysis: A Decade of Commentary on the Church and World Missions by Jim Reapsome, Evangelism and Missions Information Service, 1999.

For the Sake of His Name by David M. Doran and Pearson L. Johnson III, Student Global Impact, 2002.

Introducing World Missions by A. Scott Moreau, Gary Corwin, and Gary McGee, Baker Academic, 2004.

The Key to the Missionary Problem by Andrew Murray (contemporized by Leona F. Choy), Christian Literature Crusade, 1979.

A Mind for Missions: 10 Ways to Build Your World Vision by Paul Borthwick, NavPress, 1987.

A Missions Toolkit for Local Churches by William Smallman, Baptist Mid-Missions, 2012.

Overcoming the World Missions Crisis by Russell Penney, Kregel, 2001.

Reaching the World in Our Own Backyard by Rajendra Pillai, Waterbrook Press, 2003.
Serving with Eyes Wide Open by David Livermore, Baker, 2006.
The Vanishing Ministry by Woodrow Kroll, Kregel, 1991.
When Helping Hurts by Steve Corbett and Brian Kikkert, Moody, 2009.

24

Dealing with Church Conflict
— Randal L. Gilmore

Conflict happens. Surely this surprises no one, given our fallenness. Fallen people are notoriously self-absorbed and thereby naturally motivated to self-aggrandizement in a wide variety of life situations. In Christian contexts, other realities seem especially adept at aggravating our natural tendencies toward conflict. Churches and ministries form part of a larger kingdom at war with the kingdom of darkness. Our opponents in this war happily instigate conflict at every turn, knowing the Lord has made our usefulness in His plan largely contingent on the anointing of unity and love for one another. Their subversive activity, coupled with our fallenness, ensure that no Christian ministry will ever be entirely conflict free.

Integrating Conflict into God's Larger Purposes

Accepting the likelihood of conflict serves as the first step toward integrating it into the larger purposes God has in mind for transforming us and the ministries we serve into something better than the status quo.

The etymology of the word *conflict* hints at the possibility of God doing something transformative with it. The last part of the word comes from the Latin *fligere,* meaning "to strike." We're all familiar with the striking that goes on in conflict. It's the first part of conflict that usually catches people by surprise. The prefix *con* signifies "together," indicating that conflict-related striking always involves people who possess some type of relationship with each other. Without a relationship, they could never be close enough to strike, even metaphorically.

Norman Wakefield wrote that "the dynamics of relationship call attention to God's purposes and goals for allowing conflict among believers." Conflict has a way of humbling us, reminding us that our perspectives on any given matter are limited and often riddled with self-interest. God uses conflict to show us what is in our hearts and to invite us to change. He teaches us to rely on Him for wisdom to solve problems and the grace to live in harmony with others. Through conflict, God trains us in the character and skills of servant-leadership. He turns us into sympathetic companions for others passing through similar trials, equipping us to minister to them more effectively. Relationships are central to all of these purposes. The togetherness of conflict turns out to be a God-ordained tool for our sanctification and the sanctification of those around us.

Conflict and Biblical Same-mindedness

In *Where Do We Go from Here*, I have defined *conflict* as "perceived differences of positions and interests among two or more related parties—differences which can be biblically resolved with same-mindedness in the Lord or selfishly defended and pursued." The words *perceived differences* at the beginning stand for the many ways we become aware of conflict with others. It could be as obvious as something they explicitly say or do. Or it could be much more subtle—a look, a raised eyebrow, an inference or passing verbal reference to an opinion or perspective on some matter of mutual concern. Once the difference is perceived, it becomes something to manage.

The words *positions* and *interests* not only describe the underlying raw material of conflict differentiation, they also signal how conflict participants intend to manage things going forward. *Positions* describe what people want to see happen in relation to a conflict issue. *Interests* tell what motivates them to advocate their positions. In other words, if positions explain what people want to happen, interests explain why.

The goal for working through conflict is Biblical same-mindedness. The apostle Paul identified this goal in his response to conflict in the church at Philippi: "I entreat Euodia and I entreat Syntyche to agree in the Lord" (Phil. 4:2, ESV). The agreement Paul mentioned refers to much more than two people barely coming to terms with each other. It emphasizes understanding the mind of others and validating their line of reasoning. It involves people blending their perspectives and embracing each other's interests as if they were their own. A pursuit of Biblical same-mindedness will lead disputants to look beneath their positions to discover, validate, and fulfill each other's interests. Paul set the stage for this understanding in Philippians 2:1–21.

Some Christians fear where a pursuit of Biblical same-mindedness might lead them. The apostle addressed those fears by limiting agreement to those solutions that are in the Lord. It is as though Paul envisioned a large arena encircled by the positions and interests of the Lord Himself. The pursuit of Biblical same-mindedness involves an intentional commitment to remain in the arena of Christ's interests to discover, embrace, and satisfy the interests of others. Selfishly defending and pursuing one's own positions, or even one's own interests to the exclusion of others, lies outside the arena of "in the Lord," in territory where the self-centered status- and power-seeking ways of "the Gentile rulers" are frequently on display.

Framing—A Critical Skill

The dynamics of "together" heavily influence the positive or negative direction any conflict might take in pursuit of Biblical same-mindedness. When differences of positions and interests become salient, disputants quickly begin to frame the conflict in close connection to their view of the relationship at hand. This includes making an assessment of the morality of the other party's motives and behaviors.

Even though sin can be a dominant feature of conflict, not all conflict involves sin. Some differences in positions and interests exist for more benign reasons. Because of the way God made us, we experience the world differently. Even if we have the same or similar values overall, we might arrange those values in a different hierarchy than others. Of course, if sin is the primary cause of a conflict, it has to be addressed. Numerous Scripture passages address this.

Parties to conflict in ministry settings often seem much more inclined to categorize the motives and behaviors of others as sin when they are disputing over their more deeply held interests. Part of the reason for this could be that their counterpart truly is misbehaving. But it's also possible for both parties to magnify wrongdoing too quickly and then to begin treating each other as enemies.

Many Biblical terms could be used to frame our relationships with others. Three that stand out in relation to the development of conflict are *brother, neighbor,* and *enemy.*

- A brother is someone we feel close to and with whom we gladly affiliate because of a tie that binds us together. The tie doesn't have to be familial. It often is spiritual; as in, "I count you as my brother in Christ."
- A neighbor could be anyone we encounter in the ordinary course of daily life, anyone who happens across our path. Obviously the

relationship of neighbor is much less intimate and established than that of brother.
- The designation *enemy* doesn't necessarily speak to how close or how casual we are with others. It speaks instead to the level of enmity and animosity that we use to orient ourselves to them.

Making an intentional choice to frame our relationships with others in terms of *brother* during times of conflict holds the possibility of more positive outcomes on the path to Biblical same-mindedness. Of course, the opposite is equally true. For this reason, Jesus warned in Matthew 5:25 and 26, "Agree with your adversary quickly, while you are still on the way with him, lest your adversary deliver you to the judge, the judge hand you over to the officer, and you be thrown into prison. Assuredly, I say to you, you will by no means get out of there till you have paid the last penny" (NKJV).

The original word for *agree* literally means "be well-minded." Jesus instructed His followers to reframe their relationships with well-mindedness during episodes of conflict in order to avoid the undesirable consequences of enmity and to facilitate more agreeable outcomes.

In Matthew 5:44, Jesus gave a powerful example of how to begin cultivating the well-mindedness of *brother* toward someone we have previously counted as *enemy*. He instructed, "Love your enemies and pray for those who persecute you" (ESV). Notice Jesus did not say, "pray against them," but "pray for them." In the first part of the verse, Jesus characterized this kind of praying as "loving" your enemies. Performing acts of love for people you are otherwise tempted to treat as enemies becomes the catalyst for much more positive and mutually beneficial interaction. In Matthew 5:47, Jesus indicated that such a change might begin with the simple grace of extending the same warm greeting to your enemy that you normally reserve for a brother.

Changing the Metaphors

The Negotiator's Fieldbook points out another way to reframe the relational context of a dispute: changing the metaphors that participants use to describe their conflict and each other. Conflicts that are not going well often get depicted with metaphors of rebellion, fighting, and war: "We're battling for the soul of our church!" "They act like terrorists if we don't do exactly what they say!" "They're the ones that drew first blood!" Meanwhile, the disputants themselves also begin labeling each other with the names of some of the more infamous people in the Bible who became sources of serious interpersonal sin and strife: for example, Sanballat and Tobiah, Alexander the Coppersmith, Jezebel, and Judas. Metaphors such as these indicate frames of relationships more closely akin to enemy than to brother.

Conflict metaphors tend to reveal the feelings we associate with conflicts and our counterparts in them. They also reveal the intensity of those feelings. Metaphors can be useful if conflict participants are finding it difficult to verbalize the emotions they are associating with the dispute or with the state of the relationships they have with others. Even if someone is not having difficulty understanding his own emotions and relationship perspectives, paying attention to the metaphors used by others in the conflict might point to a better understanding of their emotions and relationship perspectives. More importantly, paying attention to conflict metaphors also provides opportunities to reframe both disputes and the relationships involved for the sake of Biblical same-mindedness. Instead of "a fight to the death," it's more like "a friendly discussion over whether to get pepperoni or sausage on the pizza." Instead of "a battle between Paul and Alexander the Coppersmith," it's more like "David and Jonathan working out the details of what to do about a common concern." Instead of "having to contend with that Jezebel-like terrorist," it's more like "Paul entreating Euodia and Syntyche."

Framing and Event Management

The framing of conflict as a particular kind of event is a skill closely associated with properly framing relationships. In leadership theory, the word *event* refers to the meaning a leader might assign to a particular episode of interaction with someone else. The emphasis is on the meaning the leader assigns to the event as interaction, not on the meaning the leader might assign to the relationships involved. For example, after talking with someone about plans for a new church ministry, a pastor might conclude, "That was serious conflict!" So from the pastor's perspective, the conversation was an event that should be framed as "serious conflict."

In their book on event management theory, authors Peter B. Smith and Mark F. Peterson encourage leaders to be aware of the perspectives they use to assign meaning to events, especially since more than one perspective is usually available. A leader's awareness affords him the possibility of more sophisticated response-strategies to events than those he turns to habitually or those that might not even be well matched to a particular event—the old "using a hammer to swat a fly."

Terms related directly to conflict are not the only words available to pastors or ministry leaders for assigning meaning to events. Author William Chris Hobgood identifies seven labels pastors or ministry leaders might typically use to interpret the conflict arising from ministry events: maintaining, reinforcing, adjusting, redefining, retooling, restructuring, and transforming. Hobgood associates a "hoped-for benefit" with each label, while also describing in each case what "resistance" generally looks like (see the chart below). Framing conflict associated with interaction using one of these labels is obviously more sophisticated than using broader, less revealing labels such as "serious conflict" or "good meeting with. . . ."

Thus, Hobgood's list provides greater assistance with understanding what the conflict is truly about, the degree to which the conflict might or might not have been expected, and what relationship and ministry strategies might be employed to move everyone toward same-mindedness in the Lord.

Describing Conflict

Initiative (Type of Event)	Range of Behavioral Responses in Resistance	Hoped-for Benefits
Maintaining	Apathy	Valuing an important program
Reinforcing	Apathy, questioning	Cooperating to strengthen good parts of a congregation's life
Adjusting	Passive disengagement to limited cooperation	Partnership to identify and address needed adjustments
Redefining	Withdrawing, friendly questioning	Congregation cooperating in craft identity
Retooling	Loyal opposition, willingness to compromise	Sharing, discerning new forms of action together
Restructuring	Loyal opposition, active disengagement/wait it out	Deep mutual understanding and work to find new directions
Transforming	Loyal opposition, threatened or real departure	Work, risking, daring to disagree, trust grows

Adapted from William Chris Hobgood, *Welcoming Resistance* (The Alban Institute, 2001).

Event management can also be helpful when the conflict is instigated by a bona fide enemy. For example, in the story of the Old Testament book that bears his name, Nehemiah seems to have employed some kind of event-management process to govern when the situation required him to be silent versus when it required him to speak or to act in some other way. Even within the speaking responses, he used different rhetorical approaches. When Nehemiah first learned of Sanballat's and Tobiah's unrealized feelings of opposition, he did nothing, with the exception of noting their feelings and keeping in place whatever device he was using to monitor them. However, when Sanballat and Tobiah began to verbally express their opposition (Neh. 2:19), Nehemiah met them head on, answering back immediately to clarify the actual nature of his mission: "We . . . will arise and build" (2:20, ESV).

Later, when Sanballat and Tobiah conspired to launch a violent attack, Nehemiah once again said nothing. Instead, he prepared the people to defend themselves while organizing them to carry on with the work (4:10–23). Still later, Nehemiah returned to a kind of verbal sparring with his enemies (6:4). Verbal responses continued in the cases of the fifth and sixth examples of opposition; however, they took on additional rhetorical purposes. Nehemiah spoke dismissively to Sanballat regarding the rumor of his impending revolt and claim to royalty (6:8). Then, to Shemaiah, he spoke emphatically against the course of action suggested to him, effectively closing the door to any further suggestions of a similar kind (6:10). All of this suggests that Nehemiah modulated his responses to conflict based on the nature or level of the threat imposed by his enemies.

The Way Forward

In the end, so much of what God wants to accomplish in our lives and ministries involves our relationships. Understanding conflict as one of the tools God uses may help us to move away from all the "striking" and toward the advantages of "together" instead. In addition to the transforming possibilities of "together," the following list summarizes five other realties of conflict to embrace:
- The priority of Biblical same-mindedness
- The obedience of discovering and satisfying interests
- The desirability of framing relationships in terms of *brother* or *neighbor* rather than *enemy*

- The power of metaphors to redirect conflict toward Biblical same-mindedness
- The wisdom of using event management to assign meaning to episodes of conflict and to adjust one's responses accordingly

Embracing these realities of conflict helps to chart the way forward in a fallen world where striking happens, a world exploited by the enemy of our souls and ministries. Thankfully, our Lord is a redeemer. If we cooperate with Him, He will use the conflict meant for evil to sanctify and transform instead, giving us a testimony at the end similar to the apostle Paul's in Philippians 1:12: "I want you to know, brothers, that what has happened to me has really served to advance the gospel" (ESV).

Take Action . . .

1. Analyze a current conflict using the realities of conflict to embrace. What new insights does your analysis reveal? What new courses of action might you take as a result?
2. Analyze a current conflict using Hobgood's classification of ministry events. What new insights does your analysis reveal? What new courses of action might you take as a result?
3. Develop a list of books and articles to read on conflict management. Identify particular conflict management ministry skills you need to develop or improve. Seek the help of a mentor as you cultivate and hone these new skills.

Discussion

1. Which of the realities of conflict to embrace are the most difficult for you to act on? Which are the easiest? Why?
2. Besides active listening, what are some other ways you can discover someone's interests in conflict?
3. In what specific ways has the Lord used conflict to promote your own spiritual growth?
4. What is your default response to conflict? How has the information presented in this chapter challenged you to think and act differently?
5. The conflict management skills explained in this chapter are not matters of personality. They can be learned and are transferable to those we minister to. Do you agree or disagree? Why?

For Further Study

Conflict under Control by Jeff Newman, Regular Baptist Press, 2007.

The Peacemaker (2004) and *The Peacemaker Student Edition* (2008) by Ken Sande, Baker.

Redeeming Church Conflicts by Tara Klena Barthel and David Edling, Baker, 2012.

Solving Problems Before They Become Conflicts by Norm Wakefield, Zondervan, 1987.

Welcoming Resistance by William Chris Hobgood, Alban Institute, 2001.

Where Do We Go from Here: The Path to Biblically Resolving Conflict by Randal Gilmore, Exalt Publications, 2007.

25

Sunday School: Boring or Soaring?
— Jack Austin

The Sunday School movement began over 230 years ago in Gloucester, England. Robert Raikes is credited with the concept of teaching underprivileged boys on Sundays, but it was a Baptist deacon named William Fox who added Bible teaching to Raikes's basic curriculum of reading, writing, and arithmetic. Even though its initial purpose was general literacy education, Sunday School soon became a great platform for drawing boys and girls to the Word of God. Over time, Sunday School became a flagship ministry of a wide range of churches and the means by which whole generations of Christians became established in their faith.

As pastors move through the second decade of the twenty-first century, they may sense a greater emphasis upon small group ministries and less on traditional Sunday morning classes. Very few new publications have addressed the use and improvement of the traditional Sunday School. Still, one would be hard-pressed to find another ministry model that can produce the educational scope and sequence for multiple generations of believers in a given local church.

What makes the difference between a healthy, productive Sunday School and one that is anemic and fighting for survival? At the risk of oversimplification, the difference is typically seen in leadership. Church leaders must fight the tendency to view Sunday School as a familiar fixture in which all staff and participants understand its purpose and direction. Any Sunday School left on autopilot will lose altitude. If it does not completely crash, it will most likely resemble Orville Wright's first powered airplane ride—a mere twenty feet off the ground, rather than cruising altitude!

Therefore, essential leadership is needed in several areas of Sunday School administration.

Purpose and Values

A clearly understood purpose shapes how Sunday School will function. If a church views Sunday School as primarily a place for enhancing fellowship and friendships, then Bible instruction is, at best, a secondary consideration. Likewise, if a church views an adult class as the place to explore the deep doctrinal truths of the Word explained by a veteran lecturer, evangelism and assimilation are likely very distant thoughts. But if the recognized purpose for Sunday School includes outreach, Bible instruction, and fellowship and service, then the church has a balanced focus by which to evaluate, measure, and adjust. If a church misses the correct purpose for drawing people to Sunday School or church services, church members will either be unmotivated to reach others or will do so only if they see some direct benefit to themselves. In either case, the unbeliever who needs Christ is the real victim. Stated values and an understood purpose guard against this kind of problem.

Curriculum Considerations

With the increasing secularization of our culture, there is a noticeable decline in common knowledge about the Bible and Christianity. Because the purpose of Sunday School includes an evangelistic element for the nonbeliever and an instructional element for the believer, churches must give attention to the curriculum they use. On the one hand, people will attend church year after year and will continue to grow in their knowledge of the Word; but if a church is doing its job in reaching new people, some of the basics will have to be retaught or reviewed periodically.

Most local ministries look to outside publishers. Here are three guidelines for choosing curriculum.

1. Same perspective

Use curriculum that approaches Scripture from the same perspective that the church does. It makes no logical sense to buy materials that are created according to a different doctrinal viewpoint. At times, someone will advocate use of a curriculum after reviewing it because they found "nothing wrong." That cannot be the only standard! Some publishers avoid specific denominational issues so their product can be marketed more broadly. For example, a Baptist church would obviously consider believer's baptism an important truth. Yet a non-Baptist publishing house could exclude the Ethiopian eunuch's baptism in its children's curriculum story from Acts 8. The story might include details about Philip running to the chariot, his ensuing explanation of Isaiah, and even Philip being caught away by the Spirit to another location. There is nothing "wrong" with the details included, but the lesson excludes the key example of a person coming to faith and being baptized. This same kind of thing can be illustrated with issues regarding inspiration, creationism, a literal-grammatical interpretive approach to Scripture, and several other areas.

2. Scope and sequence

Use a solid curriculum that provides a scope and sequence. Preschool and kindergarten-age children can grasp the simple character traits of kindness, obedience, helping others, and sharing. Elementary ages tend to connect with real people in real situations, like Daniel, Joshua, Peter, and Paul. Teens appreciate seeing the connection between the Bible and the current pressures of their everyday lives. Doctrinal, topical, and book studies garner the attention of adult learners. A line-upon-line, precept-upon-precept principle (Isa. 28:10) ensures a balanced plan for learning. You may find it tempting to jump to a new resource, but remember this: when a curriculum makes frequent departures, students can miss significant portions of Bible content and background.

3. Educational methodology

Evaluate curriculum with a view to educational methodology. Check to see that a variety of approaches and learning activities are part of each quarter's instruction. Children, teens, and even adults learn more when a new activity is incorporated into a lesson. Sunday School teachers must avoid the boredom of predictability. And do not compound this problem with a generic, unimaginative curriculum. On the other hand, keep in mind the limitations of Sunday School curriculum. Even the editors of the best materials offer ideas and application points with broad brush strokes. Ultimately, a curriculum is only as good as the teacher using it. The teacher brings the lesson alive and connects the truth to life for the learners. You can increase curriculum effectiveness by developing creative teachers.

Motivating and Equipping People

One staffing concept that has been particularly effective in various Sunday School ministries is the creation of teaching teams, and not primarily for children's classes; teaching teams work well at the adult level too. A team approach brings camaraderie in ministry that cannot be beat. It has the added advantage of providing immediate solutions when one teacher is absent. Even if another team member is called to teach with short notice, he or she knows the class and is aware of the lesson series. Shared responsibilities decrease the fatigue factor of week-in, week-out teaching that long-term teachers sometimes face.

The wise pastor intentionally guides the training of his church's Sunday School staff. The first step is to identify what a given person needs to know or learn to be effective. This list may vary from teacher to teacher according to the age group. Likely training areas include the following:

- Basic personal Bible study skills
- Communicating the gospel to others
- Developing and using lesson aims
- Age-level characteristics
- Classroom management techniques
- Child-protection and safety measures
- Developing a lesson plan
- Using curriculum materials
- Creating variety through appropriate teaching methods
- Creating appropriate lesson applications

I assume that a new or immature believer would not be recruited as a teacher for any age group. Because of this assumption, I did not include such things as doctrinal studies and Christian-living topics, although I recognize them as key components for developing future ministry workers. One effective way to help in the training of a new teacher is to place him or her alongside an experienced teacher.

Finally, in the staffing of Sunday School positions, strive to recruit correctly. Do not undersell the ministry, as a worker will undoubtedly feel tricked into serving and be surprised by the challenge before him or her. Do not motivate a person to respond out of guilt, as it is likely to create halfhearted service and a quick exit from the position. Also, it is wise to provide an opportunity for the faithful worker to step away from the classroom after a period of time to allow that person to recharge his or her ministry batteries. This is not to say that a person cannot continue, but rather it emphasizes that a worker's area of service is not a "life sentence." A pastor should cultivate a culture of celebrating, motivating, and equipping people in Sunday School ministry and enlist others in the effort as well.

Child Protection and Safety Issues

In today's ministry setting, it is critical for pastors and leadership teams to address matters related to protecting children. There is no reason for a church to delay developing written child protection policies and screening procedures for all ministry workers. The cost to a ministry for neglecting such a step can be devastating—for a child who suffers abuse while at church and for the ministry as a whole. Not only is the testimony of Christ hurt, but some ministries have had enormous financial costs as well.

A number of available resources provide sample policies, screening processes, and training materials. Christianity Today has done a commendable job creating *Reducing the Risk,* 3rd ed., which provides excellent instruction and training in a DVD format.

Churches sometimes forget that child-safety policies provide a safety net for children's workers too. When solid policies are in place and followed, accusations against a worker rarely have any legitimacy. Remember, too, that guests who bring their children to your Sunday morning ministry are much more relaxed when they see a ministry that takes extra steps to ensure their children's safety.

Facility Considerations

Perhaps you expected a chapter on Sunday School management to begin with recommendations on ideal room size and adequate teaching equipment. The reality is that unless a Sunday School ministry has a clearly understood purpose and an equipped staff to accomplish that purpose, it matters little what size room any given age group has for learning. Classes can meet in large, well-furnished rooms, but if there isn't a clear focus on what should happen in those rooms, the Sunday School will likely struggle with success. On the other hand, great things have been accomplished in a limited facility because the church has a clear purpose for its Sunday School and it intentionally and specifically equips the Sunday School staff.

One of the most helpful general resources on Sunday School planning and evaluation is *How to Have a Great Sunday School* by Wes and Sheryl

Haystead. It includes technical information on square footage recommended for classrooms, and gives ideas and advice regarding the equipment and resources for every age level. Even if you meet in a facility that has less-than-ideal classrooms, a resource like this one is worth consulting. Not every classroom need has to be met by a building expansion program. You will find it is possible to make some beneficial adjustments to your current building.

Practical Administrative Issues

Undoubtedly one of the most challenging aspects a pastor can face with Sunday School is a broad, functional coordination with the total church ministry. This integration requires regular and concerted effort. Some churches have weekly children's or youth programs that reach beyond the normal Sunday morning crowd. Have you thought about how you could draw them into your Sunday School? If your ministry reaches to the seniors of your community, what steps are necessary to get them to attend on Sunday mornings? Since missions and missionaries are often a part of church life, the church's missions program ought to connect to Sunday School in a direct fashion as well.

Practical coordination means that clear communication is needed . . . all the time! Communicate in formal public settings and in less formal settings. Communicate in meetings. You may find it helpful to communicate in written form too. If any change or adjustment is needed in the Sunday School program, communicate the what, why, and how early and thoroughly. Attempt to connect any Sunday School change to the purposes that drive your ministry. One wise mentor of mine cautioned against promoting a new idea by destroying the current one. The sage advice went something like this: Don't shoot holes in the bottom of the canoe you used to cross the river just because you desire to build a footbridge. You may want to use that canoe sometime again in the future! While there are a variety of possibilities as to how to organize and manage a Sunday School, communication and ministry coordination are essential no matter what structure your church uses.

With appropriate attention to your Sunday School's purpose, the equipping of staff, child safety precautions, facility needs, and intentional communication, your Sunday School ministry never needs to be boring; it can be soaring in its impact on people.

Take Action . . .
1. List at least five values that should guide a vibrant Sunday School. Under each one, jot down ideas for communicating these values to the Sunday School staff and then to the congregation as a whole. Choose an idea to begin implementing.
2. Write, or guide others in writing, a purpose statement for your entire Sunday School and for each department.
3. Consider sending your Sunday School staff to a Regular Baptist Press teaching seminar. Visit RegularBaptistPress.org/seminars.
4. Enlist a committee to put into place and maintain child protection policies if your church does not already have these policies and/or effective ways to practice them.

Discussion
1. In what ways have you observed a cultural decline in common knowledge of the Bible or the basic tenets of the Christian faith? How could a vibrant Sunday School address such a trend?
2. What steps can a leader take to make sure that a Sunday School ministry is not on indefinite autopilot?
3. How would you respond to the comment that a plan for child safety/abuse prevention is not needed in a smaller church setting? How might a leader set a direction for child protection policies even when there may be few physically present in a given ministry or church-planting effort?
4. How could a leader determine the appropriateness of a given curriculum for Sunday School? What could be the long-term risk of using a curriculum that avoids a literal six-day creation account, how to live the Christian life, or how to organize a local church? How can simply looking for the absence of "wrong things" not be enough of a standard when choosing Sunday School materials?

For Further Study
How to Have a Great Sunday School by Wes and Sheryl Haystead, Gospel Light, 2000.
Improving Your Sunday School by Don Anderson, Regular Baptist Press, 2008.
Reducing the Risk: Keeping Your Ministry Safe from Child Sexual Abuse, 3rd ed., Christianity Today, 2008, DVD.

Revitalizing the Sunday Morning Dinosaur: A Sunday School Growth Strategy for the 21st Century by Ken Hemphill, Broadman and Holman, 1996.

26

Dealing with the Troublemaker
— Duke Crawford

Of the many challenges the apostle Paul faced, dealing with troublemakers was close to the top of the list.

Troublemaking false teachers followed him at Corinth, prompting him to write, "But I am afraid that as the serpent deceived Eve by his cunning, your thoughts will be led astray from a sincere and pure devotion to Christ" (2 Cor. 11:3, ESV). A similar scenario occurred in the churches in Galatia, so he wrote, "Even if we or an angel from heaven should preach to you a gospel contrary to the one we preach to you, let him be accursed" (Gal. 1:8, ESV). The same was true as Paul sent Timothy to Ephesus to "charge certain persons not to teach any different doctrine" (1 Tim. 1:3, ESV).

Make no mistake: those "certain persons" are in every church dividing and discouraging the flock. The reality of their presence makes it necessary for every pastor and servant of Christ to learn how to deal with them. This is a necessary part of the ministry, and failure to deal with troublemakers will rob the pastor of joy and maybe cost him his ministry. Many churches have remained unfruitful and ineffective for the testimony of Christ as troublemakers and the problems they cause go unchecked.

See God in the Problem

Before considering a Biblical approach to dealing with the troublemaker, be encouraged with this—God is at work in and through troublemakers. He will use them and the process of dealing with them for the good of the church and His glory. Believing this will help move the church toward the battlefront instead of retreating. The young shepherd boy David rebuked the frightened armies of Israel as they cowered before the Philistine champion Goliath by saying, "Is there not a cause?" Certainly, as it relates to dealing with troublemakers, there is a cause; and that cause is part of God's agenda for changing and growing a Christian man into the shepherd of His flock.

When Paul wrote in Romans 8:28, "And we know that for those who love God all things work together for good" (ESV), he was including troublemakers and the problems they cause. Paul went on to define "good" in verse 28 as being "conformed to the image of his Son" in verse 29. Consider this: God is working to conform the believer to the image of His Son, and He knows that at times that goal is best accomplished through troublemakers and the problems they cause. No matter how severe the trouble or how great the problem, God is using this dissension for His glory. So take heart; God is on the move!

Growing through conflict with troublemakers will happen only as you open your heart to God's higher agenda for your life. Dr. Jim Jeffery says it well in his article, "How to Handle Conflict without Exploding Your Relationships." He writes, "Once we recognize the reality and danger of conflict in our relationships and are willing to allow our hearts to be exposed and changed, only then will we be ready to apply biblical wisdom to resolving the conflict in a constructive way."

Let the Gospel Be Your Guide

God knows a little something about dealing with troublemakers. As a matter of fact, He has dealt with a whole world full of them since the beginning of time! We do well to think about the ramification of the gospel in relation to our dealing with troublemakers. The Bible says, "For if while we were enemies we were reconciled to God by the death of his Son, much more, now that we are reconciled, shall we be saved by his life" (Rom. 5:10, ESV), and "Not that we have loved God but that he loved us and sent his Son to be the propitiation for our sins" (1 John 4:10, ESV).

God worked to reconcile us to Himself while we were a mess. He didn't wait for us to straighten ourselves out first. He pursued troublemaking sinners like you and me to rescue us from sin and death and to reconcile us to Him. How hopeless we would be if God had left us to our own mess before intervening with His truth and grace.

It is so easy to say, "Dealing with a troublemaker is messy. I think I'll take a pass on this one!" But every time a messy situation comes and there is work to be done toward reconciliation, follow the example of our Lord and His gospel. Friend, see yourself as the troublemaker sinner and now see the Lord reaching out to you through Christ's cross of reconciliation to deal with your sin and its consequences. Let that gospel be your guide and pursue the troublemaker, thanking God for the opportunity and ability to follow His gospel model.

Don't Ignore the Problem

Ignored problems don't go away. Ignored problems don't get better on their own. Problems are meant to be solved, so don't put your head in the sand, take a pass, or pray for another to intervene. Paul wrote to the Corinthians, "For there must be factions among you in order that those who are genuine among you may be recognized" (1 Cor. 11:19, ESV). If your faith is genuine, it's time for that genuine faith to be recognized! Remember, God has sovereignly placed the troublemaker and the problems caused by the troublemaker for the church and leader's sanctification. He has also given the pastor the responsibility to lead and protect His flock. So don't ignore the problem. With the strength of the Lord and the truth of His Word, rise up and conquer!

This is clearly the message of Scripture. In Matthew 18:15 Jesus said, "If your brother sins against you, go and tell him his fault" (ESV), and in Galatians 6:1, the apostle Paul said, "Brothers, if anyone is caught in any transgression, you who are spiritual should restore him" (ESV). Clearly the responsibility to solve the problem and move toward reconciliation is on those who are spiritual. This isn't passively waiting to see if God opens a door to talk to the troublemaker but actively going to him in the name of the Lord and the authority of His Word to bring about a God-honoring resolution.

Many times, troublemakers have been allowed to cause trouble for years. Other pastors have failed to deal with the person and the situation it brought, fearing people will get mad and leave the church. The reality is the trouble caused has kept more people from coming than would have ever left had the problem maker been dealt with in the first place.

It is also important to make yourself deal right away with troublemakers and the problems they cause. "Don't let the sun go down on your wrath" is good admonition for dealing with troublemakers immediately and not letting a lot of time go by before taking action. The more time that passes, the easier it will be to pretend the situation is no longer an issue, so move ahead and don't ignore the problem.

Get to the Heart of the Matter

James made one of the most telling and helpful observations about humankind when He said, "What causes quarrels and what causes fights among you? Is it not this, that your passions are at war within you? You desire and do not have, so you murder. You covet and cannot obtain, so you fight and quarrel" (James 4:1, 2, ESV). As you move ahead to deal with troublemakers and the problems they cause, remember there is always an idolatrous heart behind the trouble. Often, this idolatrous heart wants to control people and outcomes. This is a very common sin for troublemakers as they seek to intimidate and manipulate others in order to satisfy the desires of their idolatrous hearts.

Learn to ask questions like, "What did you want when you said this or did that?" and "What were you thinking when you said this or did that?" Use wise "X-ray" type questions to get to the heart behind the sin.

Matthew 18

The most helpful yet often neglected passage for dealing with the troublemaker is Matthew 18:15–17. Study and learn this passage well. It will be your lifeline in confronting and dealing with the troublemaker in a Biblical, God-honoring way.

Many churches contain a phrase in their membership covenants to "obey the rules of Christ," which is a direct reference to following the steps of church discipline as laid out in Matthew 18. The following is in no way a detailed treatment of our Lord's instruction concerning discipline, but these observations will get you headed in the right way.

1. Sin is the issue, not opinions, wishes, or feelings. One must be able to show the offender from the Bible that what he or she has said or done is against the will of God as revealed in His Word.
2. The sin that moves the process from one step to the next is the failure to hear. Whatever sin begins the process is not the issue once the offender fails to hear and repent. The failure to hear and obey the Word of God is evidence of an unbelieving heart, which in itself is the root problem.
3. Others may be needed to solve the problem, so do not hesitate to involve them when necessary. Failure to follow this keeps the church from functioning Biblically as a church to one another and makes the charge of "going it alone" or making the matter personal.
4. Putting someone out of the church could and should be the necessary

action if the offender refuses to hear. Putting them out of the church is not shunning but is the public removing of the brother or sister from the membership roll. At this point, the ministry of the church changes from edification to evangelism as the church seeks to win the mere professing brother or sister to Christ.

It is important to understand that long-term, habitual troublemaking could be (and probably is) a sign of unbelief. The sad reality is that many times unbelievers have caused untold havoc and damage to the church because of the failure to act Biblically. Maybe the troublemaker himself has remained in an unregenerate state or failed to grow as a Christian because no one dealt with him Biblically! Either way, the role as faithful shepherds is to deal with the troublemaker and the problems he or she causes for the testimony of Christ and the health of His church.

Precious Fruit

The writer of Hebrews gives the church this precious promise: "For the moment all discipline seems painful rather than pleasant, but later it yields the peaceful fruit of righteousness to those who have been trained by it" (Heb. 12:11, ESV). Pursuing "the peaceful fruit of righteousness" should be one of the main pursuits of ministry. Dealing with troublemakers and problems they cause will bring greater joy and confidence to the ministry and will help restore the church's testimony and a renewed desire to taste the precious fruit of God's righteousness.

Take Action . . .

1. Examine your heart. Deal with any unconfessed sin or animosity or lack of compassion toward the troublemaker.
2. Confirm the facts with two or more witnesses. Make sure your witnesses are those with no agenda against the troublemaker.
3. Choose the "X-ray" questions you will ask.
4. Be able to clearly state the sin committed by the troublemaker, showing him or her from God's Word why his or her words or actions are sin.

Discussion

1. Who is a Biblical example of a leader who had to deal with a troublemaker? How did God use that experience to mature or strengthen that leader?

2. If you are not a natural confronter, what passage of Scripture can you use to motivate you to confront a troublemaker?
3. If you are a natural confronter, what must you do to ensure that you Biblically confront a troublemaker?
4. How can you as a pastor help your flock learn to Biblically confront troublemakers under their leadership (e.g., in their homes, in their Sunday School classes)?
5. What could result from your failure to courageously and Biblically confront a troublemaker in your church?

For Further Study

Conflict under Control by Jeff Newman, Regular Baptist Press, 2007.
"How to Handle Conflict without Exploding Your Relationships" by Jim Jeffery, Sharper Iron, available at sharperiron.org.
Making Peace by Jim Van Yperen, Moody, 2002.
The Peacemaker (2004) and *The Peacemaker Student Edition* (2008) by Ken Sande, Baker.
Redeeming Church Conflicts by Tara Klena Barthel and David Edling, Baker, 2012.

27

Working with Various Age Groups
— Dave Rockwell

The presence of differing age groups in the church is evidence of God's blessing and indicates a congregation's general good health. God has surely blessed a church when children and teens gather with adults for worship and ministry. And good health characterizes a church when God's family is populated by representative adults, excited teens, energetic children, and sleeping (or crying) babies.

The presence of differing age groups, while a good thing, poses certain challenging questions to the pastor desiring effective ministry to each one God has placed under his care—especially for the man pastoring a smaller church. Among these are questions about which ministries to provide; how to recruit, train, and support the essential staff; how to select, implement, and manage curriculum; and when to schedule the various ministries to maximize opportunity and minimize "time and travel" conflicts for participants. Then there is the pervasive question of how to attend to age-group ministry needs while attending to the priority to "give attention to reading, to exhortation, to doctrine" (1 Tim. 4:13, NKJV). Either through good thinking or simple frustration, these questions generate a more foundational question: are age-grouped ministries in the church important enough for the pastor to give precious time and serious attention to them?

This question is actually the starting point for working with various age groups, and the answer is yes. The spiritual benefit of ministry to various age groups is worth the pastor's time and attention. This is true, first, because of Biblical teaching regarding various age groups and, second, because of a practical understanding of how to meet this Biblical teaching in a local church.

Biblical Foundations

Of all the references in Scripture identifying varying ages of individuals, Deuteronomy 6 and Ephesians 6 are perhaps the most well known. Both passages clearly state that the setting for the propagation of faith is the family, from one generation to the next. However, a careful look into these passages yields important information on understanding the need to consider an individual's age for an effective presentation of God's Word.

Deuteronomy 6

Deuteronomy 6 initiates Moses' instruction on the more personal nature of life in covenant relationship with God. The main command in the chapter is found in verses 4 and 5: "Hear, O Israel: The LORD our God, the LORD is one! You shall love the LORD your God with all your heart, with all your soul, and with all your strength" (NKJV). This command set the priority of a deep and extensive personal love relationship with God, the Lord. The individual was to live out the covenant through a personal relationship with God and not merely by means of an understanding of effective law-keeping. Living such a life served as an example for others and met the basic qualification for teaching the law in the family setting.

Having set the main command, Moses then directed parents to "teach them diligently to your children" (6:7, NKJV). The setting for this instruction was not the classroom, but all of life's daily happenings. The methodology for this instruction is given in the rest of verse 7 through verse 9. It can be described as all-inclusive, intentional, and visual. Nothing in life is to escape parental, covenant-based interpretation and application to a life lived under the care and protection of a loving, covenant-keeping God. While the general context for the spiritual training of children is summarized in verses 7–9, it is not all the instruction Moses had for parents.

Following a warning to the nation not to forget God when life became easy (6:10–19), Moses predicted a time when parents would need to help their children transition from observed and accepted faith to observed, accepted, and personally owned faith (6:20–25).

When the child matured in mind and heart to a place of independent thinking, parents—most notably the father—needed to anticipate a change in their spiritual interaction with their child. This interaction would be prompted by the parents' consistent obedience to the command of verse 6 and the family's faith-living practices of verses 7–9. Moses even suggested how the conversation was to develop at the occurrence of this wonderful "father-son" moment of spiritual guidance.

The son initiated the transitional conversation with a thoughtful question about the law and his personal ownership of it (6:20). Several concepts can be observed in such a question. First, it demonstrates the normal and desired maturation process of an obedient child ("what is the meaning of"). Second, it is not a question prompted by a desire to reject the law, but quite the contrary, one of personal acceptance and ownership of the law and of the God of the law ("which the LORD our God has commanded you" [NKJV]).

The father was to be prepared for this question with an answer that summarized major points in Israel's history, describing the hand of God in Israel's life, explaining the relationship between God's protection of Israel and His promises to the patriarchs, and emphasizing the implications of that protection for the obedient child of the covenant and for the whole nation (6:21–25). In short, using history and theology, the father was to explain the basis of his own testimony (6:4, 5) with such clarity and conviction that the son was urged to take personal ownership of the faith he had likely already accepted as a result of the practices enumerated in verses 6–9.

The importance of such parent-child conversations must not be missed. They affirm that true faith is not inherited, but taught by life and truth, which is then accepted by the child. They clearly explain God's place for parents—especially the father—in the presentation of faith lessons for the child. They describe the child's spiritually respectful attitude and the parent's spiritually prepared approach. The presence of such conversations in the homes of the nation was the desired outcome of Moses' teaching in Deuteronomy 6.

Ephesians 6

Ephesians 6:4 (and the surrounding verses) describes the home's place in the practice of faith-teaching for the New Testament church. Although covenant-based faith instruction has been replaced with grace-based faith instruction, the general parent-child interaction as the prime context for spiritual instruction of children has not.

The father is the principal person to assume responsibility for spiritual teaching in the home. This responsibility comes with a warning and with clearly stated instructional content. Paul's warning to the Christian father, "do not provoke," challenges the man to rethink the pagan view of family, which allows for harsh, unkind, and unreasonable demands on the wife and children. Such a view, with its unloving practices, has no place in the life of the grace-blessed, mercy-given saved man. Further, such a view is inconsistent with a recognition of the wife's place as a believer who is "in Christ" (Gal. 3:28, NKJV). Treating one's children as the pagans do denies the very essence of how Christ sees them (Matt. 19:13–15) and disqualifies the father for his responsibility to "bring them up in the training and admonition of the Lord" (Eph. 6:4, NKJV).

This "bring them up" responsibility is given to the father and cannot be wholly delegated to another, since it is predicated on the father's personal testimony. Additionally, effective implementation of this "bring them up" instructional command is possible only when the faith lessons are based on a desire for each child to know Christ as Savior and to grow up in Him (Eph. 2:8–10).

Paul, like Moses, taught that the practice of fatherly duties is itself an authentication of faith. For the purpose of spiritual instruction, the father is to approach his children with the sweetness of a godly life, a loving relationship with their mother, and sound faith lessons drawn from God's Word.

Deuteronomy 6 and Ephesians 6 set forth God's design for spiritual instruction in the faith-based home. Both passages, fairly representing both testaments, clearly state God's desired setting for the propagation of faith in the family from one generation to the next.

The church must support God's plan for spiritual instruction in the faith-based home. No church-based ministry is to replace the responsibility of parents—especially the father. An "if they won't do it, we will" attitude from the church is not to be considered or tolerated.

Church Considerations for Ministry to Various Age Groups

What Moses and Paul taught about spiritual instruction within the family does not, however, address the issues created when families and individuals are without faith or have not attained sufficient spiritual maturity to accept the responsibilities of family life in the godly household. But those very concerns are the ones the local church is privileged to tackle. For even as it is an evidence of God's blessing and an indication of good church health to have various ages in the church, it is also a marker of true ministry to have the unsaved, the spiritually immature, as well as carnal believers of all ages counted as part of the general congregation. The church is where such people should find ministry to their lives and souls.

This reality, as much of a substantiation of God's blessing as it may be, brings with it the need for serious attention to the essential elements of effective ministry. These elements include program, staff, curriculum, and facilities. These elements, never in abundant supply in a church of any size, are especially precious in a smaller church. These elements, though essential, need not be viewed as overwhelming or impossible to address. This is especially true when they are broken down into the two categories of "theological fences" and "practical fences."

Theological fences: What the church must do

The pastor and people of a Bible-based church are responsible to know, consider, and apply at least four theological truths, or fences, when addressing ministry needs of varying age groups. These truths, when understood and correctly employed, fence in the work of the church by giving direction, setting standards, and providing limits to the work of ministry. In other words, these "theological fences" establish the area of effort and set the boundaries of that work.

Family obligations. God has set the family as the primary place of spiritual instruction for children. It is never the church's responsibility to do what God has assigned to the home. It does, however, fall to the church to teach this truth to the believing family and to provide necessary training to parents—especially the father—in the means and methods for a faith-building family life. It may fall to the church to provide "spiritual foster care" for children and teens not blessed with a functioning Christian home. Additionally, it may be practical for the church to provide Bible classes for all age levels as an assist to the family. Such classes could emphasize Bible literacy and faith understanding and development. But the family, not the church, is the God-assigned, primary place for such instruction.

Teacher qualifications. God has set two qualifications for the one assigned to stand before others as a teacher of God's Word: sincerely Christian and sufficiently competent. (A glance at Moses' and Paul's stated obligations of the father reveals similar qualifications of testimony and skill.) The requirement of authenticity and skill are included and required of pastors (1 Tim. 3:2–7; Titus 1:6–9). They are further identified as essential for the "faithful men" to whom is "committed" the Word of God.

While the particular teaching responsibility may call for a greater or lesser degree of knowledge and Christian experience, the Bible teacher must be sincere in his testimony and sufficiently sound in his Bible knowledge. No church, no matter what the presumed need, is free to place an unqualified, insufficiently skilled, or, worse, disqualified individual in a teaching position.

Spiritual giftedness. God has blessed His church with "spiritual gifts" (1 Cor. 12:1). He has arranged these gifts exactly as He has thought best (1 Cor. 12:18). He has gifted every believer (Eph. 4:7; Rom. 12:3) and has determined that each one shall function as intended and not as unintended (1 Cor. 12:14–26). While it can be safely assumed that God's spiritual enabling as described in 1 Corinthians 12 refers to the universal church, each local church can rest comfortably in the assumption that God will provide the spiritual gifts needed for that church to succeed in its mission. This truth should bring great comfort to the church faced with more ministry opportunities than people and resources ready at hand to address them. While there are other factors to be considered in assuming responsibility for a ministry, the presence of gifted people, available and fit for such a ministry, is one of the most important. No gifted person, no effective ministry!

Biblical obligations. God has set His Word as both the content of instruction (2 Tim. 2:2, 15) and the only authority for Christian faith and godly living (2 Tim. 3:16, 17). The Scriptures are to be learned to the level of general Biblical literacy and applied to the place of a growing spiritual maturity (2 Tim. 3:15). Furthermore, God's Word is to be used as the basis for continual spiritual growth (2 Tim. 3:16, 17) and as the method and message of faithful Christian ministry (2 Tim. 2:15). Common sense alone suggests that the meeting of such Biblical obligations must be through a continual, progressive, and patient study of the Bible aided by qualified teachers.

These four (there are others that could be listed) "theological fences" establish the area of effort and set the boundaries for the work incumbent on each church, regardless of its size or maturity. They provide an essential starting point for the acceptance and implementation of ministries that will most likely require a focus on various age levels. The working out of these "theological fences" is affected by a consideration of important "practical fences" that must be applied locally by each congregation.

Practical fences: What the church can do or may not be able to do

The pastor and people of a Bible-based church are responsible to know, consider, and apply at least the following practical truths, or fences, when addressing ministry needs of varying age groups. When understood and correctly employed, these truths fence in the work of the church by giving direction, setting standards, and providing limits to the work of ministry. In other words, these "practical fences" establish the area of effort and set the boundaries of that work. They force a consideration of what may be reasonable for that particular church, without regard for what is possible or practiced by another church. Two "practical fences" are offered.

Theological fences. The first and most practical fence to be considered in the design of a church's age-level ministries is the package of "theological fences" presented earlier. Nothing is as practical as knowing what God requires and how well it must be performed.

Unique and essential age-level specifics. The thoughtful and prudent church will first realize it cannot do everything, but must do, with understanding, what it can do. This understanding is achieved by a reasonable consideration of the following age-level specifics.

- Children, teens, and adults do not receive and process information the same way. This, of course, is common sense. It also illustrates the Deuteronomy 6 passage, where the younger child is generally in view in verses 7–9, while the youth is the focus of verses 20–25. Paul made a similar reference in 1 Corinthians 13:11 to children's thinking. Ministry to age levels is largely prompted by this reality. Age-specific ministry must be done in age-specific settings.
- At the simplest level there are four age-specific groups, separated by a new level of thinking, that the church must address: preschool children, school-age children, teens, and adults. The wise choice to actually establish ministries for each age level is possible—even in the presence of seeming great need—only as time, talent, and treasure permit.

The presence in the church of various ages and multiple stages of spiritual life and maturity is indeed an evidence of God's blessing, but it is also a great challenge. Churches address this challenge through thoughtful consideration of both "theological fences" and "practical fences" in order to substantially achieve effective ministry to all age levels.

Practical Applications for the Pastor
1. Understand God's ministry obligations for the church and the home and seek to be loyal to both.
2. Teach the church the foundational theology related to church ministry: family obligations, teacher qualifications, spiritual giftedness, and Biblical obligations.
3. Lead the church in understanding the practical ministry considerations that age-level-specific ministries require.
4. Help the church to be comfortable in the ministry God makes possible and not compare that to another church.

Take Action . . .
1. Review and reaffirm the basics of ecclesiology.
2. Assess God's current provisions of people and wherewithal and thank God for these blessings.
3. Prayerfully and thoughtfully plan how to carry out God's mission for your church.

Discussion
1. Do you, and does your church, understand and accept God's mission for (Matt. 28:19, 20) and His design of (Eph. 4:12–16) the church?
2. What are the blessings of having all age levels present and in need of ministry? What are the challenges?
3. Are certain age groups missing from your church family? What has caused this, and how can it be fixed?

For Further Study
Children's Ministry Magazine, Group.
Church Volunteer Central, churchvolunteercentral.com.
Energizing Children's Ministry in the Smaller Church by Rick Chromey, Standard, 2008.
Regular Baptist Press, RegularBaptistPress.org.
A Theology of Children's Ministry by Lawrence O. Richards, Zondervan, 1983.

28

Handling Transition with Wisdom and Grace
— Rich Van Heukelum

To some, change is an adventure. To others, it's sheer terror. Strategic planner John Reid recalls how his mother used to say, "Life is change. Change is growth. Growth is painful." As he grew older, he came to understand how his mother was teaching him about the pain and growth that are inevitable parts of change. Pastoral transitions clearly fit into this assessment of change. For the pastor, transition is most often a matter of when, not if, and he must seek to answer, Will I handle transition with wisdom and grace? Here are some key considerations when facing a possible transition.

Be Sure to Surrender to God

"Work as if all depends on you. Pray as if all depends on God." This is great advice when you are doing the work of the ministry, but also when you are considering pastoral transition. Does it sound obvious? The obvious is often the area of failure. In seeking God's direction, five factors are usually stressed:

- *The Scriptures (Ps. 119:105).* Is the transition consistent with Biblical truth?
- *Counsel (Prov. 11:14).* Is the transition consistent with a multitude of counselors?
- *Prayer (James 1:5).* Was the Lord asked to direct?
- *The Holy Spirit (Rom. 8:14).* Was the Spirit allowed to lead?
- *Peace (Phil. 4:7).* Did the Lord's leading bring the peace of God?

The decision-making process must incorporate these factors, yet the wisdom of God is not always objectively clear even from these. What will it take for these to direct your steps? Your full surrender to the Lord.

Doulos Resources (a ministry provided by two experienced pastors) hits on this in challenging men to be "willing to be disappointed." A blog on the subject advises a pastor to move as if the transition could happen, yet to be willing to be disappointed if it doesn't come to be.

Although a pastor must work as if all depends on him, he must also pray until he has surrendered his will to God's. Then he can be satisfied in the Lord, whether He opens or closes the door.

Be Sure to Know Why You Would Leave

"The grass isn't always greener!" So why are you considering leaving? In their book *Pastors in Transition*, Dean R. Hoge and Jacqueline E. Wenger include the following motivations for transition:
- Preference for another type of ministry
- Necessary care for family
- Conflict in the congregation
- Burnout or discouragement

Logic and life reveal even more common motivations:
- Hitting the escape button
- Getting bored and needing a new mountain to climb
- Sensing your work is finished
- Sensing the need for a different type of shepherd to lead
- Sensing the Lord can use you better in a new location

The above motives may be Spirit or self led, but it's important for a pastor to ask of his own heart why he is considering a transition.

Some suggest a pastor stay until the Lord forces him out, while others suggest he leave before the congregation does. Some suggest a pastor never initiate contact with another church, while others suggest that the good health of his present ministry is an indicator of a good time to leave.

Pastors, like athletes, may stick around too long (e.g., Brett Favre). Others hit escape too early (e.g., Michael Jordan's first retirement). Many successful pastors have endured difficult days of ministry after staying too long or escaping too soon. Of primary concern to the pastor must be discernment concerning why he would leave. This must be a God-honoring motivation.

Be Sure to Look before You Leap

"He jumped from the frying pan into the fire." "Most are promoted to a level they are incompetent to handle." These two quotes give real caution to simply

moving on or moving up. The frying pan may seem hot, but the fire may be worse. Escape from one problem doesn't guarantee smooth sailing ahead. On the other hand, some offers are too good to resist, but they may be promotions to levels a man is not able to handle. Be sure to look before you leap.

Know what you're getting into. Ask, Do they need a man like me? Are they a church in which the Lord can use me? Am I really up for this?

To answer these questions, ask questions. Seek to obtain as much information as possible. Learn about the existing church through written histories and the stories of old-timers. Cover all bases in your talks with the pastoral search committee.

One may ask if the fit must feel natural to be of the Lord. After all, who'd want to take a ministry that doesn't fit like an old shoe? Yet we can all identify men who accepted a call to a church that wasn't a natural fit but where the church truly needed them.

I recently talked to a pastor who took a church that had previously been led down a broader path. He knew the task would not be easy, yet he accepted the challenge and through perseverance, preaching, and prayer, led it to a solid testimony of God's grace. He stated that those first years were very difficult, but that he sensed God could use him there.

Wisdom comes when you are led by the Spirit to transition to another church because you are confident that God will use you in that place.

Be Sure to Process with Excellence

"If it's worth doing at all, it's worth doing well." Doulos finds that "many pastors are shockingly lazy when it comes to their ministry placement." This is primarily directed to seminarians, but Doulos also finds this attitude common among pastors considering transition. Many pastors approach transition in a halfhearted manner.

A church sends a packet with a questionnaire. The pastor often doesn't really want to move, to consider that church, or to fill out the materials. This halfhearted interest leads to a halfhearted response, which gives a halfhearted impression. A pastor might even think, *If the Lord wants me to move, it will not depend on how well I fill in a questionnaire or produce a résumé.*

In reality, wisdom dictates that if a man senses that the Lord wants him to consider a ministry, he must follow the entire process heartily as to the Lord.

Be Sure to Include the Family

"The pastor is praying and his wife is packing." My father made this statement. He observed one spouse who was moving before the other was ready. Not good! A unilateral decision about a ministry move is insanity.

Remember that the first "not good" in the Bible occurred when God saw Adam without a wife? God quickly remedied that shortcoming by giving him a helper (Gen. 2:18). Not only does your wife have counsel needed for the decision, she will also have to live with the decision.

We as husbands are instructed, "Dwell with [your wives] with understanding" (1 Pet. 3:7, NKJV). Our wives have goals, needs, desires, and fears. Every transition has trauma, and if the family does not feel included in the process, it will resent the decision, especially when difficulties arise.

Be Sure to Be Yourself

"Be yourself. It's what you do best!" This statement has, time and again, saved me from trying to be or do what is not me. Each person has been developed by God to be the person he is. Yes, each of us must always seek to "grow in the grace and knowledge of our Lord and Savior Jesus Christ" (2 Pet. 3:18, NKJV), yet at any given time, each must realize who he is and live accordingly. This is especially true when traveling the road of transition.

Here are a few "nevers":
- Never portray yourself as anyone other than who you are.
- Never preach messages greater than you can normally preach.
- Never dress in a way inconsistent with the way you typically dress.
- Never leave the impression that you think a church wants to see if it is not the real you (e.g., personal evangelism, prayer life, family life, devotions, calling).

Many a pastoral candidate has left the impression that he could walk on water, only to be called and realize he is unable to live up to the expectation he created.

Be Sure to Pull the Trigger

"If you have the shot, take it." I vividly recall the day a large buck approached. I had a moderate shot, but waited for a better shot. I never got that better shot. The buck didn't take the route I expected, and I lost the opportunity. Wisdom dictates that a man must know when to pull the trigger.

Some take the shot long before they should, and some are too fearful to ever pull the trigger. They want so desperately to be sure that it's the right decision that they never decide. Like the farmer who, when asked about his crop, said, "So many things could go wrong, I played it safe and didn't plant any." Many fear failure, play it safe, and do nothing. "Status quo" is Latin for "the mess we're in," and this can limit someone from moving to greater ministry for the Lord.

If the Lord is directing, don't allow fear to keep you from moving on. Joshua's and Nehemiah's stories, as well as the parable of the talents, indicate that God wants us to obey Him, often leaving comfort zones for the unknown realm of taking new territory.

Be Sure to Say Good-bye

"Parting is such sweet sorrow." Whether a pastor leaves when all is well or when the handwriting is on the wall, good-bye will be difficult. The question is when to say the good-bye.

Recently a non-pastor friend found a new job. He felt an obligation to give his existing supervisor at least a few weeks' notice. His boss, however, said it would be best to end his service immediately. Why? The boss knew that when you are done, it's time to go. I increasingly see the wisdom in this. How can one effectively serve a company that he's leaving? His focus is on the future.

In the case of pastoral retirement, there is no new ministry to which the pastor is going, so it may be wise to let the church know months in advance and develop a succession plan. But if a pastor is moving on to a new ministry, wisdom dictates that he not drag it out. His mind is increasingly focused on his new ministry.

It's best to allow the church to make plans for its transition time. This time is often a helpful period for a church to focus on its future, and a departing pastor's presence often hinders freedom on the church's part. Like a lame-duck president, not much will be accomplished as the pastor ends his ministry, so he should take care to say good-bye.

Be Sure to Let Go of the Old

"When you leave, leave." At seminary I was taught that the number-one ethics issue among pastors occurs when former pastors don't fully leave. In pastoral transition, especially if the pastor is loved by his church, there's an overwhelming tendency to continue to connect, counsel, and come

back for special events. Yet wisdom says that one must fully leave so that the sheep can find and attach to a new shepherd.

How does a pastor do this? He tells the flock that he will no longer be involved in their lives as their shepherd. An article on this point says that "a pastor who resigns . . . no longer serves as pastor to members of this congregation. Former pastors should not agree to pastoral responsibilities that rightfully belong to the current pastor." This means that he won't return to do weddings or funerals. He won't give counsel as the church looks for a new pastor. He won't comment when the congregation calls asking about something that the new pastor is doing.

The breaking of these relations is extremely difficult but absolutely necessary.

Be Sure to Know and Embrace the New

"In my former church, we. . . ." Have you heard this line? It seems natural. After all, didn't the new church want this pastor because it valued how he served in his last church? Doesn't the new church want a replication of the other church? In truth, this is one of the most hated phrases of new pastors.

Lawrence W. Farris gives the example of a pastor named Mark taking his second congregation: "Mark set about the task of recreating that small town church in the image of his previous church experience. Needless to say, the congregation . . . did not respond positively." Farris continues by stating that the first commandment for a new pastor is, "Thou shalt be a cultural historian." That is, begin by getting to know and embrace the new. No two churches are alike, and although a church chooses a pastor because of something it saw in his previous ministries, it doesn't expect a copy of the former church. It is a new people in a new place.

Farris's other nine commandments for embracing the new ministry, found in *Ten Commandments for Pastors New to a Congregation,* go like this:
- Thou shalt spend thy blue chips for change on changes that matter.
- Thou shalt attend to thy preaching.
- Thou shalt be certain that the church's financial house is in order.
- Thou shalt not create expectations that cannot be met in the long term.
- Thou shalt take care of thyself from day one.
- Thou shalt be aware of the chronics.

- Thou shalt limit thy activities beyond the congregation that has called thee.
- Thou shalt remember what thy job is.
- Thou shalt not commit adultery.

Know and embrace the new people and place. Use your God-given skills and experience to create a new ministry. Be sure the new church senses that you care about and appreciate them.

Be Sure to Love the People

"It went ill with Moses on account of them" (Ps. 106:32, *NKJV*). In the final chapel hour of seminary, each professor gave one line of advice. Most I have forgotten, but one continues to ring in my mind: "Love your people." Ivan French gave the example of Moses, who consistently cared for and prayed for his flock until one day he became angry with them and struck the rock. We know the rest of the story. Whether leaving or arriving, an inappropriate response to your sheep may lead to God ending your ministry.

Love the people!

Take Action . . .

1. Evaluate your love for your flock. If, like Moses, you find it easier to scold than intercede, evaluate if it is time to move on.
2. Evaluate if status quo has set in—that is, you have not been moving your ministry forward—or if you find it's easier to stay than to consider leaving.
3. Evaluate how God may have been training you for a greater ministry. Evaluate whether that greater ministry can take place where you are, or if it could be at another ministry.

Discussion

1. What could happen if you leave out the Scriptures, counsel, prayer, the Holy Spirit, or peace from your decision-making process?
2. Why do some pastors stick around too long?
3. Why do other pastors leave too soon?
4. How can a man tell if it's too soon or too long?
5. What should a pastor do if he believes the Spirit is leading him to leave but his family does not want to move?

6. How can a pastoral candidate avoid leaving the impression that he is something he is not or has abilities he does not have?
7. How can a pastor graciously bow out of conducting weddings and carrying out other pastoral duties at his former church?
8. How does a congregation feel loved by their pastor?

For Further Study

Changing Pastors: A Resource for Pastoral Transitions by Thomas P. Sweetser and Mary Benet McKinney, Sheed and Ward, 1998.

"Church Transitions," Second Wind Ministries, available at secondwindministries.ca.

The Elephant in the Boardroom: Speaking the Unspoken about Pastoral Transitions by Carolyn Weese and J. Russell Crabtree, Jossey-Bass, 2004.

"The Ethics of Pastoral Transition," Metropolitan Chicago Synod of the Evangelical Lutheran Church in America, available at mcselca.org.

Pastoral Transition Blog, doulosresources.org.

"Pastoral Searches and Transitions," The Gospel Coalition, panel discussion, available at thegospelcoalition.org.

Pastors in Transition: Why Clergy Leave Local Church Ministry by Dean R. Hoge and Jacqueline E. Wenger, Eerdmans, 2005.

Ten Commandments for Pastors New to a Congregation by Lawrence W. Farris, Eerdmans, 2003.

Special Situations

29

Pastoral Internships
— Joel Dunlap

Some college interns experience just what they have envisioned: they affirm that they have chosen to enter the right field. They find out that their studies are paying off, but that they have more to learn. They acquire new tools for their toolboxes, figuratively or literally.

Others, however, find their internships fall flat. Their supervisors don't lay out any specific goals, failing to connect the interns to the operation of the business. They view the interns as the low men on the totem pole who receive only the menial tasks or, worse yet, as the gofers who fetch the boss's coffee or dry cleaning. The program does nothing to affirm, test, or equip the interns.

I trust that pastoral internship programs of local churches will more often target the former than the latter. Toward this end, the pastor finds guidance from the Biblical foundation for discipleship, the principles of contemporary internship programs, and the experiences of graduated interns and current pastors.

Pass the Baton

The Scriptures give clear evidence that Christian ministry is to be committed from one generation to another. Jesus Himself called twelve select men whom He taught and molded as His apprentices (Matt. 10:1–4; Mark 4:13–19; Luke 6:13–16). He gave them front row seats in His mobile classroom so they might call to remembrance His instruction after He departed (John 14:26). He took disciples, and they were to go and make more disciples (Matt. 28:19).

For the apostle Paul, the gospel was of first importance (1 Cor. 15:3) and its proclamation was central to his life and breath (1 Cor. 1:23).

Moreover, for Paul, gospel proclamation through others was essential to Christian ministry (2 Tim. 2:2).

Today, what is the venue for finding, training, and deploying the next gospel ministers? It is the local church—where members unite in common confession, people weave webs of accountable relationships, and believers observe and exercise gifts from God's Spirit.

Glean from Internship Models

The pastoral internship fits into the overall discipling heartbeat of the local church. The church should establish some strategic pattern of internship by which it fosters this call to the pastorate. The following models are not exhaustive, and the programs aren't meant to be replicated into every context. Each, though, stands out for one vital aspect of training that local churches can bring to bear on their internships.

Baptist Bible Seminary

For the pastor looking to get an internship program off the ground, like-minded seminaries may offer good leads about potential interns. Unique among the schools is Baptist Bible Seminary in Clarks Summit, Pennsylvania, whose Master of Divinity program requires a full-year pastoral internship. Final-year MDiv students are placed in local churches, where they are supervised, evaluated, and supported as they train on the job. The BBS internship is helpful to take a long view of ministry—that a full year on the job gives the intern a better picture of church dynamics and efforts coming to fruition.

Capitol Hill Baptist Church

Mark Dever is a leading conservative evangelical voice. He has written extensively in the area of Baptist polity and, though a scholar, he's first a pastor, serving in our nation's capital. It's no surprise that his church conducts an internship program as a "church polity boot camp," an in-depth study of the Bible's paradigm of function and leadership in the local church. The interns read five thousand pages in five months and write five papers per week as they reflect on their studies and the church's body life. The program has them consider what a healthy church looks like and how a shepherd thoughtfully cares for the flock.

Capitol Hill Baptist Church has the resources to offer six internships at a time and to involve them with a large pastoral staff. Most local churches don't have such opportunities. But Capitol Hill's internship model rightly affirms that the local church is vital in God's program, and that a pastor-to-be is wise to explore the contours of congregationalism so that he might give care to the whole flock.

Charles Simeon Trust

Charles Simeon was appointed curate-in-charge at Holy Trinity Church in Cambridge in 1782. While most congregants came to church looking for entertainment, Simeon preached repentance and faith, even when the people locked their pews shut so that visitors couldn't sit, and even when students from the nearby university hurled bricks through the church windows during services. He kept at the task for over four decades.

With the faithful preaching of Simeon in view, David Helm and other conservative evangelical expositors are convinced that the health of the church depends on the healthy preaching of God's Word. The Charles Simeon Trust conducts workshops on Biblical exposition in over twenty locations worldwide each year. The workshops help pastors and pastors-to-be shape sermons that faithfully draw out the meaning of the text and apply it to contemporary life. The Trust challenges pastors to build into their internship programs a venue in which interns learn to handle the Word of God more accurately, with support and evaluation along the way.

Ministry training strategy

Phillip Jensen has had a long ministry as a chaplain at the University of New South Wales in Sydney, Australia. In 1979, he began taking apprentices under his wing for training in local church and campus evangelism ministries, with an eye toward their further formal theological training. Ever since then, the Ministry Training Strategy has produced countless gospel-faithful church plants and ministers. MTS takes its interns to meet unbelievers, disciple young Christians, train youth leaders, and lead small groups for at least twenty hours per week of face-to-face ministry with people. Learning from MTS, the local church pastor is wise to build in "people time" so that interns catch the mind-set that ministry is about people.

God has endowed each of His churches with unique spiritual gifts, finances, members, staff, locations, and needs. Each local church must consider how it is to steward these resources wisely for internships, but may it not ignore the helpfulness of the long view of its ministry, the rhythms of its polity, the centrality of its preaching, and the people of its mission.

Cast a Wide Net

Maybe you're a pastoral major at a Bible college, and in a few months' time, you'll find yourself in an internship. Perhaps you're a pastor now looking to implement pastoral training in your church. Here are some practical tips from recent interns and supervising pastors. As you toss out your net, cast it wide.

Wide exposure

Intern, you're amped up about your first pastoral role in a church. Here's the news: it's less glamorous and less defined than you expect. Surprises will come your way. Circumstances beyond your control will turn the best-laid plans upside down. But when a teen finally shares his struggle openly, or crisis strikes a family, or children's parents are late to pick them up from your long night of ministry, embrace these as learning opportunities. God is working to produce in you what He desires of your service. See how He is exposing you to the wideness of service to Him and His people.

Pastor, you're most tempted to add staff members to take your least-desired tasks off your plate or to shore up gaps in ministry coverage. Although these are of practical value and frequent need, they aren't the focus of Jesus' disciple-making strategy. He ultimately gave His disciples the commission to take the gospel to new places and make disciples.

Take action . . .
Intern
1. You're embedded in the church, so take this opportunity to go to lunch or coffee with each of the deacons, with ministry leaders, and with families across generations.
2. Expose yourself to every dimension of the church's life. Take in the full orbit of the ministry.

Pastor
1. Teach your apprentices to embrace the same commission. If they grasp the central aim, they will see the open doors to ministry when they come.

2. Show them ministry in your church through a wide lens. Plan for them to attend one meeting of each committee or ministry team. Describe for them how each ministry fits into the Great Commission.

To a wide process

Intern, be a useful man. Talking about godliness and preaching, the apostle Paul wrote, "Practice these things, immerse yourself in them, so that all may see your progress" (1 Tim. 4:15, ESV). Discipleship is a wide process, and you play a specific role. Churches and pastors are looking for your progress. They won't be fooled by false projections of success, but when your preaching is heartfelt and faithful and you display wisdom in spiritual things, your true progress will be evident.

Pastor, you certainly play a constant role in the wide discipleship process. If you have no interns, give an eye toward the young men of your church. Watch those who respond to your teaching, who pick up on your emphases, and who with their spheres of influence begin doing what you're doing with them. Could God be stirring their hearts toward pastoral ministry?

If you have an intern, you're essential to his training and assessment. On the front end of the internship, lay out your passions and the church's heartbeat. The intern will then be able to grasp these in the moments of worship, meetings, Bible studies, and conversations, and apply them in formative bits of pastoral wisdom.

Take action . . .
Intern

1. Take initiative.
2. Show up to everything early and talk with people as they arrive.
3. Learn your supervisors' and peers' preferences, and serve them.
4. Write sermons every week even if you aren't preaching.
5. Ask others to evaluate you. "One who is faithful in a very little is also faithful in much" (Luke 16:10, ESV), so keep immersing yourself in your doctrine and conduct, not for merit, but so that others may play their roles of building into your life.

For wide learning

Intern, you're eager for four months of constant access to your role-model pastor. However, he might not have the same picture of your relationship. He already puts in fifty or more hours per week and probably has family and other responsibilities before him. He probably can't hold your hand in every task. Respect his time and energies by keeping a running list of questions, and engage him appropriately, not every ten minutes.

Learning comes by a variety of means. Some will come from direct interaction with supervising pastors. Most learning, though, is caught, not taught. Look at every task, meeting, and conversation as an opportunity to learn. I remember listening to a particular church's staff talk about its internship program. The pastors observed that most interns wanted to come because they were enamored with the senior pastor, a popular author and speaker. During the internship, though, each intern grew to love the congregation for its love and care for one another—not at the expense of the pastor, but because wide are the paths of learning.

Pastor, your intern is observing and participating in the life of the church. Live your life before him. Keep fulfilling your ministry. Strive at your tasks just as you have, and pull the intern in along the way. When he does pick your brain about how you explained a point in the sermon or why you wrote the meeting agenda that way, explain the Biblical text or the ministry values in view. In a surprising way, this articulation helps you to center in on your priorities and enhances your ministry.

Aspire to the Noble Task

Interns and pastors are now faced with the enormity of the task of ministry preparation. But Paul wrote that "if anyone aspires to the office of overseer, he desires a noble task" (1 Tim. 3:1, ESV). Ministry's pressures, battles, and discouragements are ever present, but so are its rewards as God proves His surpassing power by daily renewal (2 Cor. 4:7, 16). Aspire to the noble task, because the Bible affirms that you desire a good thing.

Pastoral internships by the Book make for a healthy church at home and healthy churches across church fellowships. You might be training someone else's next pastor, but someone else might be training your next pastor. Aspire to the noble task, because the association churches are enriched.

The church is God's display of His glory to the world (Eph. 3:21), and if passing the baton builds healthy churches, then passing the baton also spreads His glory. Aspire to the noble task, because God's name is deserving of all fame.

Discussion

1. What preconceived notions about internships have you found to be false?
2. What were three specific teaching methods Jesus used with His disciples?
3. In what passages did Paul bear out the gospel-preaching mandate?
4. Which do you find more often lacking in pastoral training: polity training, homiletic training, or ministry's people-focus?
5. What other practical tips would you give a potential intern or supervising pastor?

For Further Study

"About the Charles Simeon Trust," Charles Simeon Trust, available at simeontrust.org.

The Deliberate Church: Building Your Ministry on the Gospel by Mark Dever and Paul Alexander, Crossway, 2005.

"Internship Description," Capitol Hill Baptist Church, available at capitolhillbaptist.org.

Lectures to My Students by C. H. Spurgeon, Zondervan, 1954.

"Master of Divinity Paid Internship," available at summit.edu.

Passing the Baton: A Handbook for Ministry Apprenticeship by Colin Marshall, Matthias Media, 2007.

"Raising Up the Next Generation of Pastors," *9Marks Journal,* available at 9marks.org.

Test, Train, Affirm, and Send into Ministry: Recovering the Local Church's Responsibility in the External Call by Brian Croft, Leominster: Day One, 2010.

The Trellis and the Vine: The Ministry Mind-Shift That Changes Everything by Colin Marshall and Tony Payne, Matthias Media, 2009.

30

The Bivocational Pastor
— Kevin Subra

Why would anyone choose to work full-time or part-time and also be a pastor of a church congregation? That is a fair question to ask, and there are some reasonable, good answers to it.

A Choice for Hardship

Those willing to work part-time or full-time while leading a church are not better, smarter, or more spiritual. All pastors bear heavy responsibilities. Bivocational ministry is not a diminished way to serve but a different, viable, valid approach to pastoral ministry that brings its own strengths and weaknesses. A bivocational pastor takes the ongoing extra hardships and challenges that come with serving in that capacity (2 Tim. 2:3, 4).

What Is the Basis for Ministering This Way?

I believe we have built unnecessary roadblocks to ministry because of how our views of pastoral staffing and compensation have morphed over time. Paul said, "Those who preach the gospel should live from the gospel," (1 Cor. 9:14, NKJV), which in text clearly involves an evangelizer sharing the gospel to the unsaved (v. 22). The American church has wrongly transferred that statement to the pastoral position—a distinct and separate office (Eph. 4:11). In doing so, we have caused ourselves to focus on the position of pastor in light of a church's ability to pay a pastor fully—which has obviously severe limits—and thus we have prevented ourselves from encouraging more men to become pastors, because we simply cannot afford more.

Second Timothy 2:2 contains a clear command for leaders to reproduce teachers who can, in turn, teach others also. Our churches should be leadership development incubators. To obey this mandate, we need to be training and equipping faithful men to come alongside us and pastor. If we obey this reproductive requirement, we may well have men in varying stages of training, whether they are compensated by the church or not.

Pastoring should not be equated with full-time pay. If you think about it, Paul's command instructing Titus to ordain elders in every city (Titus 1:5) cannot be equated with those men abruptly abandoning their means of income and wholly relying upon fledgling congregations to fully support them. Working pastors were part of the fabric of the local congregations as areas were evangelized and leaders were appointed. For most, time spent studying or shepherding was time not earning income by applying their trade or performing money-producing labor. Helping pastors with sustenance was essential for them to do their tasks well and still be able to make ends meet.

Compensation was not merely a reward based upon a man's position as pastor. Rather, a pastor received remuneration in proportion to his ability, his availability, and the actual intensity of the effort and quantity of time he expended as a pastor. Some Bible passages about the compensation of pastors suggest this. Fellow believers were encouraged to share with those who taught them (Gal. 6:6). The elders that *intensely labored* in word and doctrine were to be given double honor (1 Tim. 5:17, 18).

What Are the Benefits?

Pastoring bivocationally provides strategic benefits that may make the difference or even provide the edge in a given ministry setting. Some of these benefits are financial. Some are philosophical. Some are functional. All are valuable. Here are eleven benefits of bivocational ministry:

- *Bivocational pastoring maintains traditional marriage roles.* My working an outside job while pastoring has allowed my wife to focus on her God-given ministry at home. She is free to help me minister more effectively rather than juggling her own outside job. This wonderful arrangement has allowed her to embrace the joy of bearing and raising our children as their primary caregiver and homeschool teacher (Gen. 1:28; Ps. 127:3–5; 1 Tim. 2:15; 5:14; Titus 2:3–5).
- *Bivocational pastoring keeps the shepherd in the "real world" rather than in the often-isolated church setting.* It is easier in a full-time setting to forget what real life is like for those we shepherd. Working either full-time or part-time makes it somewhat easier for me to keep a

realistic view of life (1 Cor. 9:19–22), and it tempers my expectations of the flock I lead.
- *Bivocational pastoring helps curb the temptation to rely upon government assistance.* The shepherd needs to earn his own way rather than establishing a dependence upon subsidies, food stamps, free health care, or any other form of government aid. Scripture never tasks the government to support a pastor, his family, or a church, either directly or indirectly. It is my God-assigned privilege and responsibility to work to provide for myself and my family (1 Tim. 5:8). Whether or not our congregation can assist me by reducing my need to work elsewhere, I am to exercise good stewardship and live within the means that God supplies, whether it be much or little (Phil. 4:11–13).
- *Bivocational pastoring changes the paradigm from an income-oriented position with a focus on a salary and benefits package to a ministry-focused position.* Ministry is possible no matter what the giving is in a given assembly and at whatever level feasible in positions both compensated and uncompensated by the local assembly (1 Tim. 5:17, 18). The goal of a local church is to produce disciples, not to secure full-time positions for pastors.
- *Bivocational pastoring maximizes available funds.* Instead of expending all resources to fund a single pastor, a church might consider hiring two or more men part-time, without the full-time costs of health insurance, retirement, and the like. By doing so, a church might be able to gain more productive hours and a stronger ministry impact with less money than a single full-time pastor would require (Eccles. 4:12). Having team members who can focus on differing ministry areas while sharing teaching responsibilities, exercising their unique strengths, caring for the flock, and covering needed or scheduled absences while maintaining a balanced home life is a great plan that I have seen work.
- *Bivocational pastoring actually encourages other men to consider sharing the load as pastors (1 Tim. 3:1; 2 Tim. 2:2).* Instead of becoming bystanders watching paid staff minister, spiritually gifted and mature men see themselves as those who could work and pastor to some level too, even without compensation. Many men are just waiting to serve, and need to see that it would be possible.
- *Bivocational pastoring encourages each member to minister.* Most church members cease seeing a pastor as "one paid to minister to us and for

us" and instead see him as "one of us, having the same challenges and life demands while seeking to walk with God while ministering to the body." They more easily recognize pastors as those who are given to equip the saints for ministry work until all are doing their part (Eph. 4:11–16).

- *Bivocational pastoring as a team actually adds stability to a congregation.* As seasons of life roll through, team members can share the load. If one pastor retires or is called somewhere else or is transferred because of his outside job, the church is not left without a shepherd and does not have to start searching for a leader all over again.
- *Bivocational pastoring encourages pastors to focus on essentials, helping men maximize the use of their time.* In bivocational ministry, you *have* to use your time wisely, and the demands make that very clear (2 Tim. 2:3, 4; Luke 8:14). How many pastors would be better pastors if they had *less* time available?
- *Bivocational pastoring provides shepherds for assemblies that would otherwise be unable to afford them.* It prevents placing upon these churches a burden they are unable to bear (Acts 18:3; 1 Thess. 2:9; 2 Thess. 3:8). With the extra-Biblical expenses of real estate, buildings, utilities, health insurance, retirement, and other modern expenses, churches struggle to cover all of their financial demands. They still need shepherds to lead them.
- *Bivocational pastoring allows for immediate ministry.* Working outside avoids a lengthy stint raising missionary support. If a church needs a pastor now, can it survive three or four years waiting for a man to gain enough support to become its pastor?

What Are the Challenges and Limitations?

The bivocational pastor model has its drawbacks and limitations, but you work with what you have to accomplish the mission assigned to you by your Commander (Matt. 28:18–20). Here are a few drawbacks and limitations:

- *Unrealistic expectations.* A working pastor cannot do everything that a full-time pastor can do. Church members who have experienced the ministry of full-time pastors might find the every-member ministry hard to adjust to. This is an excellent opportunity for deacons to "deek" to alleviate necessary congregational responsibilities from the pastor's plate (Acts 6:1–7).

- *Lack of broad fellowship.* Because of work schedules and time limits, my interaction is mostly limited to those within my church family. Most pastoral fellowship opportunities are geared to pastors who are full-time. Meetings are usually scheduled during the day, eliminating bivocational pastors who work normal business hours, or requiring them to take precious vacation time needed for other purposes.
- *Misunderstood lack of involvement.* Because work schedules and ministry demands prevent attendance at most meetings, the bivocational pastor is seen by his church association as nonsupportive or even disloyal to associational endeavors. This further widens the fellowship gap, and prevents invitations to fellowship and chances to participate in what he might be able to do (speak at camp, preach at chapel, etc.).
- *Difficulty getting time off.* Anyone who has worked two jobs knows how hard it is to get extended time off. Competing and overlapping demands make it difficult to get a true week of vacation. Additionally, because most evenings and Saturdays are used primarily for Sunday preparation, vacation time from work might be used up just to fix your house, go to the dentist, or even preach at a funeral.
- *Sharpening the saw.* It is hard to keep feeding yourself. Though sermon preparation is great spiritual food, it would be nice to be able to read more, attend a class, or be encouraged by a challenging conference. My outside spiritual refreshment has to come in very short snippets by squeezing in a book here or there, or listening to an online sermon.

Take Action . . .
For the pastor (and those training to be pastors)

1. View bivocational ministry as a legitimate option. It is not second-class ministry. It fills a need of many congregations that are struggling due to financial limitations. All churches need shepherds, not just the churches that can afford full-time shepherds.
2. Develop marketable skills to maximize your earning potential. It's a lot easier working for a good wage than it is working for minimum wage.
3. Focus on the Biblical priorities. You cannot do everything in any ministry role. Focus on what God requires you to do today.
4. Involve and train others. Bivocational ministry is a people-equipping ministry by its very nature. The pastor or pastors encourage, equip,

and enable others to share the responsibility to minister in every way to grow the Body (Eph. 4:11–16; 2 Tim. 2:2; 1 Cor. 10; Rom. 12).
5. Have a long-term view. Bivocational ministry is not a stepping stone, but a viable means to minister in ways often more enjoyable and flexible than just doing so while aiming for a full-time salary.
6. Have a big church view. Do what you do to benefit the entire church. God will use you. See your ministry as part of God's bigger picture.
7. Involve your family in what you do. Family time and ministry time do not have to be exclusive.
8. Develop a distance-running pace. Take small breaks to rest instead of being frustrated because of the lack of time off.
9. Understand that not all works grow into ministries that can support full-time staff. Small rural communities are an example. Areas that minister to highly migratory people groups or that carry heavy burdens—such as single mothers, believers with unsaved spouses, those from broken homes, inner-city works, stagnant locations with little movement in or out, and poor economic circumstances—all give different variables that can make bivocational ministry a constant need rather than a temporary patch.
10. Avoid accumulating debt. Debt enslaves you and steals your freedom. Don't pile up school loans, car loans, or credit card debt. Live within your means, and you will have the freedom to minister anywhere.

For the broader church (local, state, and national groups)
1. Recognize the benefit of having bivocational shepherds in your own local assembly. Augment, assist, and expand the efforts of present full-time staff and your own ministries by encouraging, enabling, and engaging men in your own congregation who display the desire, abilities, and character that qualify them for leadership (1 Tim. 3:1–17).
2. Encourage churches with only bivocational pastors by lending solid families. Instead of just praying for sister churches, help them by sharing families to assist in the work. One family that has a heart for ministry can do wonders to encourage a bivocational pastor and congregation alike.
3. Encourage bivocational pastors by involving them in fellowship opportunities as they are able to participate. Don't assume that their lack of participation means they are not interested in the association. Be willing to schedule fellowships and meetings on Saturdays rather than

weekdays. Invite them to speak at rallies, chapels, and camps. Let them participate in the bigger family, even though they cannot be your most involved supporters.

Discussion

1. What are Biblical teachings on pastoral compensation? What is required of a congregation?
2. How do the Biblical teachings differ from our common views of ministry and vocational ministry?
3. Can you name additional benefits or drawbacks to bivocational pastoring?
4. Can you think of congregations that would profit from a bivocational, team model of ministry over supporting fully a single pastor?
5. If no pay was necessary, what area of ministry would your congregation benefit from by having someone lead that area of ministry?

For Further Study

The Bivocational Pastor: Two Jobs, One Ministry by Dennis W. Bickers, Beacon Hill, 2004.

Developing Leadership Teams in the Bivocational Church by Terry W. Dorsett, CrossBooks, 2010.

31

The Interim Pastor
— Lee D. Kliewer

After serving for twenty very fulfilling years in pastoral ministry, I received the opportunity and privilege to join the administrative team of a seminary. I had no doubt in my mind that God was leading me there, and I was eagerly looking forward to being part of a team that would be shaping a new generation of men to be servant-leaders for the church. I really enjoyed the ministry that God had given me as a pastor during that twenty-year period, especially the opportunities that the pastorate provided to get close to people, be involved in discipleship, and see a body of believers grow significantly in their walk with and service to God.

God gave me a great love for the church, so when I approached the time for a change in ministry role and focus, I confess that I had one nagging question: Would I miss being a pastor? The answer was definitely yes, but God answered the longing in my heart with a great opportunity that combined my role as a seminary administrator with a continuing involvement in local church pastoral ministry: the role of being an interim pastor to churches going through a change in pastoral leadership.

How did this interim pastoral ministry get started? Soon after I arrived in my new role at the seminary, I learned that a church where I had previously served as pastor was losing its current pastor. The deacons of that church learned of my arrival in the area and contacted me to see if I would be willing to serve as their interim pastor and assist them in searching for their new pastor.

I told them immediately that I would come—what a fantastic opportunity! I was able to go back to a church body that I dearly loved and assist them for a nine-month period of preaching, counseling, and advising the church leadership in areas that would help the church grow and prepare for the next pastor.

After the church moved through the process that culminated in the calling of a new pastor, I found there were a number of churches in the area going through similar circumstances. Through the church relations department at the seminary, plus the assistance of church fellowship leaders in various states, I contacted churches needing assistance. I learned that a number of them desired help to guide them through this process. In many cases when a pastor leaves a church, he leaves a leadership void, and the remaining leaders are very open to help, guidance, and advice as they begin the process of change in pastoral leadership.

I began to study the Scriptures to see how the early New Testament church developed leaders to serve churches during times of change in pastoral leadership, and this led me to develop Paraklesis Interim Pastoral Ministries, a program that would minister to churches going through this unique period.

The purpose of this ministry was to provide Bible-believing churches that are without a lead pastor with an intentional interim pastor during the interim between pastors. Paraklesis Interim Pastoral Ministries was also intended to provide a temporary undershepherd for the church who can comfort, exhort, and come alongside a church in a *paraklesis* ministry, such as the apostle Paul did in Acts 9:31.

Over the fourteen years that I served at the seminary, I had the privilege of serving ten churches in an interim pastoral role. It was a great joy for me to connect with the believers in those churches and see God use that time to deepen their commitment to Him and to their local church!

So what does this interim pastoral ministry do? Why is it important, and how does it help churches through the process of change in pastoral leadership? What all is involved in the role of an interim pastor? Let me share some observations and things I learned as I partnered with these churches that identify the benefits, role, and functions of an intentional interim pastoral ministry.

The Biblical Foundation for an Interim Pastor

If you try to look for the term "interim pastor" in Scripture, you obviously will not find it. It is one of those terms that has developed in our era out of a practical need for this role in churches. Certainly we all understand that we employ a number of theological and ministry terms that are not found in Scripture, but for which Scripture clearly expresses their concepts or ideas; for example, *Trinity, Rapture, committee,* and *trustee.*

Some have asked me if the role of an interim pastor is really a Biblically based role if it cannot be found in Scripture; others have stated that it is a leadership cop-out or failure if a church itself does not have other capable, godly, qualified men to step into the role as lead pastor when that person leaves or retires.

Where are the other godly men, such as deacons, who are meant to be servant-leaders for the congregation, or other pastoral team members who could step into a role as lead pastor during an interim? The answer is that in some cases, those solutions are possible, but that in other situations, they are not. Smaller churches, for example, may have only a few deacons, who are already stretched to their limitations with their church, employment, and family responsibilities, and who are not equipped with the needed competencies or time resources to assume the role of lead pastor. Even in larger churches that employ multi-staff pastoral teams, each of those pastors often has a specifically designed role and ministry-leadership responsibilities that would greatly suffer if he were asked to carry the additional responsibilities of regular preaching, counseling, administration, consulting, and vision casting that are normally provided by the church's lead pastor. Hence, it is often wise and of practical necessity to look outside the present church leadership to secure an interim pastor during that time of transition and leadership void in the church.

So can this concept of an interim pastor be substantiated, or at least recognized for use in the New Testament local church? Although the term is not used, I think the concept of clearly caring for the leadership needs of a local church, particularly in times of leadership transition, is at the very heart and pattern of what the apostle Paul did. His epistles often refer to local churches "setting things in order." In fact, as we examine the letters he wrote to Timothy and Titus, which directly expound on the qualifications for pastoral leadership (1 Tim. 3; Titus 1), we find in Titus that Paul had been in Crete, that he was no longer there (leadership void), but that he had left Titus there for two functions: to "put what remained [to be done] into order," and to accomplish that goal by appointing "elders in every town as I directed you" (ESV). There is no mention of whether Paul's or Titus's role was meant to be permanent or transitional. All Paul knew was that the churches needed leadership help, he was not available, and Titus was.

Could Titus have been acting in a transitional/interim role, or could those elders he appointed also be acting in a transitional/interim role? We do not know for sure, but we do know that when Paul sensed a need to help local churches void of pastoral leadership, he helped them find qualified men to step to the plate in time of need.

From Paul's model, we can suggest two important principles for interim pastoral ministry: recognize the need and help churches when they need pastoral assistance (even if only temporarily, until permanence can be achieved); and those serving in interim pastoral roles are real pastors with all of the needed qualifications and authority in place to give quality assistance and ministry leadership in time of need.

Benefits of an Interim Pastor to a Local Church

What, then, are some of the benefits that an interim pastor can provide to a church? Here are three important ones to consider:

- He provides regular, consistent expository preaching every Sunday, which results in a consistent feeding of the flock. This also unburdens the church leadership (deacons, search committee, other staff members) from the extra time and responsibility to secure pulpit supply speakers.
- He provides consulting services as an advisor/mentor to the deacons/search committee in the process, protocol, and resources necessary in the successful search for a new lead pastor.
- He provides the outside, impartial perspective of a godly, experienced pastor for church health and growth during the interim.

The Role of an Interim Pastor: What Does He Do?

An interim pastor usually provides a number of functions for a church. Each church may have differing needs and situations; therefore, the actual functions that the interim pastor will perform should be discussed and agreed upon with the church leadership during an initial consultation appointment. These functions may include the following:

- *Preaching each week for the Sunday morning and/or evening services.* The interim pastor can also take responsibility for securing a qualified pulpit supply speaker for any Sunday he himself would be unavailable.
- *Meet as an advisor/mentor with the church staff and/or deacons on a monthly basis or as otherwise needed.* This should be agreed upon with the church leadership during the initial consultation appointment.
- *Meet as a church consultant with the search committee on a monthly basis*

or as otherwise needed to assist in the process, protocol, and resources needed to successfully secure a new lead pastor. This should also be agreed upon with the church leadership at the initial consultation appointment.
- *Help continue to develop congregational trust and confidence in the church leadership team during the interim period.*
- *Assist in the areas of refining church mission, organization, and vision; conflict resolution; and emergency counseling situations if desired by the church leadership.* This can also involve healthy discussions on the leadership level of taking the church through change by helping it identify strengths, weaknesses, opportunities, and threats plus prepare the Body for needed changes in the church's ministry operation and its vision as it looks forward to its next chapter of ministry with the new pastor.
- *Attend or lead other ministry leadership meetings on Sundays, as needed and desired by the church leadership.*

What Functions Does an Interim Pastor Usually *Not* Cover?

In some cases, the interim pastor may not be able to provide functions or leadership in the following areas:
- Leading a midweek service (Wednesday / Thursday)—this time can be a good opportunity for other church staff and/or deacons to lead an informal Bible study and/or prayer time in accordance with the regular church ministry schedule
- Teaching a regular Sunday School class
- Long-term counseling relationships, including premarital counseling

Derived Authority and Term of the Interim Pastor

The interim pastor should enter into a service agreement with the church through the written invitation/contract of the deacons or other church officers who are authorized by the church constitution. The appointment of the interim pastor by the deacons should be announced publicly to the church congregation. This provides consistent communication of the derived authority of the interim pastor and his relationship to the church. The interim pastor should serve at the request of the deacons and should be directly accountable to them. The beginning of the interim pastor's term should be clearly understood and designated at the time of the initial consultation appointment, and his term will continue until such time as the church secures a new lead pastor.

Conclusion

The intended outcome of an intentional interim pastoral ministry is that even when a church is without a pastor,

- God should be glorified through a unified, edified, and serving body of believers;
- the "table can be set" for any needed change in the church's ministry operation and its vision as it looks forward to its next chapter of ministry; and
- the church leadership and body as a whole are given informed, Biblical direction in the search and selection process of their new pastor.

When I begin a new interim pastoral ministry with a church, I often include some very intentional teaching from Scripture, including the following:

- The priorities of a local church from Christ's perspective (Rev. 2; 3)
- God's blueprint for a pastor and his combined role of *episkopos* (bishop), *presbuteros* (elder), and *poimen* (shepherd) (1 Tim. 3; Titus 1; 1 Pet. 5; John 10)
- "One-anothering" passages from the New Testament that emphasize believers' responsibilities in relationships to each other in the Body of Christ
- Pursuing lost people for Christ (personal and corporate evangelism)
- A theology of Biblical change for churches

I also continue to remind the church of some great promises that Jesus Christ, the head of the church, made directly to the church:

- "I will build my church, and the gates of hell shall not prevail against it" (Matt. 16:18, ESV).
- "Christ loved the church and gave himself up for her" (Eph. 5:25, ESV).
- "He [Christ] is the head of the body, the church" (Col. 1:18, ESV).
- "I am the good shepherd [pastor]; I know my sheep" (John 10:14, NIV).

Very often, after their previous pastor has left, churches enter a time of uncertainty, confusion, and even fear. They need someone like an experienced, godly interim pastor to model the love of the Good Shepherd and Head of the church, and remind them that the Great Shepherd will never let them down; He will guide the church through their time without an undershepherd, and as the Chief Shepherd, He already knows who their next undershepherd will be!

As a pastor, I need to be passionately committed to the health and growth of the local church. Having recently left the seminary to return to a full-time pastoral role, I have witnessed and benefited from the godly example and leadership of an interim pastor who "set the table" well for a good relationship between pastor and people.

In the role of an interim pastor, it is a privilege to partner with and encourage local churches during the crucial period of pastoral leadership change. With Christ as our example, we must love the church. I am grateful to God for the ministry He allowed me to have in helping local churches with interim pastoral ministry, and it is my desire to continue to assist and consult churches by helping them identify a qualified interim pastor to lead them during this unique time in the life of their ministries.

Take Action . . .
The interim pastor
1. Contact state and national associations of churches or intentional interim pastor ministries for contacts with churches needing an interim pastor.
2. Meet with the church leaders. Each side should spell out expectations and together decide on what your responsibilities as interim pastor will be.
3. If God is leading, enter into a service agreement with the church through the written invitation/contract of the deacons or other authorized church officers.
4. Feed the flock, guide them, prepare them for the future and their new pastor.
5. Relinquish your role as interim pastor to the new pastor.

The pastoral search team
1. Meet with the intentional interim pastor/search team consultant.
   - Target date to complete: _____
   - Search team assignments:
2. Establish responsibilities and contractual agreement between the intentional interim pastor/search team consultant and the pastoral search team.

- Target date to complete: _____
- Search team assignments:
3. Begin to develop a church and community profile and cover letter.
    - Target date to complete: _____
    - Search team assignments:
4. Begin to develop a church family questionnaire regarding qualifications and preferences for the new pastor.
    - Target date to complete: _____
    - Search team assignments:
5. Compile and analyze the results of the church family questionnaire.
    - Target date to complete: _____
    - Search team assignments:
6. Begin to develop a pastoral profile, based on the priorities of the pastoral search team and input from the church family questionnaire.
    - Target date to complete: _____
    - Search team assignments:
7. Begin to develop a pastoral candidate questionnaire: one step or two steps?
    - Target date to complete: _____
    - Search team assignments:
8. Begin to identify and contact potential agencies for résumés and references of potential pastoral candidates. Discuss and select classified advertising options.
    - Target date to complete: _____
    - Search team assignments:
9. Establish guidelines and a calendar for the pastoral search team's communications with the congregation.
    - Target date to complete: _____
    - Search team assignments:
10. Begin to compile and distribute an initial information packet (cover letter, church and community profile, first-step questionnaire) to potential candidates.
    - Target date to complete: _____
    - Search team assignments:
11. Discuss and prioritize any responses received from potential candidates.
    - Target date to complete: _____
    - Search team assignments:

12. As a potential candidate is identified, discuss procedures for follow-up with that candidate:
    - Conduct a phone interview.
      Target date to complete: _____
      Search team assignments:
    - Send part of the search team to hear him preach and meet with him.
      Target date to complete: _____
      Search team assignments:
    - Bring him to your church to meet and preach as a "person of interest."
      Target date to complete: _____
      Search team assignments:
13. When you are ready to move on a candidate, establish a schedule for "candidate week," send an information letter/announcement to the church body, make travel and housing arrangements for the candidate, and so forth.
    - Target date to complete: _____
    - Search team assignments:

Discussion
1. How should an interim pastor relate to the pastoral staff, if there is one?
2. What are the benefits of an interim pastoral role to a preacher?
3. Describe an example you have seen of an interim pastor serving a church during a transition.
4. Describe an example you have seen of a church's bad experience with an interim pastor.
5. Should an interim pastor allow himself to be considered a candidate while he serves as the interim pastor?

For Further Study
Books
Advanced Strategic Planning by Aubrey Malphurs, Baker, 2005.
Breakout Churches by Thom S. Rainer, Zondervan, 2005.
Church Structure That Works by Bill Blanchard, VMI, 2008.
Church Unique by Will Mancini, Jossey-Bass, 2008.
Leading through Change by Barney Wells, Martin Giese, and Ron Klassen, ChurchSmart Resources, 2005.

Leading with Love by Alexander Strauch, Lewis and Roth Publishers, 2006.
The Right Pastor: Seeking God's Man for Your Church by Wesley Johnson, Regular Baptist Press, 2000.
Shepherding the Church into the 21st Century by Joseph M. Stowell, Victor Books, 1994.

Online Resources

christianjobs.com
churchstaffing.com
churchstructurethatworks.com
interimpastors.com
my-pastor.com/interim-pastor.html
pastorleewiggins.com – Titus Ministries
malphursgroup.com
theinterimpastor.com

32

The Associate Pastor
— Bruce Snyder

The American Heritage Dictionary defines the word "associate" this way: "to join as a partner, ally, or friend." When God was commissioning Moses to free the Israelites from the pharaoh of Egypt, Moses pleaded with God to send someone else. God assured Moses that his brother, Aaron, would be his partner, or associate (Exod. 4:13–16). Moses also had Joshua as his associate during the wilderness wanderings of Israel.

The apostle Paul also enjoyed partner-associates in his ministry: Timothy, Luke, and others. Likewise, the disciples of the Lord Jesus Christ could well be considered associates. The Lord made it very clear to them that His work plan for the future was to "build My church" (Matt. 16:18, NKJV). The apostles in the New Testament followed that plan in establishing local churches wherever they ministered. When recognizing and addressing the local churches in Revelation 2 and 3, the Lord Jesus directed His remarks to the angel, or messenger, or pastor/elder of each local church. By this, Jesus recognized the leader of each local church to be a single person. In some cases, however, a plurality of pastors/elders appears in some New Testament local churches (Titus 1:5; James 5:14). I conclude, then, that in those churches there was a "lead" or "senior" pastor and one or more associate pastor. My task in this chapter is to examine the ministry of the associate pastor.

A High and Holy Calling

It is important that before anyone accepts the call to be an associate, he has already determined to submit to the Biblical authority of the senior pastor. If he cannot surrender his own preferences or opinions, he should not take the role of associate. The role of associate pastor has been construed in many cases as a secondary or lesser important position in the local church. Nothing could be further from the truth. While it is true that the senior pastor is the one whom God will ultimately hold responsible for the leadership in the local church (Heb. 13:17), the call of God to be an associate is a high and holy calling. In many cases the success or failure of many a senior pastor can be attributed to the ministry of his associates. In my fifty-three years of ministry, I have been a senior pastor thirty-two years and an associate pastor twenty-one years in the same church to four separate senior pastors. None of the pastors with whom I have been associated ever treated me or looked upon me as secondary or inferior. The role of an associate should not be viewed as a stepping-stone to the office of senior pastor. Commit to the role of associate, not always looking to the future.

Loyalty to the Senior Pastor

This brings me to a very important point, the matter of loyalty. If the associate pastor will be loyal to the senior pastor and treat him and refer to him with respect, he can expect to be treated with the same respect and loyalty. If the associate pastor has difficulty or has to adopt a tongue-in-cheek attitude toward the senior pastor, it would be best for him to prepare to leave and seek association with a senior pastor whom he can respect without reservation. The associate pastor should never have an ear for those who might oppose or dislike the senior pastor. He should remind people who might want to vent their frustrations and disagreements to him that if they have an issue with the senior pastor, their Scriptural duty is to go to him directly to discuss the matter openly and honestly (Matt. 18:15, 16).

Necessary Qualities
Faithfulness

The second important subject in this chapter is reliability, or faithfulness. The apostle Paul testified that God used him because He counted him to be faithful (1 Tim. 1:12). The associate must be faithful to his Lord; to his leader, the senior pastor; and to God's leading, that is, the local church where he serves his Lord. One of my professors in Bible school emphasized that we must be "truthful in what we relate and faithful in what we promise."

Responsibleness

The associate must be responsible! Because the associate pastor generally is not required to punch a time clock for his ministry, he could easily procrastinate or become lazy toward his ministry. An associate pastor might argue that he does not get paid very well, so what will it hurt if he is lax in his work. The answer to that attitude is simply this: the associate does not work for the church or for the pastor; he works for the Lord of the church and is directly responsible to Him in all things (1 Cor. 10:31). The associate should be looking forward to hearing our Lord say, "Well done, good and faithful servant" (Matt. 25:21, NKJV). He will not be able to say such if it is not true of his ministry! The associate who honors the Lord will work long and hard for His pleasure alone (2 Tim. 2:3, 4).

Even though the work of the associate is not necessarily for the local church but for the Lord, he must also be loyal to the local church in which he serves. Remember that the local church is the work of God in the world today. The associate must respect and commend the local church to which he is called. The associate must agree wholeheartedly with the church's and the pastor's doctrine and philosophy of ministry. It is wrong for the associate to bad-mouth his local church to his friends, to his family, or even to his foes. To be complimentary to the work of God is always best.

Truthfulness

The associate must always be truthful. If a sinful or unscriptural situation exists in the local church, the associate must be wise in his comments about these sensitive matters. In other words, he must be tactful as well as truthful. Remember, this is the Lord's work!

Pastoral Changes

Another sensitive, and in some cases controversial, subject is what happens to the associate or associates when the senior pastor leaves the local church. The senior pastor is the God-appointed leader. When the leader leaves, an associate pastor must be prepared to leave as well, but the timing of his departure may not necessarily be until after the new senior pastor has been called. The associate or associates can be an invaluable resource to the local church as they seek the will of the Lord for a new senior pastor. The local church would be remiss if the associates had no part in the calling of a new pastor.

A new senior pastor should always have the prerogative to choose his own staff. He may well desire to have the associate or associates remain in ministry with him. If he chooses to make changes, those changes must be tactfully and Scripturally done with complete openness toward the church and the associates. If the new senior pastor desires change in the staff, those associates who are not to be retained must, in all cases, both public and private, be gracious, kind, and supportive of the new pastor's desires.

Disagreements

Controversy in the local church should be avoided at all cost! Remember, it is the Lord's work! How should the associate react and respond when he disagrees with the senior pastor regarding a policy or program? The first response is to go to the senior pastor privately to openly discuss the disagreement. If the senior pastor feels strongly that his policy or program is both Scriptural and relevant, the associate has only two recourses. He must respectfully express his disagreement and then both publicly and privately support the pastor. Or, if the associate cannot support the pastor, he must discreetly and swiftly prepare to leave.

The leadership of the local church cannot be divided: "If a kingdom is divided against itself, that kingdom cannot stand" (Mark 3:24). If the associate decides he must leave, the well-being of the church is paramount. The associate must never, under any circumstance, undermine the senior pastor or create a situation whereby the church may be divided. No matter how strongly the associate may feel, it is always better for him and his family to leave the church rather than create an environment whereby other families may leave the church. Remember, the Lord is in the business of building the local church, not dividing it!

Ministry Enrichment

Another important matter to be considered is the associate's working to improve his knowledge and ministry skills. Books, seminars, conferences, and other growth opportunities should be used to sharpen the focus and extent of ministry. The local church would do well in encouraging and financing the associate toward improvement, since both will definitely benefit from those improvements. The apostle Paul made it very clear in his first letter to Timothy: "This is a faithful saying: If a man desires the position of a bishop, he desires a good work" (1 Tim. 3:1, NKJV).

Being a pastor is indeed a good work. Being the associate with a good pastor is also a very good work. It is such a great privilege to be directly involved in the work of the local church and see firsthand what God is doing in ministry. To all associates, I echo the sentiments of Paul's first letter to the Corinthians: "Therefore, my beloved brethren, be steadfast, immovable, always abounding in the work of the Lord, knowing that your labor is not in vain in the Lord" (1 Cor. 15:58, NKJV).

Take Action . . .
1. Prayerfully consider accepting the role of associate pastor.
2. Evaluate your opinion of the role of associate pastor. Do you see it as inferior? as a stepping-stone to the role of senior pastor?
3. Practice faithfulness, responsibility, and truthfulness.
4. Work toward having an open, honest, mutually respectful relationship with your senior pastor.
5. Practice discretion.
6. Always be learning and growing in the areas of ministry for which you are responsible.

Discussion
1. Why is the role of associate pastor just as "high and holy" as the calling to senior pastor?
2. What should an associate do if his senior pastor does not respect him or treat him with respect?
3. How can an associate find the balance between truthfulness and tactfulness?
4. Should an associate pastor resign when his senior pastor resigns? Why or why not?

For Further Study
Becoming a Healthy Team by Stephen Macchia, Baker, 2005.
Church Staff Handbook: How to Build an Effective Ministry Team by Harold J. Westing, Kregel, 2012.
The Leadership Baton by Rowland Forman, Jeff Jones, and Bruce Miller, Zondervan, 2007.
Leading from the Second Chair by Mike Bonem and Roger Patterson, Jossey-Bass, 2005.
Leading Leaders by Aubrey Malphurs, Baker, 2005.